# DANCING NAKED

Stripped, Whipped and Set Free
to Survive Divorce

DANCING NAKED
STRIPPED, WHIPPED AND SET FREE TO SURVIVE DIVORCE
Copyright © 2007 by Alice Belt
Edited by Lyrysa Smith, 2007

First Edition - 2007

Manufactured in the United States of America

Cover design by Susanne Murtha
Cover photograph by Brian W. Benson

Library of Congress Cataloging-in-Publication Data is available.

ISBN: 978-0-6151-4985-1

This book is dedicated to:

Deborah J. Mendelsohn, M.S.W.,
    San Diego, California

and

Victor M. Meyers, Esq.
    Hudson, New York

*Heroine and hero, standing on opposite shores,*
*saved a life -- mine.*

Note: Because I burned my earliest journal notes, some of the journal entries in Chapter 1 are based calendar notes and on my memories. Some of these entries may have discrepancies with the events of a specific date, but all represent my experiences as honestly and as factually as my understanding allows. – A.B.

# DANCING NAKED

## Stripped, Whipped and Set Free to Survive Divorce

by Alice Belt

Lyrysa Smith, Editor

# Table of Contents

# Glossary

(some names have been changed to protect privacy)
<u>People</u>
me, myself and I - Alice
my husband, him - Garrick
the filing clerk, his employee, his girlfriend - the other woman

Children:
daughter - Michelle, born in 1960
married to Pierre, my son-in-law

daughter - Molly, born in 1961

son - Jeffrey, born in 1965
    married to Starr, my daughter-in-law
    and Justin, their son, my grandson

Lilly - my sister, married to Neal

Deborah (Debbie) Mendelsohn, M.S.W. - my counselor

Tom Griffin, and then, Victor Meyers - my lawyers

Brett - an accountant who worked in my husband's CPA office

Friends:
    Falls Town, New York: Nancy, Pete, Ed, Flora, Margaret, Lyrysa, Brian, Jean, Betsy, Ruth, Cathy, Debbie, Ana, George, Galen, Audrey, Pastor Esther, Marilyn, Kit, George, Paul, Russ, Shirley, Sarah, Mike, Pat, Sue, Marty, Kent, Sue, Newell, Jack, Barbara, Paul

    In Stockbridge, Boston and Otis, Massachusetts, and Chappaqua, Pleasantville, New York City, NY, and New Canaan, Connecticut: Ruth, Diane, Stu, Ann, Gerry, Norman, Bev, Tony, Judy, Dayse

    In Atlantic, Iowa: Betty, Judy, Joan, Bob, Jill, Susan

    In Barrington, Illinois: Alice, Catherine, Gerry, Alice, Kathie, Jane, Barb, Joy, Earline

From the Army days: Gwen, Barbara

In Seymour, Indianna: Malinda, Mary, Betty, Tricia, Doug, Myrna, Carl, Glenna

Pets
Tootsie (Roll) - a chocolate Labrador. She produced a litter in 1993.
Spooky - a black Labrador from Tootsie's litter.
Chicken Feet - a long-haired domestic, outdoor cat.

Places
Falls Town, NY - a small rural town in Columbia County in upstate New York.

our home, marital residence - The home we built in 1984, just outside of Falls Town, designed to be our cozy, romantic retirement home.

the Big House - Purchased in 1987 and extensively renovated. It included my husband's office and I operated it as a weekend Bed & Breakfast inn.

the farm - the property that surrounds the Big House, purchased in 1993. It contained the farmhouse and lovely hills and rolling fields acreage. We built a greenhouse near the farmhouse.

the church - The United Methodist Church of Falls Town in the village center on Church Street, which is named for this beautiful old church.

Church House - The Victorian house next door to the church, which the church owns. The house needed to be completely renovated and we needed to add on a fellowship room. I got the ball rolling and the project was paid for with funds raised while the renovation took place. Now, the building serves as a site for many community gatherings and church social functions.

Church Street and Main Street - The two main streets in Falls Town on which most of the businesses are located and that intersect in the center of the village at the Memorial Clock Circle.

# Time Line

1/20/35 - I was born in Indiana

5/12/56 - I secretly married Garrick. I was 21, he was 22. He was my first and only lover.

1957 - I graduate as a registered nurse. I was president of my class each year.

1958 - I move to Germany to join my private first-class husband. I had a miscarriage. We didn't have a car and I didn't work. I was president of the enlisted men's wives club.

1960 - Michelle was born in Chicago. Garrick began his professional career. He passed the CPA exam, got a job with Price Waterhouse and traveled a lot.

1961 - Molly was born. We bought our first house in Lombard, Illinois.

1964 - We moved to Atlantic, Iowa. Garrick worked for W.R. Grace.

1965 - Jeffrey was born in Iowa. Garrick worked and played golf. I was active in charitable work. We enjoyed a "couples" social life.

1967 - I had another miscarriage. I supervised the construction of a new home in Atlantic and we moved in.

1968 - We moved to Memphis, Tennessee; a career advancement for Garrick. Within six months, he accepted a new job in Chicago with Peat, Marwick & Mitchell.

1969 - We moved to Barrington, Illinois. Car pools, children's lessons, charitable activities and social functions filled my time. Garrick worked long hours and traveled a lot.

1976 - Garrick worked for Ward Foods in Chicago. I supervised the construction of a new house in Barrington, Illinois, and we moved in.

1978 - Garrick commuted to New York City for his new job with Ward Foods at their headquarters office. The family was together on weekends.

1980 - We moved to Chappaqua, New York. Ward Foods was sold. Garrick took a new position with Viacom. I was involved with new neighbors and our church. We had a rather glamorous social life.

1984 - I supervised the construction of a country home in Falls Town, New York, designed to be our "retirement" home. Garrick commuted to New York City until Viacom was sold. He was chief financial officer of the company.

1987 - Garrick retired and we took a three-month vacation in our RV. I supervised the construction of a log house, which was sold when we bought the "Big House." I supervised the renovation of the Big House, with the purpose of it being an office for Garrick. He established a CPA practice in Falls Town.

1988 - I operated a summer weekend B&B in the Big House to serve the community and to utilize the furnished space.

1992-93 - The "girl" (30 years old, married with one child) was hired as a part-time filing clerk for Garrick's growing CPA practice. She replaced a part-time college student. We bought the farm that surrounded the Big House. I supervised the renovation of the small farmhouse, which was converted into Garrick's new office.

1993 - Garrick moved into the new office in the farmhouse, next door to the Big House. The "girl" had become a part-time student and still worked part time for Garrick. I continued with community charitable projects.

# INTRODUCTION

At the time of the divorce, it was a 40-year marriage, sustained with love and loyalty until the 38th year. In the trial, I testified to my married life -- committed, loyal, supportive, steadfast and happy. My husband was my confidant, lover and best friend. My sex life began with my marriage and I remained faithful to my husband for our entire marriage. I willingly carried the responsibilities of homemaker, dutiful wife and mother. I worked very hard to create a happy home and to smooth the way for my husband's career. While placing him on a pedestal for family and friends, I trusted him completely and I felt loved. But after almost four decades of marriage, things changed.

There are many theories of what happened to him, but my story tells what happened to me: How I lost confidence in our relationship, became suspicious, acted upon my instincts, was validated in my beliefs and finally, survived divorce. Trashed, whipped, stripped of self-esteem and abandoned, it took years for me to rise from the ashes of my marriage.

When my husband began to block every effort of communication I tried with him, I instinctively turned to writing about my feelings. At first, I left my notes out for him to see, but as he rejected my efforts to communicate, verbally or on paper, I poured out my emotions in my journal. This book is a result of that survival tactic. My "journaling" enabled me to view my daily situation, express my entire range of feelings, plan strategies and eventually, witness my own progress.

My counselor informed me that devastating divorces after 40 years of marriage were not very common and that there is a lack of published material dealing with the subject for people in my age bracket. She encouraged me to keep writing for my own therapy and also suggested that my honest accounts of my experiences could help others in similar situations, including people age 60 and older and younger folks, too. This idea motivated me to work toward a goal of publishing my story.

Journaling has been an extremely important tool in my recovery. Extending the same frankness about my feelings and my situation to my family and friends has enriched my relationships and my place in my community.

Writing has helped me to clarify my thoughts as I struggled in a vast, unknown, emotional wilderness. Writing also documented that my instincts were on target, even while my beliefs, constructed over a lifetime, were shattered.

Through this painful experience, I have become comfortable with myself. I feel decent and strong. I will not be controlled or shit on. I stand taller, laugh often, cry, curse, pray, and I dance naked.

# SUSPICIONS

## June 3, 1993

I bought a back-washer yesterday. He's stopped washing my back when I'm in the tub. After all these years together, I'm still a little shy naked, so it felt particularly racy to enjoy the warm water trickling down from the cloth pressed against me with his strong hand, the up and down stroking. Then he stopped. I began asking him to wash my back a few weeks ago and he would come in grudgingly and do it without effect.

This past weekend, we held Jeffrey and Starr's wedding reception at our house. He and I were both acting as hosts to our son's and his new bride's friends and family, but he performed a little ceremony for Jeffrey and Starr at the reception without asking me about it at all. I wasn't included in any of it. I am Jeffrey's mother after all.

In his presentation to them, he recited lyrics from a romantic Elton John song. A friend leaned over to me and whispered, "You know, he's reading that to you." I gave her a little smile, but my impression deep down was, No, no he's not.

Recently, he also seems reticent to show pride in my accomplishments. A couple of weeks ago, I was awarded the DeWitt Clinton Masonic Award For Community Service in recognition of outstanding service to the community. It was a very special honor to me. At the ceremony, I looked to my husband for his approval, but he just glanced up and seemed detached, as if it was no big deal.

Then at Jeffrey and Starr's reception, a friend from Iowa noticed the award on the bookcase and said, "Garrick, this is fantastic. You must be so proud of Alice." He let the comment drop. My heart sank.

He used to be my greatest fan. He would brag about my smallest accomplishments to his business associates and friends. I would hear complimentary comments from them that fed my self-esteem and confidence. I felt cherished.

Now it's like walking on eggshells. This morning when I tried to get him to talk about what's happening between us, he didn't have anything to say and he left to go to work. He has a new immediacy about getting to work in the morning. Why has he stopped treating me like I'm special? It isn't like him at all and it seems so strange to me. So many things feel weird.

**June 14, 1993**

He turns away from me to sleep instead of us "spooning" together, which is how we've slept for as long as I've known him. It's like we're coming unraveled. Sex that used to be spontaneous and fun is now full of anxiety and hassles. Maybe it has to do with his prostate problem and the drugs he takes for that. I haven't wanted to direct too much attention to his impotency. My body has been going through changes, too, because my menopause set in about the same time that his prostate troubles began. But when I tried to ask delicately about his impotency, he fired off at me, saying I was way off track. I told him that I was OK with it and that sex isn't the point. Togetherness and romance are what really count.

He didn't respond and the conversation was left hanging. Our communication, which always felt effortless and inspiring, is now stilted and awkward. And he's grumpy. Our home has always been a place of humor and sensuality; candlelight dinners at the kitchen table almost every night, and plenty of giggling at his surprises and one-liners.

OK, I have to keep my head straight. In 37 years, I've never seen him act this way. It's out of line. Since he won't speak to me about it yet, I'm hoping to get some clarity by using this journal and writing down what I'm feeling and what I see happening.

It's so bizarre to read what I've just written. I can't believe it's me. My stomach feels disconnected. My handwriting looks knotted and uneven. Deep breath. Be calm. Keep writing.

Gotta get my thoughts organized. Use my instincts as a guide. OK, here are some changes:

- The once-common fanny pats are few and far between. The standard one was every time we'd go upstairs, he would allow me to go first and he would follow and grab my behind. Now he makes an effort to go up the stairs ahead of me. Also, it used to be that when I was standing at the kitchen sink he'd come up behind me and caress me. Now he passes through the kitchen behind my back, like a ghost. I watch him go by in the reflection in the kitchen window in front of me.

- He's stopped helping me with chores or with my charity work. Normally, he would pitch in, but last week, he wouldn't even help me put up the tent at the church fair. Now he won't commit to helping me with anything, even though he really does have spare time.

- He's stopped being generous. A couple of years ago, he gave me a very lavish gift for our 35th wedding anniversary. He was in cahoots with our youngest daughter, Molly, who drove in from Massachusetts where she lives. They lead me with my eyes closed to the garage. When I opened my eyes, I found a brand new red

3

convertible with the top down and the whole car filled with red roses. Molly gave me a tube of bright red lipstick to go with it. It was amazing, I was stunned. I felt loved. And he was delighted with my reaction.

- He's not considering me anymore. On our 36th wedding anniversary, just last year, he wanted to take a cruise to Bermuda. He'd wanted to take a cruise for our 25th anniversary, too, but it wasn't my idea of an active vacation, which I prefer, so I talked him out of it. We did a great canoeing and camping weekend instead. This time, however, he insisted and booked the cruise. Maybe he thought it would be nice, or romantic. It wasn't. This year, we were so busy getting ready for Jeffrey and Starr's reception, we didn't do anything special at all.

- My 40th high school reunion was earlier this month, and although we had always gone to each other's reunions together, my husband said stuff at work was too hectic. He said, "You could go... You go ahead." So I went alone.

- He now questions whatever money I spend – for the dry cleaning, a wedding gift, a charitable contribution, car repairs, whatever. If I'm wearing a new outfit or buy a gift for one of our kids, he'll say, "So, how much did that cost?" He's never done that before. I'm certainly not spending extravagantly, but now he's complaining about whatever I spend.

- He only tells me what he's doing or where he's going on a "need to know" basis or at the last minute. He used to regularly share his schedule and consult with me so we could fit our schedules together. Now he wants to make his own arrangements. He often leaves me uncertain of any definite plans until the eleventh hour.

**June 20, 1993**

I just saw my friends, Mike and Marianne, in town. We were talking about church and we got around to talking about a couples' workshop we'd all attended in the spring of 1989. Can it really be four years ago? Anyway, we recalled an incident at the "Tres Dias" weekend.

After having been separated, the men and women came together at the end of the workshop to discuss their experiences. Individuals were asked to present to the group something they'd learned. My husband was incredible. In front of everyone, without saying a word, he hugged and kissed me passionately to the point that Mike exclaimed, "Hey, you two! You'd better stop or we're all going to have to leave you alone." It was intense and wonderful.

Today, the three of us had a laugh together talking about it. Marianne said, "You have the marriage that we want at your age."

**July 31, 1993**

We've just returned from vacation. First, we visited with my sister, Lilly, and her husband, Neal, at their cabin on a big lake in Minnesota. Then we went to Chautauqua in Western New York with three other couples who are friends of ours from Iowa.

I had made the plans for both of these trips and they turned out fine. Our trip to the cabin reminded me of when we all went canoeing at the Boundary Waters Canoe Area last year. On that trip, my husband didn't want to canoe much or go fishing. He just wanted to hang out at the campsite and he seemed bored. However, the weather was perfect, the mosquitoes didn't come out and the food was great. It's a relief when everything works out because I worry if anything goes wrong, my husband will get really crabby.

I know where this fear comes from. Last fall, I did all the planning and arrangements for a trip to Europe. My husband would say almost everyday, "Things don't get better than this." It became our rallying cheer. The other two couples on the trip also used the phrase throughout our travels. From then on, even on our recent vacation with them, someone would say it at a good moment and we would all laugh.

But it was during our trip to Europe I felt abandoned by my husband for the first time in my life. We arrived in Munich one night earlier than we expected, in October, in the midst of Oktoberfest, and we didn't have a hotel reservation. Throughout the first part of our travels in Germany, finding a "zimmerfrei" (room for rent) in towns along our route had been easy. But in Munich the pressure was really on me and I had to work out our lodging crises by myself. My husband didn't even offer encouragement.

In the end, I did solve the problem with the cooperation of our friends. But I had worked very hard by myself in an adverse and stressful situation. In the past, my husband definitely would have helped me.

**August 4, 1993**

It's been my lifelong habit to confide solely in my husband -- he's my lover and my best friend. So, for several months now, I've been trying to talk with him about my concerns. I've talked to him about what I feel to be a "distancing" in our sex life. I've also expressed my concerns about his relationship with his new filing clerk at the office and how it's affecting me. He says there's nothing to it. But I can't shut down my gut feelings and I sense something is unusual. My concerns and my expressions of them are becoming increasingly intense. All he says is that his relationship with his filing clerk is normal and professional. My instincts are screaming at me. I have an urgency to deal with this.

**August 6, 1993**

I'm writing down my feelings and observations because it's the only way I can effectively get them out. My husband is quiet and always has been; it's never been his way to be really chatty. He doesn't like to talk about personal stuff or about anything that's going to hurt. He's happy to talk at length about other things like politics or business.

My attempts to have conversations with him about our situation have been unsuccessful. Since he's not really communicating with me about this, I've written short notes to him and left them at the breakfast table a few times.

Mornings have always been our best time together, even lately, when things have been strained. He's always witty in the morning and we'll have a few laughs over breakfast, with good conversation, too. Then I'll get a big hug and kiss and he's off to work.

But my notes aren't helping. I'm still not getting any response from him and our mornings are becoming quieter. He'll read the note to himself and then lay it aside. My notes say how much I love him and how important our long and happy relationship is to me. I say that my instincts are flaring over what seems to me to be a too-close relationship with his filing clerk. I say that I can't deny my instincts but I'd be thrilled to learn that I'm wrong.

I'm really hoping for some solid reassurance from him. He hasn't given any yet. Even his "I love yous" in response to mine as he's leaving sound hollow. Once he's gone I destroy the abandoned notes.

**August 15, 1993**

Ruth Carlin was going to come to Falls Town for a visit, but instead she called and asked that I join her in New Jersey to help her find a building site for their new home. So, we spent last week roaming different communities in New Jersey, looking at land and at rental homes for Ruth and her family to live in while they build their own. She's hopeful they can find something soon and get their plans together over the winter months. We had fun looking in different places and imagining what it would be like to live there. We had good talks and good laughs together, like best friends do. Still, I held off and didn't tell her about my concerns with my marriage.

Unfortunately Ruth's back was hurting her quite a lot, which was very worrisome to both of us. She's going to set up an appointment with her cancer doctor as early as possible this week.

**August 16, 1993**

My husband seems totally uninterested in what I'm doing or thinking. I've been leaving my notes in different places around the house for him to read but we're not getting anywhere. It's maddening. He reads my notes and knows everything I'm feeling -- all my fears and my hopes. And yet, he's not giving me feedback of any kind. It's as if these exhibitions of my deepest, most anxious feelings are being read by a stranger who doesn't know me or care about me at all, as if they'd been washed up on the shore in a bottle from some faraway, unknown place.

**August 17, 1993**

My place in our marriage is deteriorating. I feel unwanted and suspicious, feelings I've never experienced in 37 years.

He seems confused about what he's doing. He used to seek my approval or ideas on personal issues, like his hair, his clothes, his employees, the development of his business, his charitable contributions or our kids. Now his hair is growing long and I asked, "Do you need a cut?" He said, "I like it long."

He used to say looking "professional" was very important, but now he dresses in shorts or jeans for work. I think, "Well, it is the country, he's semi-retired, it's comfortable and he still looks good."

He started reading the newspaper when we eat together -- even in restaurants. When I finally objected, he became defensive and short-tempered. He put the paper down in a huff and turned his eyes on me like lasers. I didn't know what to say. Now his solution is to read right up to and immediately after the meal and he's eating faster. As a result, eating out has become empty and we haven't eaten by candlelight at home in many weeks.

And even though he knows they make me sleepy, he wants to watch videos almost every night now.

**August 19, 1993**

Today there was a "bankruptcy sale" on the county court house steps. County officials were auctioning off properties that belong to people who are now in bankruptcy. My husband and I decided to attend because we were curious to see what would become of the farm property surrounding our Big House. We were not there with any notion of purchasing the property ourselves, but when no one was bidding on the farm property, even at the minimum bid, my husband looked at me, asking with his face, "Well, should we?" The auctioneer's gavel was banging, about to come down for the final time. I looked at my husband and nodded, saying with my eyes, "Yes, I guess so." We won the bid and suddenly owned the property. It was very impetuous.

The auction ended and I stood there and cried as the people started to move away. I felt for the farmer and his family who had owned the land we just bought. I felt sad for all the people there who were bankrupt and losing their land. My husband began organizing the purchase and I heard him direct that the property be in his name only.

**August 22, 1993**

We spent the weekend in Saratoga Springs. My husband attended a tax seminar and I spent most of the weekend dreaming up a concept for the farm property we bought on Thursday. I came up with a neat plan, but it hinged on whether my husband wanted to continue his CPA practice in Falls Town or at all. When I asked him about it, he seemed enthusiastic and convinced that he wanted to keep his CPA business going.

I then suggested to him that he should conduct his business from a more serious, professional location than the room in the Big House. I said his current office feels more like a personal home office rather than a true public business. I said he should place his CPA business in a space at street level, like the other businesses in town, and not in an upstairs room in a residence that serves as a B&B on weekends.

I proposed that we renovate the small farmhouse on the farm property to become his office. I said it would be perfect for his business because it's right on Church Street and visible from the road, unlike the Big House, and fixing up the little house would also improve the neighborhood. My husband seemed to like the idea and I told him I'd draw up some plans and he could check them out.

**August 28, 1993**

We've started cleaning up the farm property, removing the junk and debris that have been laying around it for a long time. I want to show the town that we plan to take action quickly and that we're not going to sit on it for years.

I took measurements at my husband's office of all his furniture, equipment, bookshelves, etc. We've been discussing what arrangements at his new office would be most ideal for him.

It was awkward there in his office, though. I felt strangely out of place. But I'm trying to go beyond those uncomfortable feelings and stay focused on my project.

**August 29, 1993**

I've begun to figure out some of our plans for the farmhouse. Don is such a super-capable builder; he can work from a straightforward line drawing, without all the levels and other architectural stuff drawn in. This will be the seventh project I've worked on with him. Hard to believe.

I've been checking all my ideas with my husband and, so far, he's approved of everything. He's been offering his comments, too, particularly with electrical items like the placement of switches and outlets for computer equipment and the location for phones, stereo speakers, etc.

**September 3, 1993**

My husband agreed to take off from work Monday and Tuesday so we drove to Vermont and visited with our oldest daughter, Michelle and her husband, Pierre, for a couple of days. It was beautiful there and we had a wonderful time with them, very relaxing and very warm.

11

## September 4, 1993

Well, OK, so he doesn't want to do this or that. I'm not going to make a big deal of it. I'll just put on my best face and put forth my good nature. I think I see all of these changes in him, but I should just go on and get over it. I'll make a fresh start and try a new approach on my outlook. After all, my husband has always been nice to his employees and he's occasionally enjoyed being a sort of teacher to younger people in his office.

Even I have helped his filing clerk adjust to working in an accounting office. I also coached her on how to handle my husband's work habits. When she first began, some months ago, she was always telling me how much she loved the Big House and how much she admired my decorating. She asked me about my Bed and Breakfast operation there and she would tell me about her daughter and baby-sitters -- the usual small talk.

After a while she would ask me for advice or what I thought about different things. She was inexperienced in office situations like dealing with angry clients. After my husband left her with a difficult client one time, I tried to encourage her by telling her I thought she'd handled it well. Another time, she was almost in tears because my husband had snapped at her about something. I took her aside and comforted her. I said, "His bark is worse than his bite," and that he'd cool off and she shouldn't take it personally.

She's shown gratitude to me and treats me like a friend. She found an exercise class for us to take. She brought in pickled eggs, a traditional American Indian dish, for us to share at the office. She is American Indian. She's frequently spoken about American Indian issues and about her mother and grandmother. The two stone pillars at the bottom of the driveway of the Big House have statues on the top of them of an American Indian chief wearing a feathered headdress. As far as I know the statues have been there for many decades. I asked her if they offended her and if so, I would have them removed. She said, "No, not at all."

I have been a very nice boss's wife. I shouldn't feel that she's a threat to me. She is married after all, she's younger than our daughters and she's just my husband's filing clerk.

**September 8, 1993**

Running my B&B at the Big House is becoming too crazy and I'm feeling uncomfortable there. When I pass through my husband's office it feels awkwardly hushed, as if I'm interfering with their work.

I've had a steady stream of weekend guests this summer. In the past, my husband and I would spend the night together at the Big House so I could prepare breakfast in the morning. Then, a few weeks ago, my husband said he didn't want to stay over any more. I spent the night there by myself a few times, but I didn't like that. So I've really burnt myself out this summer running back and forth between our house and the Big House to take care of guests and make breakfast in the morning. It's been exhausting.

**September 9, 1993**

Today, I learned from Ruth that her cancer is back and in new places in her body and she is not well at all. She became very sick over Labor Day weekend and still isn't feeling better. We had a good long talk and I plan to visit her soon. I'm frightened for her and I feel so sad.

**September 10, 1993**

I've occasionally been attending Overeaters Anonymous meetings because I've felt like my weight was getting out of control and I seem to be eating compulsively. I'm feeling very sensitive about it so I thought I might learn some useful pointers about controlling my weight at the OA meetings.

I've felt fat, ugly and repulsive to my husband and I've thought maybe that's why he's distancing himself from me. It's such a cycle of frustration. I feel like I'm trying to hold it together when it's totally falling apart.

**September 11, 1993**

I'm noticing changes in my husband's office behavior more and more. He's been putting in longer days, claiming a busy time and an intense schedule, but when I'm at the Big House and go into his office, I see newspapers opened, coffee cups, CDs, snacks and basically the clutter of "hanging out." He wasn't one to chum around with his employees, but with this filing clerk, he's suddenly into chatting and hanging out.

He used to choose separate lunch times from his employees so the office would be covered, but now he often takes his lunchtime to coincide with hers and they eat together. He seems to be maximizing his time with her.

I overheard her tell him the other morning about the accounting course she was taking in college and she asked my husband to look at her homework. He offered to pick up lunch for the two of them and talk about her homework over lunch. Later when I "happened" in on them, he asked if I wanted lunch, too, (even though he'd only purchased two). I stayed anyway and felt like a fifth wheel.

**September 13, 1993**

It's very weird. I'll stop by the Big House to refresh the refrigerator for my B&B guests or go to my desk in the living room to write a check or look over my calendar. I use the Big House frequently for meetings with

14

Falls Town Flowers and other organizations' social functions. But little by little, I feel the filing clerk's comfort level in the Big House moving up to meet mine. She works there for my husband, but it's my house. The sensation of her in his office is unlike any other employee he's ever had.

The other day she told me she's interested in an accounting career and her goal is to become my husband's business partner. I mentioned this to my husband and told him how I had guided her regarding him. He said, "You don't help her -- she's my employee!"

**September 14, 1993**

My husband and I spent some time today in the farmhouse walking through and discussing ideas and plans for his new office there. The filing clerk also came along and had one suggestion; that we make the general bathroom downstairs have a large handicapped-accessible door. That's fine with me as I'd like for any of his clients to be able to use a bathroom at his office comfortably. Besides that, the bathroom is located along the hallway between what will be the filing clerk's office and my husband's office. I'm designing that hallway to be wider than usual so that two people can pass in the hallway without having to come in contact with each other, and it will also be able to accommodate a wheelchair easily.

**September 16, 1993**

The mood at my husband's office is intense and obvious. They start their "chummy" day with coffee. She stops in the kitchen for her first cup of coffee and then she drapes herself along the frame of the doorway to his office (like Rita Hayworth would in an old movie if she was in a bedroom wearing a beautiful nightgown), coffee mug in hand, facing his desk, holding his eyes, laughing, cooing and talking about everything except business -- the weather, the news, her sleepless night, her headache, her

15

need for a housekeeper, how hard it is to keep house and take care of her child, her husband's uncertain working hours (he's an undertaker), her child care needs, etc. She said she needed a vacation and was planning one without her husband.

They also talk about working out and losing weight. He started exercising at home before work during the same time period that she started exercising in her home. Then, over coffee in the morning, they discuss their workouts.

Normally, my husband and I work out together. We inspire each other when we feel out of shape. We start eating better, taking walks together and we establish a routine of exercising on our exercise machines at the same time. When I tried to join him in his latest morning exercise routine, he stopped working out.

I've also noticed that she's wearing sexier clothes to work; lacy tops, shorter skirts, tight leggings -- bordering on unprofessional dress, actually. When I enter the room, it almost always feels like I've interrupted something. Their locked-in eye-to-eye link gets broken by my presence.

I can feel these things. I can see them, I'm not blind! It's beyond intuition. I can feel the two of them connecting in a deep way and I can sense them nurturing it bit by bit.

**September 17, 1993**

She has an unusual mannerism for holding eye contact for a longer-than-normal span of time when speaking. Her dark eyes are stronger than her voice and I'm learning to read messages that are more clear than her spoken words -- furtive glances, sparks of anger, concern, begging, flirting, mocking, questioning, coaxing.

Her voice is syrupy sweet and she's a talker. I've noticed that when she talks to my husband, his voice becomes kind of giddy and musical. Perhaps babbling better describes the small talk that I overhear. She giggles and complains and usually manages to extract a favor. "My daughter is sick, I need to be home early." Or "I'm sorry I'm late, it was a bad morning." Or "Would you mind if my daughter stays in the office with me and watches TV?"

**September 21, 1993**

Coffee and donuts have always been the norm around my husband's office, but now I notice that he and the filing clerk have suddenly become addicted to the same treat -- cinnamon hard candy. They unwrap a candy, plop it in their mouths, watching each other, sucking together. Here again, she is often draped along the doorway to his office. They gaze at each other, sucking on the candies.

The body language is blatant. He's never cared for hard candies before. In fact, in the past he kept stashes of chocolate candy in his own desk drawer and ate it privately. Now both of them go to her desk drawer throughout the day for the cinnamon hard candy supply. Is this professional behavior?

Their ongoing episode with the hard candies has become a tangible ritual of intimacy, a clear display of unusual behavior from my husband on many levels and red flags of warning are going up all around me.

**September 23, 1993**

Planning a tax seminar for clients with his employee is not out of the ordinary, but to "practice" in the evenings after office hours and be told that I should not be there is definitely atypical. He's also said he doesn't want me at the Big House when he and his filing clerk, or "assistant," present the seminar. He's taken to calling his filing clerk his "assistant" these days. He made it sound as if I would interfere. He <u>has</u> asked Molly to come to the seminar to help serve refreshments.

Fortunately, I have plans to visit Ruth in Westchester on the evening of the seminar anyway. She is still very sick and her doctors are running tests.

This whole ordeal with the seminar is really rubbing me the wrong way. It feels particularly unnerving because I know she wants to become his business partner. It feels like he's really grooming their whole situation at the office.

**September 25, 1993**

This morning, my husband announced he was going today to an American Indian Pow Wow in Albany. My cousin, Ann, is visiting for the weekend and he said to us, "You can come, too, if you want to." He said his filing clerk would be at the Pow Wow.

This is a new avocation for him. Ann and I decided to go along even though we felt awkward and not really included. At the Pow Wow, my husband suddenly revealed a major new interest in American Indians and sought out the people in charge of the event and spoke at length with them. Ann and I felt very out of it the whole time. We watched the dancing and looked at the crafts while my husband hobnobbed with the Pow Wow organizers.

**September 28, 1993**

Ruth was told by her doctors that she is terminally ill with cancer. She and her family are determined to make the best of it and they're looking toward the future. Ruth insists that the construction of their new home continue and she plans to be involved every step of the way. Ruth is in a lot of pain and the doctors don't know how long she has to live.

I'm crushed. She's my closest friend. My heart is twisted with sadness and tears have poured out of me all day. I wish I felt I could count on my husband for support, but I don't.

My responsibilities seem to be getting greater and greater. My usual work at home and at the Big House of cleaning, cooking and organizing go on and my husband is doing less and less to help. He doesn't want to assist me with my community projects and does so only if I ask him to. And now my best friend is dying and he seems disconnected to what I'm going through. His support of me is growing weaker while my work is increasing and the stuff weighing heavy on my emotional side is becoming excruciating.

I've allowed him to call all the shots. He decides that we'll eat out and where we'll go. He chooses to come home and watch rented videos at night. I'm beginning to feel like I'm being dragged around by his decisions. His insistence to control what we do is pulling us apart. I must take a bigger role in our plans and in our decisions.

**October 7, 1993**

Tonight was my husband's tax seminar. I was at the Big House before the seminar began and my husband knew I was there and would be leaving shortly. I spoke with Molly, briefly, and said hello to several of his clients who were arriving as I was leaving. Then I drove to Westchester to visit Ruth.

I so wanted to tell my dear friend what I feared was happening in my marriage, but it seemed selfish to burden her with my troubles. It would have been wonderful, though, just to talk to someone who might respond in a supportive way. It's such a small issue, though, compared to dying.

**October 11, 1993**

The broken, dilapidated silos on the farm property were torn down today. A caved-in, old storage building, a deteriorating greenhouse and lots of other debris have been cleared away. It feels good to be moving ahead on cleaning up the farm property. I've got time to work on plans for the farmhouse and shop around for materials and interior furnishings since Don won't be able to put much time into the renovation before early spring next year.

**October 17, 1993**

About a year ago, I developed a rash on my finger from my wedding ring. We had both noticed that our rings had become too tight on our fingers. So, I haven't worn my wedding ring for some time. It wasn't a big deal, I felt very secure without the symbolic ring to prove I was married. A couple of months ago, my husband also removed his wedding ring. I did not feel secure when he removed his ring at this time, so I decided to have our rings enlarged so we could comfortably wear them again. A month or so ago, I presented the enlarged ring for him to wear and he put it on. After a few weeks I noticed he wasn't wearing it. I asked him about it yesterday and he said, "Oh, it gave me a rash so I took it off."

**October 26, 1993**

I am so acutely aware of my husband and the filing clerk now that my "detection antennas" are up constantly. It probably shows. Each time I walk into the Big House I take a deep breath and brace myself. Even when she's not there, like today, I said to my husband, "I can smell her." He said, "That's crazy." But I'm wired for every clue and I'm a changed person when I'm there. I peer into trashcans looking for how many wrappers from cinnamon hard candies there are, I analyze her handwriting on phone messages, I look over his business calendar, I even scanned his checkbook for unusual expenditures or checks written to her.

**November 1, 1993**

To make Halloween more exciting for the trick-or-treaters this year, I suggested we leave the lights on at the Big House, which is near the town center, and stay there to welcome the kids with candy. I offered to dress like a witch and greet them.

Last night, children and families we know from town made their way up the long driveway to the Big House. When the filing clerk, her child and a friend of hers with her child came to the door, my husband suddenly took charge. He has never given a hoot about Halloween before, but he'd anticipated his employee's visit and went into his office for the special treat he'd prepared for her child -- a $5 bill and candy. He presented the treat to her child and gave the other child a quarter and candy.

When they left, I said I didn't think it was fair to give such an unequal gift when two children were together. He shrugged and said that he didn't know there would be somebody else with her and besides, she's his employee after all.

**November 2, 1993**

I asked my husband about what I sense to be abnormal generosity towards his filing clerk. In the past, my husband would often come to me with questions about how to compensate his employees; he'd say, "What do you think? What's appropriate?" Now he is secretive. He hasn't asked me anything about her compensation.

But today, after I asked, he told me about his plans for his filing clerk's pay and I wanted to squelch them instantly. I questioned him about his intent to give her a Christmas bonus <u>and</u> a raise in pay, especially since he's already given her a lot of time off with pay, anytime she wanted it, in addition to eight weeks of paid vacation. I said, "It seems like she gets pretty special treatment." He said, "I haven't completely decided yet. It's none of your business, anyway. You can't control what I do, so stay out of it."

He went on to say that I was trying to control his work and his employees. I said, "No, I've never done that. I don't know anything about your work."

I'm starting to feel like I am too nosy, but no -- I'm not going to deny my instincts. With any of his employees in the past, getting him to give something to them, even a little Christmas bonus, was like squeezing blood out of turnips.

I've become valiant and dogged in my attack. I told him that his relationship with his filing clerk is causing tension between us and that we are at a turning point in our marriage.

**November 7, 1993**

While scanning over his business calendar with my antennas up, I noticed a luncheon date around Christmas time with her initials. In all of his business years, I have never been aware of him planning a Christmas lunch with his assistant alone. I have always been invited and he has always asked me to purchase a gift. But now there appears to be a Christmas lunch planned and I haven't been told or invited.

**November 10, 1993**

Today, I went into a closet in the attic searching for a folded cot and I found a framed photograph I've never seen before. It is an antique photo of a group of American Indians in front of a teepee. My heart was pounding as I realized it was a gift, probably a Christmas gift, for the filing clerk.

The sales slip said $400 -- ten times more than he allowed me to spend for gifts for loyal secretaries in the past.

I was distraught. With sudden cramps in my stomach, I replaced the photograph in the closet and went to the bathroom with diarrhea. His secret, expensive gift feels subversive to me.

I've decided that I will ask my husband about it, but I'll wait a day or two. I'm really hurt and I need to think.

**November 11, 1993**

I was doing some cleaning around the house today and out of nowhere I remembered something my husband told me when he retired from his position as chief financial officer at Viacom in 1987. He said, "The first 30 years were mine, the next 30 are yours."

Even at the time, the remark fell very flat with me. I pushed it aside and really haven't thought about it all these years because it didn't feel like a warm or caring comment. Instead, it felt like it was his own regret that he was finished and there was nothing more for him. The next 30 years are mine out of default. It wasn't that he wanted to give me support like I'd supported him for the past 30 years. His plan was to retire and just be around.

This is how his comment struck me in 1987. And today, I'm remembering the way it felt when he said it.

**November 12, 1993**

I feel horrible. I'm sickened in my stomach as I write this. I had a real shocker yesterday.

My husband has always beckoned me and our children with a unique whistle. When we heard that whistle, we knew it was for us. In 38 years, I have never heard him beckon another person with that sound.

Then yesterday, at the Big House, he used it to call his filing clerk who was across the driveway. I was in the kitchen and I heard him whistle nearby outside. I instinctively responded and went out the back door to find him. Then I saw her turn around, responding to his whistle, and he was on his way over to her since he'd gotten her attention. I stood there disbelieving what I was witnessing. I felt like I'd been shot.

How could he use his family whistle for her? I'd stopped what I was doing and went to find him. It's a whistle for his family, I'm used to responding to it.

He didn't know I was nearby -- then he saw me standing there. I'm sure I looked ashen. I broke down and cried uncontrollably. He came over and walked me towards the back and took me in his arms and held me. We stood by the back fence and I cried in his arms. He acted benevolently, as if it was no big deal, so what.

Our family relationship has been loving and private. His whistle to her ripped apart through our protective barrier and pierced my heart like a cold, poisoned arrow.

I had a horrendous nightmare last night. In the dream, birds awakened me in the morning with the same distinctive whistle, as if even they were taunting me, mocking my husband's penchant for the filing clerk, who is, apparently, revered by him as "family," or is replacing "family" for him. It was as if even nature had turned against me. I awoke feeling panicky and alone.

**November 14, 1993**

What used to be my normal life is now caged in anxiousness and doubt. An ordinary trip to the Big House to take care of my business now makes me shake to my core. I dread being there. Since the whistling incident, I look and listen to my husband and his filing clerk with utter distrust and fear.

**November 16, 1993**

Yesterday, I wrote this letter to my kids. I don't plan to send it.

*To Michelle, Molly and Jeffrey,*

*After all these years of married life, I'm sad to say another woman (actually a young girl, your age) has invaded my space and is systematically destroying my marriage and my life. Perhaps she doesn't even know she's doing it. I just know it's happening.*

*Dad is enamored of her youth. He has reached a stage of middle-life crisis -- denial of his age and grabbing for youth. The girlfriend is looking for security, money and a relationship with her boss. Everything is clicking for them. She wants to be a CPA and become Dad's partner. She plays romantic music at the office. She wears sexy clothes and talks about trying to lose weight. She is very chummy with him. Maybe she doesn't know that she's heading for a close personal relationship with Dad, but it is my feeling that she is. She is taking college courses in accounting and Dad helps her with her homework. Dad bought her an unusually expensive Christmas gift, which he has not shown me. I accidentally found it in a closet in the attic. He seems to be giving her more and more; higher salary, bonuses, time off, etc. He wants her at his side for each business meeting and the private meetings in between.*

*I feel shaken, nervous, often sleepless, upset stomach, suicidal. I don't know what to do. She seems to be gaining self-esteem and says she's happier than she's ever been. I'm losing self-esteem and I'm the most insecure and unhappy I've ever been.*

*When I try to talk to Dad about it, he says I'm crazy. I'm exploding inside and he won't hear me.*

*I want you kids to know that I love you and that whatever happens to me has nothing to do with you all being the family I wanted and have been proud of. Dad has not wronged me intentionally; he doesn't see the situation as I do. I can't help myself. If I kill myself, don't feel guilty. You didn't know. You couldn't help. All the things I have belong to you. I hate to think of her in my house with the only man I've ever loved.*

*My life has been dedicated to a loyal marriage and my family and friends. But I'm helpless to sustain a level head when my heart scares me to death. The idea of the new office frightens me, too -- longer hours, more togetherness, cozier situation and privacy. If I continue to terrify myself, I know I will find a way to end it.*

*Don't blame Dad. He didn't set out to create this problem. He's not guilty of anything but his own quest for self-esteem, masculinity and youth.*

*Love to you,*

*Mom*

**November 17, 1993**

I confronted my husband, very calmly, with my knowledge of the photograph. He confirmed that he wanted to give it to his filing clerk as a Christmas gift. I told him I thought he was being entirely too generous to her and I thought it was strange he hadn't included me in his Christmas lunch plans with her. He shrugged all of this off as if it was nothing. He was feeble and didn't offer any explanations. Eventually, he said I could come to the lunch with her, too, and suggested that I wrap the photograph as our gift.

**November 19, 1993**

I retrieved the photograph from the closet. I did the very best job I could of wrapping it -- beautiful Christmas paper and a large velvet bow. Then I went shopping in a southwestern store for an Indian-style outfit to wear to the lunch date. I bought a denim shirt and skirt that will look good with my western belt, my cowboy boots and a denim jacket I have that has a colorful Indian blanket fabric insert on the back. I also bought some silver and turquoise jewelry.

**November 20, 1993**

My husband is insistent that we do not have a party or do any kind of celebrating for his 60th birthday in a few days. I can't help but feel that he is in total denial about turning 60. It makes him very irritable and angry if I mention anything about celebrating his birthday.

We plan to drive to North Carolina with Molly and meet up with Jeffrey and Starr there at Starr's father's home for the Thanksgiving weekend.

**November 25, 1993**

It's Thanksgiving Day and my husband's 60th birthday. But we're focusing on Thanksgiving only. For days now, he has demanded that we not do anything to celebrate his birthday. He's been so adamant he's actually frightened me. He's been absolutely intense about it.

So I haven't breathed a word about his birthday today. He already seems very edgy.

**November 29, 1993**

Driving back home with Molly today, we stopped and had lunch in a restaurant. I was in a freaked-out state of mind, ready to burst with anxiety. I couldn't hold back any more and I just poured it all out. I complained about the filing clerk and I told Molly about my concerns with her father's relationship with his employee and his many uncharacteristic accommodations for her. I told Molly what I felt was happening to my marriage. I was extremely upset and couldn't stop crying. It was awful. Molly comforted me and put her arm around me. My husband did nothing, said nothing, he just stared into space while I exploded with feelings he hasn't responded to.

Molly suggested that we see a marriage counselor. She said she'd noticed flirtatious behavior between the two of them at the tax seminar she'd helped with. My husband said that I, alone, needed a counselor and that there was nothing unusual about his relationship with his employee.

**December 10, 1993**

I shared my feelings about my marriage with Michelle and Jeffrey. Michelle also suggested I "should talk to someone." I told her, "I am talking to someone, I'm talking to your father."

I've kept all my sadness and concerns between my husband and myself for so many months. It feels good to tell my children.

**December 17, 1993**

Our Christmas lunch at the Swiss Hutte with the filing clerk was strange. We all went together in one car and I felt very awkward right from the beginning. We were seated in a nice room; I carried the wrapped gift. I tried to "make nice." During the meal, I extracted conversation from both of them. My husband didn't carry any weight of the conversation; I carried it all. Only occasionally would the filing clerk come up with something other than a response to my questions.

I handed her the gift and she opened it at the table. Her reaction was not at all right to me. She wasn't effusive or curious about it. Other than a flat "thank you," she didn't have anything to say about it. It was very odd, especially for a one-of-a-kind antique photograph featuring American Indians. She was obviously uncomfortable and very cool. It occurred to me that perhaps they had actually seen the photo together somewhere before he bought it as a gift.

## January 2, 1994

We drove with Molly up to Michelle and Pierre's house in Vermont for Christmas weekend. We stayed at a very nice B&B. We all went out to dinner one night and we had dinner at Michelle and Pierre's another night. We celebrated Molly's birthday on the 26th, which was fun. It was all fine; we didn't have any friction.

On New Year's Eve, we went to Diane and Stu's party at their place in Stockbridge, Massachusetts. At midnight, we kissed each other rather perfunctorily. Parties hosted by other people have never been my husband's favorite thing and it was my choice to attend. His impassive behavior wasn't atypical.

## January 13, 1994

I learned today, without a word to me, my husband gave his filing clerk the go-ahead to use our Big House anytime during her "off" hours to do her homework. She had complained to him how noisy her house is and he told her she could use the Big House as a quiet place to study. She's told me before how nice and quiet the Big House is. I've also learned that my husband continues to involve himself in her homework by looking over her assignments, checking her papers and reading parts of a textbook she's working with.

**January 21, 1994**

I turned 59 yesterday. I spent the day with Ruth in Westchester. It was a quiet time of sharing. And it was good to be with her but also difficult.

Two nights ago Molly came over and prepared a beautiful birthday dinner, which the three of us ate with relish and joy. It was a wonderful gift and a wonderful evening. Tonight we're going out to dinner with John and Cathy and that should be really fun. They're such lively and interesting people.

**February 8, 1994**

I got assertive with my husband and demanded to know what his filing clerk's schedule is. I said, "What exactly are her hours? Eight to four, nine to five -- whatever! What are her hours? I expect to see her at the Big House working during that time only and she should not be there any other time. She has a home and she should be in it, not in ours. It's none of your business to deal with her and her homework."

He seemed to want to placate me and said, "I'll establish definite hours for her," as if I had made a good point.

**February 11, 1994**

He has displayed her "To The Boss" greeting card an inordinate amount of time. It's says, "I like you so much I'd work for free" And then in her handwriting, "Ha, ha, ha." It's still there on his desk in his office and has been for months. Bosses' Day was in mid-October! Meanwhile, cards from his own children for his birthday or for Christmas barely come out of the envelopes and are not displayed.

**February 18, 1994**

Apparently, he allows her to shop at his expense for "shared office needs." Along with standard office supplies, this also includes packages of cinnamon hard candies and CDs of romantic music. Fuming with anger yesterday afternoon, I clutched several of the CDs. My husband was in his office so I carried them up, stood in his doorway and slammed them to the floor. I said, "I don't like this music being played in the office. It's not professional!"

My husband offered a calm appeasement. He said they belonged to his filing clerk and that he would return them to her to take home. I cracked a couple of the plastic cases when I threw them down so I switched the cases I had broken with some unbroken cases from my own CDs.

**February 24, 1994**

My husband acknowledged to me that he sometimes permits "flexible" work hours for her so that she can bring her child and her sister's child to work with her and baby-sit them while she "works." He said, "She asked me if it was OK." By now I have noticed that she gets anything she asks for, despite my request that he set standard business hours for her.

**March 10, 1994**

A small incident became cataclysmic today. While at the Big House before working hours I found a phone message left for my husband in the filing clerk's handwriting with a one of the cinnamon hard candies taped to it. I stormed out in a rage.

As I was driving down the driveway, my husband was driving up, arriving for work. I jumped out my car and ran over to his car window. I was aware that my behavior was in plain view of the town but I didn't care. I was extremely upset, I felt out of control and I angrily asked him about her notes with candies on them. He didn't say anything. I screamed, "I've had it, I've had enough!"

Just as I was ranting my legs completely turned to rubber. My husband was looking at me like I had five heads, like I'm totally nuts, and my legs gave way beneath me. I collapsed into the snow next to his car. My head was light and my body was limp. I was only down a moment or two, though. I got up crying and said, "I'm going to Diane's in Pleasantville." He said, "Be careful driving down there."

I drove 90 minutes straight, steeled, trying to control my emotions. When I arrived at Diane's she greeted me saying my husband had called and sounded concerned and I'd better call right away. I called him and totally made it seem OK. He asked how I was, I said in a cheerful voice, "Oh, I'm fine, just fine, no problem with the roads." When I got off the phone, Diane asked if everything was OK and I said, "Oh yeah, just fine."

**March 11, 1994**

When he arrived home this evening, my husband told me that he'd asked his employee about the note with the candy on it. He said the filing clerk told him that her daughter was in the office and that it was she who had taped the candy to the note. I don't buy it.

None of these incidents over the past nine months between my husband and the filing clerk would mean anything to me if they were single isolated events. But they have accumulated; they're snowballing. I feel the magnitude of them.

**March 20, 1994**

Falls Town Flowers had a fundraising potluck dinner last night that we called the "Pot of Gold" dinner. We all worked very hard to make it a success and it was. The tickets sold out and everyone from the community participated. My husband and I had a very good time talking and laughing with friends and really enjoying the activity and each other.

**March 29, 1994**

Last night after we'd gone to bed, we got a phone call -- a wonderful announcement. Jeffrey and Starr are expecting a baby in November! Our first grandchild! I was wide awake instantly and elated with this great news. My husband remained rather sleepy and seemed nonplused by the announcement, although he said, "Oh, I'm glad for them. They sounded very happy."

**March 31, 1994**

He claims over and over again that he has a purely professional relationship with his employee and that they only talk business. Today, however, I went to the basement of the Big House to retrieve some clay pots to bring to the greenhouse and I knew they were in the kitchen above me so my antennas were up and tuned in. Although I couldn't see them, I could definitely hear what was happening. I heard 45 minutes of laughing, chatting, cooing and "having coffee" with no talk of "business." As far as I know, he's never carried on like that with any of his employees before. It's unprecedented behavior.

I came up from the basement and slammed the door on my way out. I went over to the farmhouse and called him. He answered the phone in the strangest way, like he was singing, "Hel-looooo..." I yelled, "Go to hell!" and slammed the phone down.

I ran over to the greenhouse and he followed me there very quickly. I was crying and screamed at him when he came in, "This is it. It's over. She's gotta go, now! Not one more day, not one more minute!"

My husband said, "If I let her go, will you still love me?"

I stopped cold and looked at him directly and said, "Yes. That's the point. I still love you and I can't stand her."

He said, "Trust me, I'll get rid of her."

He left and I waited. I began filling pots with soil, without looking, on automatic pilot, unraveling my tangled thoughts and staring into space. His response was a surprise to me. I've suggested in the past that he fire her and he's always had some excuse; he saw no reason to, it's none of my business who his employees are, or even that she might sue him for discrimination if he did.

He came back in a while and I asked him how she took it. He said, "Pretty well. We'll settle on the final date soon." Then we hugged and kissed and embraced some more. It was the best contact I've had with him in many months. I feel completely uplifted. I'm so happy.

**April 6, 1994**

Don and his team have begun the renovations on the farmhouse/new office. They're working on the roof, the siding and some framing problems. It's great to have that project underway.

**April 8, 1994**

I realize that I have become more and more extreme in an ever-increasing effort to get a nonevasive response from my husband -- a true reaction, a real heart-to-heart conversation. I want him to be honest and straightforward with me. Just show me that much respect.

I still feel red flags fly up, but I'm encouraged because at least my most recent outburst seems to have finally reached him. I wish I didn't have to explode to get him to respond truthfully to me, but at least it feels now like he's beginning to get it.

**April 14, 1994**

Two days ago, after I prodded him about it, my husband told me that he and the filing clerk were planning a trip to Albany today to deal with a client there. At the time, I said that I thought a third person should also go with them and he agreed to invite Evelyn, too. She used to work with my husband and I knew that she was more strongly connected to this client and his case than my husband's current filing clerk. Still I couldn't stomach the idea of this trip, so this morning I went to the Big House to do some of my business and check stuff out.

I went up to the filing clerk's office, really just to scope her out. She was agog with excitement about their trip. She was wearing a too-short-for-business skirt and told me that she'd tried on three different outfits this morning before deciding what to wear. She said her husband just laughed at her and couldn't believe what a big production she was making out of it. I said, "You look fine."

They all went together in my husband's GMC Suburban. I watched them go from an upstairs window. I noticed as they went down the driveway that Evelyn sat in the back seat. With the filing clerk in her short skirt and the GMC not having any running boards to accommodate someone like her with short legs, I visualized my husband having helped her into the passenger seat and what that must have looked like.

They came back this afternoon high as kites because they had been successful with the client and his case.

Once we were home tonight I told my husband that I didn't think her short skirt was appropriate to wear to a professional meeting and I knew what a big hike it was to get into his car and that I didn't like it at all. He said, "All young women dress like that. She looked fine."

Boiling over I said, "You think she works hard and is smart. I say she's opportunistic and she's using you. I see her sucking up to you and you're sucking back! Her syrupy sweetness makes me gag -- it's bullshit! You're acting like a school boy; you're acting like the cat that swallowed the mouse!"

He didn't say anything and walked away.

**April 18, 1994**

I had specifically expressed to my husband that I didn't want the filing clerk in the new office for any reason. I told him the renovations were going along fine and the plans were all set. I told him it wasn't necessary for her to be in there -- she'd been fired, she wasn't going to work there, she'll finish up her work at the office at the Big House and that's that.

Then today I saw him taking her into the new office. Later I pleaded with him, "Why?" He said, "Well... she asked." I said, "OK, but no more."

**April 20, 1994**

Perhaps we're making progress. We had another good talk today. I asked him if a final date for the filing clerk had been set yet. He said that they're still sorting it out, but in order to make me more comfortable, he has agreed that he will phase her out of the business very soon. He didn't share his plan of action or involve me in how he would do it. He said, "Trust me, I'll work it out."

**April 24, 1994**

About a month ago, my husband said he wanted to play bridge at the Church House on Sunday evenings. So I put the word out and for the last three weeks a group of us gathers on Sunday evenings to play bridge. What's odd about it is my husband's behavior, especially since the bridge games were his idea. As soon as the two hours are up, he slaps his cards together and says, "That's it" -- even if we're in the middle of a game. It's so abrupt it's rude. I feel like a buffer between his domination and what should be amicable gatherings.

After he did the same thing at tonight's game, I began to see him as very controlling; he's taking charge whether he's considerate about it or not. It makes me wonder if he came up with the idea of playing bridge just to kill time on Sunday evenings between 5 and 7 p.m.

To my surprise, I've actually enjoyed playing. We haven't played bridge since we lived in Germany when my husband was in the service. And although my husband plays for two hours, he doesn't seem to enjoy it and he keeps an eye on the clock constantly. It feels like another way that I am powerless over our situation.

### April 29, 1994

Ruth's husband called early this morning and asked if we would come down to see her today, or as soon as possible. I told him I'd leave now and be there right away. My husband wanted to go with me. He said, "Ruth has been my friend, too." So we both went. I was glad he decided to come.

Ruth seemed to comprehend that we were there with her. She was semi-comatose with only slight facial movements. Still, it felt like our chance to say good-bye.

### May 2, 1994

Falls Town Flowers held a short "unveiling celebration" this afternoon for a beautiful handcarved sign which stands on a grassy knoll at the north entrance of town. Our group raised all the funds for the creation and installation of the sign that says "The Hamlet of Falls Town, established in 1824." George, a member of Falls Town Flowers, has a landscaping business and did beautiful plantings around the sign. It really looks great and it's a wonderful addition to our town.

The local newspaper, the town supervisor and other Falls Town notables were there. My husband and I went together, but while I stood outside in the grass with the rest of the townspeople, he wanted to stay in the car and watch from down the street. His filing clerk was also there standing nearby with some friends. I'm sure his behavior must have seemed odd to other people there. I knew that if he were to stand with the crowd, the filing clerk would stand beside him and who knows what I would do then. He must have feared I would embarrass him by losing it and crying or becoming distraught.

## May 3, 1994

Ruth, my best friend, died yesterday. I have known her almost 15 years. I'm a wreck. When I walked into the Big House this morning my body rebelled with diarrhea and nausea. Even when one knows the death of a loved one is coming, it hits hard when it finally does.

Every cell in my body is throbbing in sadness. I need some tenderness and consolation. My husband has not shown any sympathy to me. I feel adrift. I couldn't tell Ruth what was going on with me, now I've lost her and there is no support from my husband.

Ruth's illness has been excruciating. The intense painkillers she was given would sometimes distort her perceptions of reality. Her mental state would fluctuate wildly. Sometimes, she would become most frustrated with, or even bizarrely paranoid of those of us who were closest to her. At times, I had to muster incredible mental strength and determination to be rational and understanding. Even so, it always hurt when she would get accusatory and lash out at me. Even when I knew in my head it was the drugs causing her behavior, my heart would ache after such incidents with her. And now I realize that coping with Ruth's condition magnified everything going on in my life.

My husband has found many ways to distance himself from me. Mostly, he is a wall of silence. He did tell me he wouldn't go to her funeral or memorial service. He has never been comfortable with hospitals or funeral homes and I think he feels he made his peace with her before she died. So that's it, he's done. I also recognize that his going with me to Ruth's funeral would mean supporting me and I believe he's unwilling to do that.

For my part, I cry hysterically, I collapse from weakness, I smash cups and dishes into the fireplace.

**May 7, 1994**

Today was the memorial service for Ruth. I went alone. It was very, very difficult.

**May 13, 1994**

Last night we went out to celebrate our 38th wedding anniversary. Since 1956, May 12th has always been a day of great romance, great lovemaking and great joy. Yesterday, however, was different.

My husband arranged for us to have dinner at the Columbia County Golf Club restaurant where our friend, Nancy, is in charge of the dining room and the chef is our cleaning woman's husband. Knowing it was our anniversary and seeming delighted that we'd chosen to spend it there, a fabulous meal was prepared.

Shortly after we were seated with a glass of wine, my husband presented me with a card and a tiny package. First, I opened the card -- it wasn't what I expected at all. The cover was a realistic painting of an empty couch with an open book laying on it, binding side up. There was also a teapot and two cups on the table in front of the couch. The printed words inside said:

*With love on our anniversary... On this special day, I'm thinking of all we've been through together... as parents, making a warm, loving home for our family... as partners, sharing so many rich meaningful times... as best friends, always being there to help each other... On this special day, I'm thinking of how very grateful I am for you and your love. Happy Anniversary.*

Beneath that my husband wrote: *Love! Me.*

It immediately struck me how perfectly unromantic, unsexy and unpassionate the verse was. Also, the words "I love you" do not appear anywhere and "Me" is a signature I've never seen my husband use before. It felt cold. I quieted my distress signals, said, "Thanks, sweetie," fronted a little smile and proceeded to open the small box.

My husband has always given me beautiful gifts on our anniversary and it has been our tradition that he gives me a gift only. I anticipated that the small box might contain jewelry, maybe something in gold. But I could hardly conceal my disappointment when I saw a cheap pair of earrings from Hallmark -- little metal, enamel-painted flowers. I was stunned. Still, with my knees almost buckling underneath me, I rose from my chair and leaned over to thank him with a kiss.

Nancy came across the room to see what the gift was. She is known to be quite direct in her opinions and even she only said, "Oh... hmmmm." I felt embarrassed. But I instantly decided to brush all of the strange feelings aside to allow for a pleasant dinner and a mood for romance. I actually put the earrings on for a while until the tight clasp became unbearable, then I put them in my purse.

We thanked the chef and Nancy and drove home with little to say. There was no romantic mood. Sleep was not difficult. I felt worn out.

This morning, I put his card in my bedside table to save it -- just as I have saved many cards and special letters from him in the past. My overwhelming feeling, however, was how our 38th anniversary was such a sad contrast to our previous anniversary celebrations. Then I remembered a note I'd written for my husband on a past anniversary and I went looking for it in his "treasure drawer" where I thought I'd seen it. I pulled it out and read it again:

*Our 30th wedding anniversary -- where did the years go? How can I feel more satisfied with you? Why do I feel happy with myself? At 52, why do you look so good to me and feel so good to me? How do you make me feel loved completely?*

*Better than newlyweds -- a steady progression in every aspect of married life toward a perfection which seems to be ours. Choosing you 30 years was the beginning of a love affair.*

*I love you. Alice.*

**May 14, 1994**

We received an especially high phone bill this month for the Big House, which includes the office phone lines. There were phone calls to Massena in upstate New York. This is the town where the filing clerk's mother lives. It appears my husband has given her total freedom to make phone calls anywhere she wishes as often as she wants. It is not characteristic for his employees to do that.

**May 16, 1994**

I learned from my husband that he used his one remaining contact at Viacom -- his secretary of eight years ago -- to get free tickets for Universal Studios and Disney World in Florida for his filing clerk and her child. Apparently they're planning a trip to Orlando over the upcoming holiday.

I found myself assessing the filing clerk today, trying to understand why my husband seems to be attracted to her. Her most impressive physical feature is her eyes -- dark, clear, almond-shaped with a hunter's quick glance. Her appearance supports her American Indian heritage -- long straight black hair, a prominent jaw, thick waist and hips and heavy legs. Some of her clothes hang from her shoulders, but she's recently been choosing snug tops and tight-fitting stirrup pants or leggings that do not flatter her figure. In fact, "dumpy" comes to mind.

She is two generations away from the reservation where her grandmother still lives. Her father was Italian. My husband says he admires her for being a "feminist." I don't think either one of them has a clue what that really means.

**May 17, 1994**

A ray of hope today. She will be leaving her job at my husband's office. According to my husband, she believes her husband is an alcoholic and so she'll go to school full time to accelerate her job possibilities. I hope she begins school soon.

**May 18, 1994**

I spoke to my husband in his office today and asked for the specifics about when she would be leaving. He said since she planned to go to school full time, he intends to replace her with someone else very soon. He didn't give me any dates, but he was somewhat reassuring.

**May 20, 1994**

Work has begun on the interior of the farmhouse, so to help with the renovations I cleaned out the attic a few days ago. Amidst all the ratty junk, I found a stack of old children's books about American Indians. I was delighted to discover that they were in good shape and really interesting "time pieces." I thought they might also be collectible and valuable. I carried them over to the Big House. I was excited about my little treasure so I showed them to my husband. Then I put them on my table.

Today I discovered that without a word to me, my husband gave the books to his filing clerk. When I asked him about it he said he didn't think we wanted them. He said I could ask her to give them back to me if I wanted to.

**May 22, 1994**

These days, while standing in the grocery store line, my eye is drawn to all those magazine articles about ways to arouse your man, revitalize your marriage, tips for spicing up your sex life, etc. I've never paid much attention to these articles before, but now I think I should get all the help I can so I've been buying the magazines and reading them so that I can try out stuff. I look for anything that might give me insight. I even clipped out an article about older men with young women.

Last night when we were in bed I tried some of the advice for exciting my husband. He turned away from me and said, "Don't -- that doesn't feel good." I ripped off my nightshirt and yelled, "I want sex now!" He didn't move. I went into the guest bedroom and slept alone.

**May 24, 1994**

It's become unbearable. Today I demanded that he never speak to her outside the office again.

Later on he said, "Her husband is an alcoholic. I would think you'd be sensitive about that and be more sympathetic."

I said, "No, just the opposite. I see her husband's car at the bar almost every night and I see her clinging on to you! I know their marriage isn't good. So don't tell me she's not looking for something better."

He seemed pissed I couldn't "embrace" her.

## May 25, 1994

Nothing is working for me. My tears leave him flat. His benevolent responses to my outbursts seem to accelerate my need to make him see me and understand me. This morning I heard music booming from the basement as I awoke and I knew my husband was resuming his morning exercise routine. I jumped out of bed, splashed some water on my face to freshen up and went down to join him.

My nightgown was not the best outfit to exercise in so while I was doing a few warm-up stretches I stripped it off, nonchalantly, trying to be seductive. I wanted to feel the freedom and I was hoping my husband would notice. He looked at me and said, "I pity you."

The music stopped in my head, a pall of rigidity and piercing cold instantly gripped my body. I almost crumbled to the floor, but instead I picked up my nightgown to cover myself. I didn't cry or scream. I just went upstairs and got dressed. Later, after he went to work, I cried hard. His words kept beating in my mind. They were words that had never been spoken to me by anyone before.

## May 26, 1994

After scouting his calendar at the office, I transferred his Albany trips to my calendar at home. I designated them as "G.A." -- Garrick Albany. Apparently, he's noticed them on my calendar for when I asked him what his plans were for today, he said, "You know I'm going to Albany. It's on your calendar."

Sometimes he takes his filing clerk on these all day excursions to Albany and sometimes he doesn't. I am never told one way or the other.

**May 31, 1994**

The filing clerk left her husband a few days ago. She's renting an apartment in Falls Town East, the next village over, about two miles away. She was going to move in with her sister in Albany so she'd be near her school, but rumor has it that she had a major blow up with her sister over the weekend. Now she says she'll stay in Falls Town East.

Several accountants have responded to my husband's ad. He's decided to go for someone with a degree in accounting, a local and preferably a male. The most promising candidate was approached the same way these things were done in the past. I was asked to read his resume, which I did, and commented on it. When the young man came for his interview last week, my husband brought him over to the greenhouse to meet me. It felt like the dust was settling on the filing clerk issue and that soon our lives would feel comfortable again.

Besides, we are both anxious to take off on a three-week vacation to California to see Jeffrey and Starr. Yesterday, my husband said, "I can't wait to get out of here." I suggested that we camp in his GMC Suburban on some of the travel nights at the parks in the west and he went along with the idea. He said, "Yeah, maybe a few nights, but not every night." He prefers hotels since he's not much of a camper. I'm envisioning romantic nights with campfires, beautiful scenery and cozy cuddling in the back of the big truck.

**June 1, 1994**

Today my husband told me that the filing clerk would have to stay on through June. This news makes my heart sink and my stomach twist. I detest feeling suspicious. It's an awful way to live. I dread what I will discover next or what will send my instincts reeling today. My husband gives me no reassurance or comfort. I've waited weeks for her last day on the job to arrive and she's still there. Meanwhile, my husband is annoyingly impervious and speaks to me in a condescending voice. I'm sure I can't go on this way.

To me, the red flags are everywhere and if this marriage is to survive, I must deal with them and with my husband.

**June 3, 1994**

Today when I asked my husband when her last day would be, he said near the end of this month. He also said that she will have to come back for a few days in July and he may have to talk to her from time to time about certain clients.

Is he keeping his options open? Is he somehow deciding between the two of us? Does he intend to keep fueling his relationship with her while he keeps me close enough to be his wife, but distant enough to carry on with her? He tosses me a "cookie" every now and then to keep me happy, like a warm hug or kiss, or he'll cooperate willingly with a plan -- even small things feel like a big piece of hope to me. Part of me can't help but wonder though -- Is he staying on the fence until he can solidify his position one way or the other?

**June 4, 1994**

My husband finally admitted to me that he finds his filing clerk attractive and enjoys working with her. He depicts her as very smart and hardworking. This is not easy to hear, but at least we finally had a fairly honest discussion and that gives me hope. I'm not crazy after all. My instincts are good. And we have a place to move forward from now.

**June 9, 1994**

We're traveling across the country stopping occasionally to visit family and friends. It should feel good but I feel a barrier. I don't trust him when he makes a phone call from a gas station. I feel his irritation if he's not in control and I tread carefully with what I say and when I say it. We're avoiding talk of his work or the filing clerk. He chooses our overnight stops. There is no sex.

**June 19, 1994**

Sleeping a couple nights in the GMC resulted in being crowded and stuffy since the windows of the truck were up. My husband was concerned about security. There was also very little said around the campfires. So much for that idea.

Now we're in California at an excellent motel near the ocean. I feel paranoid about the phone in our room. Will he try to call the office and talk to the filing clerk? We are both happy to see Jeffrey and Starr, but I feel the strain between us. I wonder if Jeffrey notices. I hope not.

**June 21, 1994**

Molly called our motel room yesterday morning. She was concerned about a phone call from the filing clerk inquiring about the sale of the Big House. Molly said the filing clerk told her that a Realtor planned to show it today. I went bonkers. What the hell! Behind my back, there is a plan to sell my house and the filing clerk has the information to handle it and I don't even know about it!

I blasted out of the motel room and took off down the beach with fierce footsteps. The waves crashing on the shore were mild compared to the fury within me. Suddenly I felt someone behind me. My husband had followed me, running to catch up and then walking my ferocious pace beside me.

He didn't have anything to say, but I exploded with accusations and foul language. He cringed at my display of anger, but we kept walking. We went in one direction for a couple of hours and then at his urging we turned around. Back at the motel, exhausted, we went to sleep. By this morning our kids were our focus again and we were OK.

**June 27, 1994**

The days of driving through the west to return home were spent in isolation. My husband planned a stop in Las Vegas and we saw Tom Jones perform. I read three books while we drove through constant reminders of American Indians -- billboards, Indian jewelry shops, reservations.

He asked, "What are you reading?" But I don't feel he really cared. He said, "What you say about her gets under my skin."

I am trying to say nothing.

**June 28, 1994**

Our friends are asking, "How was your trip?" I say, "Great. We had a good time with our kids and we really saw the country." I've noticed my husband does not attempt to conceal his lack of enthusiasm for this vacation.

**June 29, 1994**

Granted, we had talked before about selling the Big House. We have too much property and need to sell something. And yet, it was a surprise when a Realtor stopped by my greenhouse a few weeks ago and asked, "How much do you want for the Big House?" Put on the spot with one of my friends present, I asked, "What do you suggest?" The Realtor threw out a ridiculously high price and I said, "OK," knowing it would never sell for that amount.

The Realtor assumed I knew what was going on and would have never thought my husband would be handling the sale on his own. When I asked my husband about the Realtor's visit, he didn't say anything. I was out of the loop on purpose again.

That was all I knew until Molly's call when we were in California, from which I realized that the filing clerk knew all about selling the Big House and I still didn't know anything. During our long walk on the beach, my husband said that the filing clerk didn't know anything about it. I snapped back, "I say she does."

Today I saw real estate information about the Big House on the filing clerk's desk.

## June 30, 1994

This is supposed to be her last day on the job, and yet her things are still in her office and on her desk and there are no signs at all that she's left.

I'm not at my best with all this back and forth stuff coming from my husband. I'm being jerked around. And in the height of this frustration and fear over my husband's uncommon actions, my behavior is desperate and irrational. It's been building over months now and I feel it cresting inside of me. Never in my 38-year marriage have I seen him act this way and my reactions are sometimes violent and unrelenting -- hysterical crying, uncontrollable angst, diarrhea, upset stomach, depression. My self-confidence and self-esteem are shot. I'm sad and frightened. My feelings are acted out in coarse talk, fast driving, convulsive physical behavior and screaming.

**July 1, 1994**

It's the beginning of a new month. Looking back over the past months in this journal, I realize my suspicions and concerns would be irrational if my husband had always behaved the way he is now, if he had treated other employees in similar ways. But he hasn't. He's never behaved this way to any of his other employees.

Suddenly and totally, I am thrown out of the rhythm of our former relationship. I think I'm in shock. I'm always adjusting to his new reasons, his new actions, this new way that he is. I'm constantly adapting to keep my sanity. I'm definitely confused. All I know to do is to keep trying to communicate with him and keep writing. It's like hanging on.

**July 4, 1994**

Over the weekend, my husband finally verbalized some of his feelings and I was able to speak to him about mine. He said he was confused about his emotions. I thought, good, if he can just open up, then we can deal with the problems and work to solve them. It felt like a breakthrough. Several days have passed with a positive feeling for me.

**July 7, 1994**

He told me he was going to a seminar in Albany as he left the house this morning. He gave no indication of the time of his return, as had been his habit in the past. So, it's now 6:15 p.m. and I feel squeamish and unsure.

At 6:16 p.m., just as I was writing, he called from the Big House. He's in a good mood. He explained his day and that he left Albany in a torrential rainstorm. His explanation makes me feel better.

For years, I was the most informed wife, now I'm lost. It's scary to be so suspicious. I wish a magic wand could bring me the serenity of former days. At least I feel better after his call.

**July 9, 1994**

A friend told me that a mutual friend had run into my husband at the post office. Our friend had congratulated him on becoming a grandfather soon and she exclaimed how wonderful it is to be a grandparent and how much she enjoys <u>her</u> grandchildren. When she asked him if he was excited and looking forward to becoming a "granddaddy," he apparently really put her off and responded in a gruff and negative way to her question and enthusiasm.

**July 10, 1994**

Something else I have to deal with now is my husband's mood. If I don't hear what he's saying, he's irritable; if he doesn't hear what I'm saying, then I'm not talking clearly.

We played tennis with Molly and her fiancé, John, and my husband threw his racquet and stormed about missing shots a number of times. His behavior made everyone else uncomfortable. Later, I talked him into going skinny-dipping at a friend's pool. He insisted that I bring his bathing suit, but when he actually got there, he did skinny-dip, but he stayed far away from me. I feel our natural personal space has developed into a large unfamiliar circle. I carefully do not enter his space and he stays a cool distance from me.

**July 11, 1994**

The filing clerk has <u>finally</u> removed her things from the office. My husband attributes his frustrations to the amount of work he has. The move into the new office in the old farmhouse has begun gradually. There is no joy in it. My orders are to stay out of the office unless asked. Without sex and without romance and very little conversation, I feel discarded. Should I understand that it's been uncomfortably hot and that the pressures of work and moving into the new office explain irritability and distance?

**July 12, 1994**

I believe he lied to me about the sudden appearance of his travel toilet kit in his car. It was bouncing around the floor at my feet in the passenger seat this morning. I reached under and pulled it out. He explained that he uses it to freshen up before meetings after a long day. I don't believe it. Again, he's never done this before. It makes me shake with anxiety.

**July 13, 1994**

The telephone company called me early this afternoon to report that it was possible someone had stolen our telephone credit card. They said many calls were being placed from Albany to a number with our local prefix, but not our home or office number. I knew my husband was in Albany today and I told the telephone company I would check it out.

First, I called the number they reported to be receiving the excessive calls -- I thought it was hers and indeed it was. I then called my husband at his seminar in Albany, got him out of his meeting and asked him about the calls. He said he had called her for help to remove paper stuck in the office fax machine.

So I drove to the office to ask Brett, his nice new employee, if the paper had been a problem in the fax machine. He said, "No, not really. It got stuck once this morning, but it's no big deal. There's nothing to it. I fixed it myself."

**July 14, 1994**

For a few days, I've noticed the absence of our "important papers" box, a small portable file box that we use for tax papers, information on our stocks, our properties, etc. It was removed from the office closet and I've looked everywhere for it. In the past, the key was kept in the lock on the box, but I had noticed recently that it was locked without the key being left in the lock. Then the whole file box disappeared. I haven't asked because I'm afraid it will be taken as snooping, which it is, but my suspicions are that either his former filing clerk has it or it's hidden. I don't understand why it would be hidden, but I'm concocting a theory that she has been given a project to do at her home and it's our taxes. If I'm right about this, I'll be angry. If I'm wrong, I'll hate myself for being so suspicious. But, it is odd.

**July 15, 1994**

The locked file box is in the attic, so I'm wrong. But I still don't know why it was moved, where the key is or what's in our box these days.

The move to the new office is complete and it went smoothly. I'm relieved she's not around. It seems there's a little less tension between my husband and me.

**July 18, 1994**

For some reason when we woke up this morning, he got an erection. It was the best for us in a very long time. It came short of a climax for him, but it was very close and I felt great emotional satisfaction. I don't know how he felt, he didn't say.

He asked me to make some suggestions at the new office and I helped make some organizational changes, too. It's a more functional space now. There are still some details and the last little dregs to sort out. I cleaned out her desk in the old office and that was a "stomach-in-knots" time. She left the drawers in a mess.

**July 21, 1994**

Today her car is parked next to his at the new office and it makes me queasy. I am keeping an eye towards the new office while trying to do some of my B&B work at the Big House nearby. My husband had told me that he and Brett were going to meet with her to learn about her so-called "clients" from the business. I asked him to leave early and not be around for the "hanging out" talk afterwards, but he refused, saying it was important for him to be there and he needed to review the work. It feels like the evil monster is flaunted in my face. I've vowed to try to stop referring to her as "bitch" or "fucking whore" to myself, but when I look at her car over there my heart pounds. My instincts screech, "fucking-Indian-whore-bitch." My fear and anger are at record levels of intensity.

Today is supposed to be the last time she comes to the office. What will I do if she ever comes again? What excuse could allow her to invade my space again? He said she would be gone by 4:30 p.m., or at the latest, 5:00; it's 4:25 and I'm waiting to see when she goes.

As I'm waiting, I'm wondering what happened to cause his erection the other morning, pretty much sustained, but just short of climax. Then he retreated to a cool distance with no pillow talk and also no comments about the success or failure of something that has been and continues to be a problem between us. The strange fact is now that I know he can do it, I realize it is truly a matter of mental or psychological interest, not just part of his aging or a side effect of his prostate medicine. So, that brings me back to me -- am I old, fat, repulsive? And is she young, pretty, exciting, and now, available? He and she so perfectly fit into the "mid-life crisis" syndrome; he is aging and freaked out about it, she is the new model cozying up to him. I fit the discarded older woman scenario. It doesn't matter that I've been faithful, loved him, and been the woman behind the successful man all these years.

Life isn't fair. I can't dream about my many good years because they have been shattered like a delicate goblet thrown against a stone wall. The past is gone and I have just this moment and today. Instead of making this moment good, I'm torturing myself by looking out the window at her car parked next his, knowing that they are inside the office, laughing, talking and cooing. She's gazing deep into his eyes, he's responding with admiration and possibly lust for her.

It's 4:45 and she hasn't left. The thought crosses my mind that she might ask for her job back and my husband and Brett might say, "Gee, that would be nice." If that became a reality, my feelings are already in place. I want to break every dish in the house, smash every one into the fireplace and scream until I can't. I want to explode. This is how I feel with no basis. Just a passing thought. A scenario that is likely not true and not even in anyone's head but mine.

**Later --**

At 5:05 p.m., he finally came over to the Big House. I was visibly shaken and I asked for this to be the last time she would ever come to the office. He hedged on the commitment and said it "probably" would be. At 6 p.m., she left the office.

At home this evening, we changed the topic of conversation and life went on.

## July 23, 1994

I saw the business checkbook yesterday and there was nothing unusual in it. I believe I am wrong about her doing our taxes and about any money being diverted to her. I don't think I'm wrong about his admiration for her, but I think I'm wrong about an intimate relationship behind my back.

The move into the new office is a big help and it seems to be working. It's nice to know she's not there and the new location has already attracted more business. My trauma from the day before yesterday has diminished. I overreacted. I still detest her in a violent way -- stomach cramps, pounding head, wild anguish.

I'd like to have good sex, but I don't see it happening.

## July 24, 1994

One of my husband's former employee's wedding and party were fun. We probably appeared to be having a good time, but I never felt we were really "together." I didn't receive the special, loving hug or feel his awareness of me being there with him. Even our dancing was estranged and felt bizarre to me.

It hurts because dancing with my husband has always been magical. I remember so clearly the Lion's Club Christmas dance, just a year and a half ago, our dancing was intimate and close and sensual. We moved in step, connected harmoniously to ourselves and to each other. It was beautiful.

When we danced at the wedding it was uncomfortable. He was tossing me around, spinning me out wildly and I was trying to hold on. He didn't want me to hold on or to be connected. He didn't hold me closely or intimately. The contrast in our dancing between these two events is striking and painful to me.

I did feel the atmosphere of new love from the bride and groom and much happiness from the families and friends, so the occasion was joyous. Maybe my romantic expectations are too high. Maybe we're both too old. Maybe I'll never have that "cherished" feeling again.

As soon as we got home, he was tired. I did the laundry and picked up around the house. I figure he'll be sleeping when I go to bed and when I wake up tomorrow, he'll be sleeping. And during the day, we'll be busy and then he'll be sleepy again. Is that "old?"

**July 27, 1994**

He had a routine appointment with his urologist. I thought he'd ask about his problem with erections and maintaining them, but he said he didn't. That makes me wonder. I think things like -- he already knows, so why would he ask his doctor; or he's embarrassed and doesn't want the doctor to know; or he doesn't know and doesn't care.

**July 28, 1994**

Since I had to pick flowers at 6 a.m. for the concert tonight, he got up early and went to The Hub for breakfast. It felt like he was using the opportunity to "get away." He brought a video movie home for the evening "get away."

On the plus side, I'm feeling fairly OK, with her gone from the office. She's pretty much out of sight and out of mind. I do hear the scuttlebutt about her -- mainly negative. There's talk about how she never cleaned or cooked for her husband and probably wasn't much in bed either. Her husband is having overnight girlfriends. A few refer to her as that "crazy Indian." Since she's trying to rent a house in town, it's possible she'll be around and I dread that.

I just re-read my writing and got really queasy and had diarrhea. I am looking forward to going to the Falls Town Flowers concert tonight with my husband and I hope the nostalgic, sweet songs will help bring us closer.

## July 29, 1994

The concert was a good success, but my hope to connect with my husband through the romantic songs didn't happen. He stayed glued to the music and then socialized separately. When I got home after cleaning up, he wasn't sleeping, but he had no interest in intimacy, so we went to sleep.

This morning I got up, brushed my teeth, came back to bed and commented that I was hoping I'd "get lucky." So he tried but no luck. I felt lonely and fat. But it's a busy day -- cleaning the house, preparing for guests, driving to the train station.

## August 6, 1994 -- morning

We went out to dinner last night with two couples, our neighbors, and today I'm still trying to understand why my husband acted so belligerent and ugly in front of everyone. He came home in the afternoon with news that he'd been asked to chair the next Chamber of Commerce meeting and was also approached for the presidency. Both ideas were great ego-builders and his spirits were raised considerably.

The evening with our friends was going well until we were on our way home. He had been drinking pretty aggressively during dinner, and while we were driving back in our friend's car, he announced his role in Columbia County development and he became domineering, loud, opinionated and very unpleasant. He was argumentative and did not allow for a fair exchange of ideas with the others present in the car. I poked him several times to help him realize he was out of line, but he pursued his loud, one-sided tirade on the needs of the county. Then he scolded me out loud, "Stop poking me!"

He launched into the availability of health care, adamantly insisting good health care was within 20 minutes in three directions. He shut out everyone else's comments, especially one of our neighbors who is a doctor. I thought he was drunk. I was very uncomfortable in a situation I couldn't escape. I tried to validate the others' comments, but to no avail. When we got home, I told him I thought he had been loud and rude and he got angry, so I just said OK and went to bed.

I'm wondering if this was intended to do what it did to me – push me away, give me another emotion to overcome? I can't cozy up to him if I've just been embarrassed and treated as if I'm not worth decent behavior from him. The problems here are impossible for me to understand -- is it me? is it him? It will be hard to erase the events of last night.

**August 6, 1994 -- late evening**

Although his timing was bizarre, I signed the income tax forms he presented to me tonight at a clearly awkward time -- I was doing dishes and dinner guests were present. He brought them to the sink and demanded a quick signature from me. It was another blow to my trust. Can I believe what he says, what he does or how he loves?

We file taxes jointly, the extended late form. I stayed up late tonight to write and to review our copy to see exactly how much money was coming in and going out. I guess I don't understand exactly what our taxes mean for us financially, but I've already signed them. For the first time, it smacks of coercion.

It appears that his business is being subsidized by money that is considered "ours," like our jointly held bonds, etc. Even though he's told me that he pays all the bills out of his business, the truth seems to be that he paid her, bought a lot of equipment and poured money into his business -- mostly paid for from our joint funds through his business account. It comes off looking as though his business made nothing but the exodus from our joint funds seems to be about $300,000.

Now that I've checked out our taxes from last year, I'm wondering about my part of this year's finances. Running the Big House B&B is a good write off and it has much more potential for profit, but it's not the kind of work he likes or is interested in. Furthermore, her presence in the Big House when it was his office has made me grow to hate the house so I'm happy to sell it. I don't think it will sell easily though, so I'll keep the B&B going for now.

Also, I earned charitable contributions for the Roe Jan Choir, the Methodist Church and Falls Town Flowers this summer by selling plants and flowers I grew in the greenhouse. I handed the $900 in cash that I earned to my husband and he wrote checks to each of the groups for the amount they were due. I wonder if he'll take the $900 next year as a charitable deduction write off.

I'm remembering, too, how he complained about the money I spent this spring on the renovation of the farmhouse to become his new office. Every single item that was done was demanded by him or cleared through him. But I was questioned on every expenditure.

He now calls all the shots. He spends as he wishes, I spend with his permission. We go where he wants, walk if he wants, play tennis if he wants and watch the video that he chooses. If he snaps or grumbles, I smooth the situation. This doesn't sound like a very good relationship, not to mention the absence of any sex life.

I'm an emotional yo-yo, jerked around first by his fear of turning 60, then devastated by his amorous behavior with his filing clerk and finally a loss of confidence in my own place in our relationship.

I believe I've been treated dishonestly with his relationship with her, dishonestly with our finances and dishonestly emotionally. I'm angry and I don't want to take it anymore.

**August 8, 1994 -- early morning**

I'm lying awake at 3 a.m. thinking, "What kind of living hell am I in?" I'm unable to express myself to him because he's unwilling to hear me. I'm talking a blue streak and he's shutting me out more and more. I held my tongue yesterday in conversation with Molly and I've been trying not to make more of an issue of things I've already said.

Last night, after I told him about a chat I had with Michelle, he said, "Let's take a day and go up to Vermont to see her." Surprised, I said, "After we do the canoe trip?"

As is often their way, our kids gave us a romantic excursion as a gift for our anniversary this spring; a canoeing and B&B trip scheduled for mid-August. But my husband said he didn't think he could do it because, according to him, there was no time in his life before the end of August (which is bullshit, but nevertheless). I suggested that I could call and try to change the date, but he didn't want me to. It seemed to be a problem with his control of what we do and when we do it. So, now the canoe trip is a difficulty and so is finding time to visit Michelle, and he leaves me with the impression that it's my fault, I'm the uncooperative one.

It's sad for me to think that our relationship, which was friendship and trust, has become control and deceit.

My instincts have been sending up red flags that I haven't ignored. I keep bringing them up. I'm not sure if I've been a very slow learner or whether I'm timely in picking up on the change from respectful and truthful to bully and manipulative.

In the past, in the days that I received respect, there were others that were treated shabbily by him -- toll collectors, elevator operators, cab drivers, sales people, waitresses, etc. I always spoke up for the rights of those people to be treated decently. Now I'm speaking on my own behalf.

**Later --**

Before he left for work this morning, he asked me why I was not receptive when he wanted to have sex in the middle of the night last night. I explained that when I'm not receiving any closeness, companionship or romance from him during <u>any</u> of the rest of our time together, and when I feel his expectations for sex have nothing to do with "making love" with <u>me</u>, it's a lot to mentally overcome so we can just "do it" in the middle of the night. He doesn't seem to get it. Now, he thinks he's damned if he does and damned if he doesn't.

**August 8, 1994 -- late evening**

Because he won't talk to me about us anymore, I sometimes do what I tried in the past and leave my handwritten journal notes out on the table so he'll read them. It's the only way I can fully communicate my feelings to him at this time. I know he read my notes from a few days ago (about the argument after dinner with the neighbors) because the pages had been moved from where I'd left them. He may have read them this afternoon. He said nothing, but his behavior with me has improved slightly. He has been kind and pleasant and loving. It seems like an unspoken apology.

I haven't seen the former filing clerk around lately and I have no reason to believe she's in touch with the office so that's a relief. I seem to be better informed about activities at the office and Brett seems to be getting along fine. The whole environment is more comfortable.

However, my trust level is low so I'm always looking for foul play. I hate that because I used to trust him completely. Now, it's a feeling of guilt if I snoop and a confirmation of distrust when I discover he's not been totally honest.

However, I don't cry these days, I don't scream and I don't break things. In fact, I haven't smashed anything into the fireplace in weeks. That's an improvement.

# DISCOVERY

I knew my husband would be away from his office this afternoon; he had a meeting with the Chamber of Commerce. I had dog obedience class with Spooky tonight so I decided to stop by the office on my way there just after 5 p.m. when I knew Brett would also be gone. It was a perfect opportunity to search for the key to a locked file cabinet that's in his office. As long as I've known him, he has never locked the file cabinets in his office. However, I had noticed, just recently, that the one next to his desk was locked. In fact, I don't think he had this file cabinet before he moved into the new office. That locked file cabinet has burned in my mind.

I left Spooky in the car and entered the office as nonchalantly as I could since I was in clear view of anyone passing by. I was also aware that anyone might stop in if they noticed my car parked out front. I was on a mission and I steeled myself to be direct and swift in my purpose.

I quickly checked the desk drawers, behind the computer, behind the file cabinet, along the windowsills and a lot of other places before I haphazardly ran my fingers along the top molding of a floor-to-ceiling, built-in bookcase in the reception room and felt a key on the corner edge! I froze. It was a complete stroke of luck! I knew immediately it was the key and it was, without a doubt, a deliberately hidden key.

I don't think I breathed as I went up the steep stairs to the file cabinet. Trembling with apprehension, I put the key in the lock. It fit perfectly. It was tricky to hold the latch and maneuver the key, but it clicked and turned. I paused for a moment hoping I was wrong about my suspicions and about his secrets. Then I slid open the top drawer. I reeled with a boiling panic as I peered in. I discovered the awful truth -- I am right. My suspicions became documented facts.

Suddenly, I felt the burden of everything on me. I tuned in sharply to my entire surroundings, every sight, every sound. I was under a time pressure and felt crushed. I felt real terror. It felt life threatening. I felt totally by myself in the world, all alone.

In the file cabinet, I found an oil painting, a portrait of an American Indian, purchased for $400 at an auction. I found several books about divorce. I found the filing clerk's address in her hometown in upstate New York. I found notes my husband had made to himself about negative aspects of our marriage and the potential of a relationship with "NC," the filing clerk's initials. There was also a slip of paper that seemed to be a reminder for an appointment he'd made with a marriage counselor and it seemed to be her marriage counselor. There was also a bank statement page of almost daily $200 cash withdrawals from an account through an ATM. Where is that money going and who's getting it? Why would he lock all of these things in a file cabinet and hide the key? It's obvious he wanted to hide them from me. It's utterly deceitful. I found all of the things he's never told me and that he's kept locked away.

It was as though I had found toxic waste. It was oozing in my hands, burning, and I had to save myself and everything around me with no experience or knowledge of how to do so. I willed myself to absorb what I was confronted with and think clearly. The time had flown by, I had to go. I had only gotten a quick glimpse, I needed more time to sort through it all. I decided the safest thing to do was to put the stuff back, shut the drawer, lock it and leave. The cabinet was hard to lock again and that scared me, but I finally got it after a little jimmying. I replaced the key in its hiding place and scooted out the door. Spooky and I went to obedience class and came home.

Now, several hours later, I'm still shaking with my discovery as I write this; of how right I was and how very scared I am. My pulse rate surges. I don't know if I should confront him now or wait until I can document more stuff. My worst fears are true. He has lied to me and I'm not sure he hasn't already had an affair with her. He was surely taken with her in many ways and, even now, with her no longer at the office, I doubt it's over between them. I'm really terrified. My mind is a blur, I feel sick and aching all over. I love him. What should I do?

**August 10, 1994 -- early afternoon**

I cried a lot last night and he held me. I said I loved him, he did not say the same. We didn't have sex but he held me in a very warm way. I guess he's used to my crying because he didn't ask me anything. So, I didn't speak, I just wept.

This morning we chatted, there were some warm kisses and then I played tennis. I am emotionally shot. However, I did formulate a plan: I will photocopy some of the information I found in the locked file. My thinking is if I need it for documentation later, I'll have it. Maybe I'll decide to confront him with the situation and see what happens. On the one hand, I think honesty is the best way to go, but I'm afraid it will make matters worse. I'll wait until I see more of what exactly is in the file. Maybe I'll wait to see if he becomes honest with me. I don't know. My stomach is in knots.

The cleaning girl asked recently if someone had slept in the B&B at the Big House because a bed was used during the week when there aren't guests. I wondered then, and especially now, if it was him.

Another thought: On our anniversary in May, he gave me those cheap flower earrings. This compares to a car, a cruise and other pretty substantial anniversary gifts in the past. Yet, I find hidden for the filing clerk a $400 Indian painting. This follows the $400 antique photograph gift at Christmas and all of his other unusual generosity to her as an employee. And what about those daily $200 cash withdrawals from an account accessed by an ATM? This problem is so big I don't know how it will go away. I am devastated.

I saw the signs, I spoke up, I cried, I offered to listen. I have felt suicidal and murderous. I've felt angry and wronged. I also feel I've made my life a failure. I know that some fault belongs to me. I feel like I've ruined my life as I approach 60. Only eight years ago, I wrote how satisfied I was with my marriage -- how good it was to have sex with my husband and how I've never loved him more. Today, everything has changed. He doesn't love me, we have no sex, I'm fearful and totally without confidence. I talk stupidly because I don't know what to say. I'm trying to make a rational plan but I don't know what to do. I'm thinking of calling Molly or Michelle for advice, but I hate to drag them into this and cause them pain. I want to call Jeffrey and tell him, too, but I can't. He doesn't need this extra stress. So for now, I'm going it alone.

**August 10, 1994 -- late evening**

I went back this afternoon to the locked file cabinet. I knew my husband would be away again and Brett was gone. I worked with the efficiency and smoothness of a well-paid spy on a dangerous assignment. I only needed a few minutes to search more thoroughly through the file cabinet and photocopy his pages of notes, the bank statement and the other bits of paper that seemed important. I made my own notes, too, of the book titles and other details about the stuff in the drawer. The titles of the books in the cabinet are "The Art of Staying Together," "Women Men Love -- Women Men Leave," and "Crazy Time Surviving Divorce."

I put all the stuff back, but at the last moment before closing the drawer I pulled out the Indian painting and decided to take it with me. I locked the file cabinet and carefully placed the key back in its hiding place.

I returned home with the photocopies and the oil painting. I chose to hide my photocopied evidence in my kitchen cabinet where I keep maps, wedding invitations, business cards and brochures.

I held the painting with my left hand and grabbed my kitchen scissors with my right hand. I stood near the dining room table and tightly gripped the long cold scissors just below the finger holes. The scissors were slightly opened. I stopped for a moment because I found it hard at first -- not to destroy the canvas, but to destroy an artwork. But once I plunged the scissors through it and began gauging, it felt good.

Soon the canvas was pretty much in shreds and while I caught my breath and looked at what I'd done, I noticed that the frame was OK and since I knew it was old I thought it might be valuable. I decided to keep it thinking I might use it at a later time. I separated the frame from the canvas and stuck it in my wrapping paper drawer.

When my husband came home I held up the tattered canvas and said, "I found this in your office." He actually sobbed, but through his tears he said, "That was my gift to my friend." Then I said, "I saw those books about divorce in your office, too. Can I read them?" He said, "Go ahead." I did not mention my other evidence.

Pain has gripped me like an iron clamp that all of my crying does not ease. I am weak and nauseated. I wrote on my calendar, in capital letters, BAD DAY. What an understatement.

**August 11, 1994 -- morning**

Now that I've had a chance to study the photocopied stuff from the file cabinet, my whole body aches and convulses with what is really the sharpest stab of pain -- discovery of my husband's clear intention to divorce me and his long-term deception; all of his lies.

Remarkably, most his handwritten notes to himself that I found in the cabinet are dated "August 8, 1994" -- one day before my discovery! It's as if they emitted some radioactive signal and led me to the file cabinet like a Geiger counter. It's bizarre. He must have written them on Monday, put them in the file cabinet and locked it -- perhaps being particularly careful since he knew he would be away from his office some on Tuesday and Wednesday. Maybe he put the key on the top of the bookshelf on his way out the door.

It seems some of his notes are about him and some are referring to me. They are all about us. Some bits and pieces of notes say:

- ran its course

- no longer trust

- no more second guessing. I always seem wrong. Others are OK or right.

- Our interests are totally opposite

- We are not a team

- Not leaving for someone else, would consider splitting regardless. Subsequently would look into sharing life with another.

- TIMING

- She is a saint, difficult to be married to a saint

- not much in common

- no passion in relationship

- have no desire to tell her my feelings

- do not want to grow old with her

- Indifferent, I'm just going through the motions

- NC unwilling to give up other

- love as my children, not as wife/lover

- respect her highly

Another note says:

- Some risk -- better than to die and wonder what if I had done...

# DISBELIEF

I drove in the direction of Sheffield, Massachusetts, today, in the hope of finding the marriage counselor my husband had listed in his secret notes. I had a name, a telephone prefix and a boggled head. I eased along with a Ouija board mentality, believing I'd be pulled toward a professional-type building or a house with a plaque with the name on it. I thought I'd walk in, introduce myself and ask for help.

I wondered if a police officer might pull me over for confused driving. I was as lost as any person could be -- driving in a desperate search for help in an unknown place in an emotional wilderness. What road? What building? What am I doing here? I decided to stop at a little deli and ask to look in their Yellow Pages under "Marriage Counseling." A place called The Option Institute was listed with a Sheffield phone number and I remembered a sign for it near an intersection a short distance before, so I went back and followed that road.

Just before I gave up hope, there was another little sign, a gorgeous driveway and a mansion on a hill. I turned in and read the message at the bottom of the sign; "Miracles Can Happen." It seemed a higher power was guiding me. I parked and walked up the beautiful hill to the mansion.

"It looks like you could use a hug," said Willow, when she looked up from her desk and saw my face. She called Richard from his office and he immediately came to talk with me. I blurted out, "My husband wants to divorce me."

We took a walk and I talked and cried. At one point Richard said, "Why is it bad that your husband wants to divorce you?" I said, "What if I lose the keys to my car? Who would help me?"

In our 50-minute "session," I gained enough strength to start to deal with the shattering news that I had unlocked and I became clear about my desire to save my marriage. I drove home feeling grateful.

For a little while, later on today, I actually thought maybe I'm grateful to the filing clerk for bringing this problem to a head. If there's time to resolve it, I will really be happy, and if there's not, at least I'm moving in a direction to help myself.

**August 12, 1994**

Today I made a decision: I'm not going to look again for lies and cover-ups. It only hurts me and nothing productive can come from it anymore. I've uncovered all I need to know and that information has given me the power to look at myself, help myself and be sane. I've made an appointment to talk with the dialogue counselor again and I have hope. My daughters also have hope. I told them that I'd received good help from The Option Institute and that I was encouraging their Dad to go, too.

I said to my husband, "Something good happened to me yesterday. I found a place in Sheffield to get counseling help and I plan to go back. I think you would like it, too."

He said, "How much is it?"

"It doesn't matter if it helps," I said. "Besides it's very reasonable."

I also told him that I was going to try to stop referring to his former filing clerk in any way whatsoever. I told him I was going to look on the bright side and be non-judgmental.

Since all this stress began, I've often deteriorated into what I don't want to be -- foul-mouthed, explosive, always crying and desperate. It felt good to talk to my husband in a clear, strong and positive way.

## August 13, 1994

Molly came over today and I told her all about the file cabinet and what I'd found. I told her I had stashed my photocopied information in my kitchen cabinet. She calmly accepted the news and clicked right into her strong sense of logic. She suggested that the photocopies would be safer if she locked them in the trunk of her car until I could resolve the problem. She didn't want to read the papers and said she wouldn't.

I think she thought my husband would go into orbit if he found the papers or knew that I had them. I think she felt that it wouldn't help anything for him to know about them and she wanted us to have a chance to work out our difficulties without him going bonkers over this stuff.

Shirley arrived for our tennis game this morning. I wasn't sure I could play but I walked onto the court and immediately said to her, "I have a problem." I started to cry and said, "It's my marriage." She hugged me with compassion and said, "If there's anything I can do... I'm sorry. I'll pray for you." We played an easy game. She's my first friend to know.

I've decided to share what I'm going through with the people I like and trust. I know the gossip will start soon and in a way it already has since people are asking things like, "Who pays her rent?" in reference to the filing clerk.

I feel pretty good. My husband held me again last night and when I feel his energy go into my body, I know it's good; and when it doesn't, I know there's a difference.

I'm on a more level playing field yesterday and today, like I've got a life. And with a life of my own, I can be me. I'm so grateful for The Option Institute.

## August 15, 1994

It was an OK weekend. I fluctuated from feeling happy to feeling sad. We played tennis on Saturday, and since it was rainy on Sunday, my husband offered to play a game of Scrabble with me. He played his best and won. I have shared my problem with my kids, my sister, several friends and my neighbors. Molly came over Sunday evening. She has been a rock of support. She's been absolutely wonderful.

I am held and kissed and I feel loved, but I know that until my husband tells me that he loves me, it won't be the same for him or me. I have come to believe, in these last few days, that what I want is my marriage, my lover and my best friend. If I can't have that, then I want my marriage and my best friend. And if I can't have that, then I want my best friend.

Last night, as we lay next to each other in bed, I told my husband everything that I talked about at The Option Institute. He was curious and somewhat suspicious about the type of counseling I'd found, but my excitement about the place intrigued him enough to listen. I tried to explain all of my feelings and how I was willing to strip away layers of old beliefs and look at choosing happiness.

He said, rather benevolently, "Well, you know, I'll always be your friend."

It wasn't what I wanted to hear, but it is today's reality. It makes me sad, but it still gives me hope. After all, almost 40 years ago, we started out as friends and became lovers.

## August 18, 1994

I've been thinking about our beginnings, so yesterday I went to the attic and got out the old photos taken at the time of our marriage and the love letters from our days when my husband was stationed in Germany. I thought I'd cry, but I laughed. While reading those letters of 38 years ago I thought, "I'm still married to the same guy."

Later, I showed the letters to my husband and he read them and he laughed too, but his laughter didn't feel so good. It felt as if his recollections of those early feelings were that they were part of a humorous history; as if the things expressed in the letters were ridiculous. He said, "That was then, this is now." I thought, "Maybe I'm not married to the same guy."

This morning my husband kissed me good-bye with the most intensity and passion I've felt in two years. Over breakfast I'd said, "I'm not allowing myself to be controlled anymore. I know what I want and I plan to do what it takes to change what has happened to me. I signed up for a weekend called 'Happiness is a Choice' at the Option Institute and I want you to go with me." He said, "I'll think about it."

My new support system of my kids and friends has grown and I feel the power. Today, I feel attractive and strong.

**August 22, 1994**

My emotions go up and down. I cried at a neighbor's wedding reception on Saturday and had to exit quickly. I was overcome with envy for them and sadness for me. Later on, after we were home, we felt good together. It's a yo-yo.

**August 29, 1994**

We've had sex and a few attempts. It's felt hopeful, but not complete. It's missing passion. I feel like it's a test -- it's up to me to deliver the goods. I better come through or else. Of course, it doesn't work that way, and it's not.

**August 31, 1994**

A second session today at The Option Institute helped me discover and articulate my need to have it all -- trust, love and good sex. After my one and a half hours with the counselor, I decided I would try to be stronger about my "wants."

I came home feeling powerful and boldly said, "I need to know more about our finances. I want access to all our accounts and I'd like to plan a time to discuss them with you." He was clearly uncomfortable with my request. He didn't refuse, but he wouldn't participate in the discussion I was trying to have with him and he wouldn't set up a time to talk about our finances together.

I feel shaky again. I called The Option Institute this afternoon to schedule another session.

**September 1, 1994**

I realize I have no idea what's going on with our finances. I'm not informed, I'm not calling any of the shots, I'm totally in the dark. And I don't feel I can trust my husband.

When I asked for full knowledge of our financial affairs yesterday, my husband said, "You can always look at the Merrill Lynch mailings." I said, "I mean all the accounts," for there are several other accounts other than the Merrill Lynch ones. He said, "Sure, whatever." I don't know where to find everything but I know it's all sequestered at the Big House, so I've decided to go and look around.

**September 1, 1994 -- late evening**

I went to the Big House and found our Merrill Lynch statements. They were mixed in with our personal bank mail, which was thrown, unopened, in a large pile on a shelf in a cabinet in his old reception office. I felt like a criminal opening months and months of my <u>own</u> financial records. I'm not accustomed to reading him or zeroing in on the bottom line, but I did find something unusual in the August 1994 statement. There were two Visa charges from New York City on August 3, 1994 -- a store in Trump Tower of almost $350 and a "Sea Grill" restaurant of almost $100. I felt cheated on and lied to again. It was the day he had gone to NYC for his ear doctor appointment. I was led to believe he had gone alone.

I also found three checks each in the amount of $5,000 written over this past summer which transferred money from our savings account into his CPA account. I wondered if it was some type of "loan" he had given to his business or to his filing clerk.

We were in bed earlier tonight when I said, "I want to know the details of the 'loan' you gave her. I want to know exactly where our money is."

Then I also confronted my husband about the Visa charges in New York City. He admitted he had taken her to the city, bought her clothes for school and a fancy lunch. This new knowledge sent me into a rage. It was more than I could handle. I reached for the phone and said, "I'm calling her now. She must return the clothes to me." He grabbed the phone away and jerked it out of the wall outlet. I went downstairs to the kitchen phone and dialed her number. I noticed on the kitchen clock that it was 9 p.m. She answered in her syrupy voice and I let her have it. "I know you went to New York City with my husband and he bought you clothes with <u>our</u> money! I want the clothes returned! You must also return the money he lent you!" And I hung up.

## September 2, 1994

My husband called her this morning to apologize and make amends -- or so he said, I didn't hear it.

77

According to him, she said she was sorry she went to the City with him and she would return the money as soon as she got her "Indian" grant. I told my husband I wanted the money given to our kids and the clothes burned.

Later, actually at noon, when I came home for lunch, the clothes from the Trump Tower shop were cut up and thrown on the porch floor. I knew right away that the clothes sprawled there were the Trump store purchases; leggings and a jacket -- brand new and cut up into ribbons, a pile of destruction. I felt the anger behind the action of his destroying this gift to her because I had demanded it. It looked like he came home with the shreds of clothing, opened the porch door and tossed them in.

I took the pile of cut up clothes to the burn barrel and burned them, wondering as I watched the flames if the price of this outfit could account for the entire $350 he spent in the Trump Tower store.

**September 3, 1994**

We are on the waiting list for the weekend session at The Option Institute. I explained to the folks at OI that I didn't know if my husband would do it or not. They're being extremely accommodating.

It feels like our last chance of getting ourselves together. I encouraged my husband to join me in choosing happiness through this program of self-help, but he really seems to be vacillating about his feelings for me.

I'm fluctuating between optimistic and scared. We played tennis with Molly and John. My husband is reading "Happiness Is A Choice," a publication from the Option Institute that I'd purchased and asked him to look over. He went to his office to read so he could be alone.

We are living in a nightmare with periods of what looks normal.

## September 4, 1994

It was a gorgeous day and my husband suggested we walk the dogs on our land near the office. I added a plan of my own and packed a picnic and blanket with the idea of sex in our secluded field. Once we got there, I took off all my clothes and stretched out on the blanket in the sunshine. He was reluctant at first but he gave in to the idea and was able to have good sex under the blue sky. The two dogs watched. It was a happy feeling for me. He was quiet afterwards and I wasn't sure what his feelings were. I'm hoping we get to go to the OI weekend starting on Thursday. My husband is still noncommittal about it.

## September 11, 1994

The "Happiness Is A Choice" weekend at The Option Institute was an 11th hour decision for my husband. Prior to going he said he was unsure about our marriage and that his "passion" was an issue. He said he would make a decision about our marriage by the end of this weekend.

I feel pretty good. Considering my husband said he would not sleep over at the OI with me, he decided once we there that he might as well -- they had single beds. After saying he was not interested in the reading material available there, he browsed the bookstore and purchased a few things. Then he also altered his decision about a dialogue session for himself and did schedule one. We had separate sessions with different counselors at the same time.

So even though he stayed physically distant from me, I think there are positive signs because he chose to participate in the program. I'm watching for miracles.

**Late evening --**

I waited for my husband to follow through on his promise to tell me his decision about our marriage, but when it started to get late this evening, I asked, "So, what did you decide?" He said, "I need more time." I said, "You must tell me on Tuesday, September 13th."

I think two more days is fair and more time just prolongs the agony.

**September 12, 1994**

Bursting with frustration and unable to sleep, I left our bed last night. The only thing I could think to do was to go outside and find a safe place to walk in the dark. Instantly, I thought of our tennis court -- to walk the inside perimeter of the court next to the fence. It was the perfect place -- a flat, solid, sure surface. I could walk barefoot, outside, in the dark, mindlessly.

I alternated walking fast and jogging some. I felt alive to breathe hard. It was relaxing. The repetition of the confinement of the court's surface felt good. I could see the stars. I took off my nightshirt so I could feel the fresh air passing over my bare skin while I felt the strong surface beneath my bare feet. I felt human. I felt free.

In a while, my husband came out and said, "Come on back to bed." I was drained of emotion so I was pliable. Stripped and whipped, I went back in to sleep.

Today, when I think about last night, I marvel at what a simple and effective solution the tennis court was for me. I was able to get fully relaxed and release all of my tension without alcohol, without medication and without screaming. It was the healthiest thing I could I have done.

## September 13, 1994

Early this morning, my husband said, "C'mon, let's build the porch." He said we should arrange to have it built on the front of our home right away. He wanted me to call Don, our contractor, before Don left home for work.

I was shocked. It was so sudden. But it's what I wanted to hear and it made me feel so hopeful that I called Don at 7:30 a.m. to slate his time to work on it. Don agreed to alter his schedule to do this fairly small project.

I believe my husband's desire to quickly build the porch means that he, too, is ready for the pleasures of a wicker chair, watching the sun rise over the distant hills, evening chats with friends or just the two of us, outdoors.

Then, before he left for work, my husband confirmed to me that he wants to work on our marriage. His decision makes me very happy, but I find I'm in self-protection mode, too, and my survival instincts are peaked. I'm looking at all the possible ways to interpret what he says. I feel myself braced to ride the waves -- possibly to be tossed around, smashed into the sand or, perhaps, glided smoothly into shore.

I started a list of what I absolutely need if I have to leave here suddenly. I washed and organized my car. I put a few important items in a box. I'm not going to make any social commitments.

## September 22, 1994

Yesterday, my husband suggested that we take today off and go shopping in Vermont. I liked the idea as an opportunity for time-away-together, so I agreed.

We had a pleasant drive up this morning. As I browsed in the stores, he drifted out to the street in that "I'm bored waiting for you" shopping-mode that's not unusual for him as he is generally not a shopper. I bought an outfit for myself at a discount outlet store and when my husband looked at it, he complained about it costing more than $100. I thought to myself, he's just spent close to $350 on his filing clerk at the Trump Tower boutiques and now he's complaining to me, his wife, about my purchase!

During the drive home this afternoon, he stated a sudden need for "space," and that he thought separate vacations would be a good idea. Then he dealt a final blow to me. When I asked about the status of his passion, he swapped back on his notion of building the porch and everything else that had seemed hopeful recently and said he wasn't sure about his passion. He said, "It comes and goes," and he doesn't know.

I said, "Fine, you need space, you got it. I'll need 20 minutes when we get home and I'll be gone."

I had braced myself emotionally and prepared myself physically for this. I was ready to go. I'd been to our safety deposit box and taken my things out of it. My car was prepared to leave immediately. In it I'd packed a little clothing, a towel, a sleeping bag, an L.L. Bean folding cot, my boom box and my most essential things. I had also carefully packed the treasures from my life in a small box: a toy sewing machine I'd received as a child, a valuable sculpture of a carved bird, a Waterford crystal bowl my mother had given me and various little mementos from my kids.

It took me less than 15 minutes once we got home. Meanwhile, my husband went outside and walked around the inside of the tennis court -- just like I'd done before when I was so upset. I left our home and came here to the Big House to spend the night. In a little while, my husband came and found me here and said, "Don't go, I'll make it up to you. I'll start earning you back right now." I said, "I'm already gone."

Just a while ago, I made my second phone call to his filing clerk. I wrote down what I wanted to say to her and I read it to her over the phone and then hung up. This is what I said:

*I had a great marriage until you came. Since you were here, my husband has lied to me, hid from me his gifts to you, began treating me like old merchandise and treating you like a princess. He gave you our money without my knowledge, he took you on a New York City spending spree and he lent more money to you, and hid the records in a locked file cabinet. He went to you to find a marriage counselor. He became totally infatuated with you. And now he questions if he wants to stay married. I have left him tonight.*

*You have seduced my husband at his most vulnerable time, when he feared getting older and when he feared the loss of his masculinity. In my opinion, you have wrecked my marriage. You have driven me out of my home, my town and my church. It's too much for me. I've tried to be patient, I've tried to forgive the situation and I've tried to make myself stronger. I hope you'll never speak to my husband again and never come to his office or our house. I hope you'll leave him alone to find himself. And I want our money back. Our kids are all aware of your part in the destruction of our once great marriage. I don't like you at all and can't accept you in our lives. Stay out.*

## September 23, 1994

This morning, I called a few people to cancel scheduled obligations or other social things I needed to get out of. I went to the bank for money and I stopped at the pharmacy to talk to Russ about Falls Town Flowers. I broke down and cried a lot there.

Then, as I was leaving Falls Town, I saw the most spectacular rainbow I've ever seen in my life. It was a gift from nature. It was singularly beautiful and rare. I took it as a good omen, a positive sign.

I drove to Michelle's house in Vermont. I'm staying overnight but I've determined that I must be on my own even if it means camping. Tomorrow I'll start my search for place to live.

**September 24, 1994**

Somehow I found Otis Reservoir in Massachusetts and, by a total stroke of luck, I also found a place to live!

I was walking around the reservoir looking for "For Rent" signs and saw a small cottage with a "For Sale" sign in front and a truck parked in the driveway. I wondered if the owners would consider renting it for a while. As I walked to the front door, a large German shepherd trotted up to greet me. I knocked on the front door and no one answered, but I felt sure someone was home. So with the friendly dog at my side I wandered around to the back door and found Tony and Bev in their kitchen. They looked surprised to see me standing there, petting their big, happy dog. Bev said, "I'm stunned. I can't believe he didn't bark. I've never seen him not bark when anyone but family comes to the house, much less be so friendly to a total stranger!"

Tony and Bev are a lovely young couple and they're willing to rent me a second charming cottage they own on the Otis Reservoir across from their vacation home. I told them I'd like to stay there a month. They said I could move in tomorrow. Tonight I'll sleep in my car at Camp Overflow.

So, I'm set to be in Otis for a month. At the end of October I have plans to go Indiana and then on to California in November for the birth of my first grandchild. After that, I don't know.

### November 2, 1994 -- A catch-up on my life

My emotional yo-yo goes on, even while I'm here in California with Jeffrey and Starr, anticipating the birth of their child.

On October 25, I completed one month in my rental cottage in Otis, Massachusetts. I felt Tony and Bev should know if I planned to return after my trip to Indiana and California. I decided to be fair to them and protect myself. I would commit to another month after my anticipated return in late November and leave it open after that. So, I extended my renting time until January.

Tony and Bev like me as a renter and treat me like a "mom-friend." We've had dinner at their home with their kids and they've frequently stopped in to see me. They've both worked on the cottage to make it more comfortable and they plan to enlarge the bathroom while I'm away.

During the month of October, I had an extensive social life -- friends coming, calling and meeting for lunch and dinner. I tried to let go of my judgments regarding my husband's behavior and I reached out to my family and friends. The telephone next to my bed was my security blanket. Sometimes Molly would talk to me until my tears dried and sleep came.

Still, my emotions raged as I desperately tried to sustain my life. Sometimes my emotional pain was so great that I craved release, anything to escape it. One of my notes says: How can I end it? Every idea I come up with seems flawed somehow. My kids -- I need to make it as least traumatic as possible for them. OK, I'll think about it and wait.

One beautiful mid-October morning I was in this type of dark, anxious mood. This is what I wrote at the end of that day.

## October 17, 1994

Tony said the reservoir is lowered each year in October and the force of the water going over the dam, into the falls and over the massive rocks roars with an unbelievable sound. Forewarned, I knew the sound when it happened this morning. It was like Niagara Falls.

I walked out to the dam. The water had so much force it was shooting straight out over it. Then I walked down the trail to where I could look up and see the water surging over the dam, bending, and finally, crashing violently onto the rocks below, just in front of me. I stepped up to the edge and stared out into the water. My face and hair were damp from the heavy spray. I thought how good it would feel to be slapped with that cold water and smashed against those sharp rocks, out of control, unrelenting, beaten and beaten and beaten. No one was there but me. Just one step and I could be there. I turned away quietly. Maybe tomorrow. I walked back to the cottage and made coffee.

After two weeks at the cottage, my husband came to visit a few times. We had pleasant outings and talks, some sex and bouts of crying. When I asked about the filing clerk, he defended her and his friendship with her and I cried uncontrollably and hysterically. He then became critical of the way I acted and said it made him feel "drained." I said that I had experienced emotional pain so severe, I wished for physical pain to alleviate it. He didn't understand what I was talking about.

He said, "Down deep, I know I love you. But I think I'm trying to self-destruct." He also admitted that the problem is in him and that he can't seem to let go of his infatuation with her.

The next day, Flora called to say that my husband had written a "Letter to the Editor," published in our local paper, supporting the American Indian. After I hung up with Flora, I cried. I felt shunned.

Several friends have urged me to line up a good lawyer. A few days after my husband's last visit, I searched the Yellow Pages and located the name of a lawyer I had met once at a dinner party. I recalled that he seemed smart and he was fun to talk to. I called him and explained a bit about my marital situation and said I wanted to contact him now just in case things don't work out in the future. He said, "Well, Mrs. Belt, I hope I never have to hear from you again." I said to myself as I hung up the phone, "I hope he doesn't either."

Since I had long ago planned to have a surprise party in Indiana for my mother's 80th birthday, I was determined to see it through. We chose to do the party in late October even though her birthday is in February because of weather-related travel concerns in the middle of winter.

I told my husband that his attendance at the party was critical in terms of his commitment to our family. At the last minute, he decided he would go and would drive separately, on his own. He also wanted me to drive to Indiana and then fly to California from there to wait for our first grandchild to be born. This plan made sense since he would not commit to going with me.

At my mother's party on October 29, my emotional state was so on-the-edge I didn't think I would make it. So far, only my sister knows what's going on. But I made it through the day. My husband slept with me at the motel and I cried so hard all night. The next morning, I looked terrible with puffy eyes, but I met my family for breakfast and then left for my flight to California. My husband followed me to the airport exit and signaled me to stop by waving his arm out of his car and blinking his car lights at me. I pulled over to the side and he got out of his car, came over to my car window and said, "I feel like hugging you. This is crazy. I'm going to set up an appointment with the marriage counselor." I got out of my car and we embraced on the side of the highway. Then he got back in his car and drove to New York. I got on a plane and flew to California. It was a strong, uplifting send off.

A few weeks ago, Michelle and Molly decided they had to do something to try and help their parents' marriage, so Molly had asked some of her friends for a recommendation for a marriage counselor. She turned up one in Stockbridge, Massachusetts. Michelle and Molly then told my husband that he must do the marriage counseling for their sake. He did not agree to do so at the time. I had already agreed to the counseling a while ago, so my husband's declaration on the highway felt like a positive decision.

**November 6, 1994**

My husband called me here at Jeffrey's house last night. He wanted to talk "nice," about his work, who he'd run into and chatted with, the good movie he'd seen and his life in general. I then asked if he had seen or spoken to the filing clerk and he said, "Yes, I see her from time to time." I went bonkers. I hung up and went to the pay phone on the street and called him back. The upshot of that conversation was that I said "I don't understand why you continue to speak to her when you know how I feel." I asked him to promise me he would never speak to her again and he said, "Never say never." He said he would work on it, but he would not promise. I said, "Don't call me if you are still speaking to her, and if you do call, then I'll know you're not." His last words were, "Don't call me," as I hung up on him.

I'm staying quite near the Pacific Ocean in the trailer park where Jeffrey and Starr are living and where Starr's mother, Paula, and her mother's husband, Joe, also live. We all wanted to be in close proximity to each other so we can respond quickly and be nearby to help out when the baby is born.

Paula and Joe live next door to Jeffrey and Starr. Joe parked his "truck camper" for me to use in one of the vacant sites a couple of rows away from their place. The bed is up over the truck's cab area and the mini-kitchen and bathroom are hooked up to the water and sewer. I have all the comforts of home except for a telephone. It only took a day to get organized with groceries, a plan to cook dinner for my "extended family" in the camper, to find the pay phones on the street and to establish a routine.

Paula said, "You're a good sport to adjust to the truck camper and trailer park life." I said, "It's perfect -- a place of my own with everything I need -- plus I can entertain!"

The trailer park has an outbuilding that has a Laundromat. I did some laundry and noticed the laundry room could use a good cleaning. Since I have a little extra time I bought a broom and a bucket (handy, practical things to leave behind) and I scrubbed the Laundromat top to bottom -- the machines, the floor and the folding tables. A few tenants in the trailer park came in and saw me cleaning. Many of the residents speak Spanish so I just smiled and said, "Hi."

After a day or two here I also decided I could make myself feel more worthwhile if I carried a plastic bag on my morning and afternoon walks and picked up litter along the way. I walk through the trailer park, along the street near the donut shop and to the beach. My plastic bag is almost always full when I return and drop it in the trailer park's dumpster. Several more people have noticed me picking up trash and say, "Buenos dias," or "Hello."

The manager of the park asks me daily, "Is there a baby yet?" I'm pleased how quickly I feel comfortable in my lifestyle here. I am getting a life, period -- at least temporarily.

Jeffrey and Starr just joined the Encinitas Y.M.C.A. and we all went over a couple of days ago to check out the facilities, which include a fabulous indoor pool and many beautiful tennis courts. Joe's work schedule allows him some free time during the day so I asked if he plays tennis. He said he had a racket and he had hit against a backboard from time to time. I said, "Let's try it. If you don't like playing with me, it's OK. Nothing lost." He agreed to play and we've had a lot of fun. He is a natural athlete and I've enjoyed returning some good shots.

Today, while I was waiting for him in the Y's lobby after our game, my thoughts roamed through my phone call with my husband last night and returned to my personal life crisis. I stared into space for a moment, remembering and thinking and then I looked around the lobby. I noticed a poster on a door across the room that said "Family Growth and Counseling Center -- Magdalena Ecke Family YMCA." In what seemed like an involuntary physical reaction, I got up, walked over, opened the door and went into the office.

A woman looked up from the desk and asked if she could help me. Without hesitation, I said, "Do you do marriage counseling?" She said, "Yes." I asked, "Would I have to be a member?" She said, "No. We can schedule you and your husband." I said, "No, it would be just me." She said, "Is there a phone number where we can reach you so we can set an appointment with the next available counselor?" I said, "I'm staying in a truck camper in a trailer park and I don't have a phone, but I can give you my son's phone number."

It feels good to be taking active positive steps on my own for my own life and wellbeing.

## November 7, 1994

Today one of the Y.M.C.A. counselors called for me at Jeffrey's. Her name is Deborah Mendelsohn. We set an appointment for me to see her tomorrow.

## November 9, 1994

I met my guidance counselor, Debbie Mendelsohn, yesterday. She is a beautiful young woman, very bright and warm. She greeted me and led me into her office. At first, she was confused about my circumstances -- the trailer park, a baby due any day, no phone, what was I doing in there, where was my husband, etc. She asked me to explain some of this before she designated the fee for the counseling, which is based on one's ability to pay.

I told her everything. I told her about the past several months and how I'd left home, wandered through Massachusetts following signs to Camp Overflow, slept in my car, walked along the reservoir the next day looking for a place to stay. I explained how I'd found Tony and Bev and how their German shepherd had not barked at me. I started to cry when I related how I'd broken down when telling Tony and Bev why I needed a place to stay and Debbie had tears of compassion and joined me in taking a tissue for our tears.

When I finished she said, "I know how that German shepherd felt walking with you to the back door."

She said she'd never heard a more disturbing case. She believes I've been terribly emotionally battered and that my feelings are compatible with such abuses. She said it is amazing I'm able to get out of bed in the morning and she sees me as an exceptional person.

When she asked me where I placed my anger, I said mostly on the filing clerk. I explained that my husband says the filing clerk has nothing to do with it and Debbie said, "Oh, yes, she does! The filing clerk is a needy person and she uses your husband. Your husband is guilty, too, and some of your anger needs to go to him."

She said she saw him as a classic case of "fear of growing older" -- grabbing for youth as if it will change things and also looking for excitement. She suggested I get a lawyer.

Debbie told me that my emotional pain will not go away quickly and it will crop up even much later. She commended me for keeping up with my friends, staying active, picking up litter to make myself feel worthwhile and spending money on myself.

At the end of our session, Debbie asked if I felt at all concerned or inhibited talking with a younger person about my marital problems because there might be another counselor available who is closer to my age. I responded quickly and said, "No, I like you." Debbie said, "Good." We made another appointment for the day after tomorrow.

**November 10, 1994**

I'm going back for another session with Debbie today and this time it's to trash the filing clerk. The other day, Debbie said that my husband is the one who should leave town and take his "damn business" with him. I should have my life and my greenhouse in my community. She also said there were legal implications to "moving out."

I'm taking it all in, bit by bit. It's a lot to assimilate. I felt an immediate and deep connection with Debbie. It's amazing and a relief. I feel perfectly free to spill my guts with her. Her statement that I have suffered extreme emotional battering at the hands of my self-centered husband keeps running through my mind.

In a moment of intense frustration when we were together in Indiana a couple of weeks ago, I told my husband that I felt like "doing him in" and that I had a weapon -- the truth. I said I would write a letter telling the truth about our whole situation and I would send it to everyone. He said, "If you do, it's over."

I have written a letter with the truth of what my husband and the filing clerk have done -- the lies, the cheating, the locked file cabinet, the secret payments to her, etc. I'll send it to all of his clients, the Chamber of Commerce, the Lions' Club, the church, all my friends and family. Then I will be free to start a new life. I feel stronger today knowing I'm right. I have done nothing wrong and I have suffered a great injustice, which is recognized by my kids, my friends and the professionals.

### *My Weapon Is The Truth*

*For more than a year, I have shared my personal agony and emotional pain with my husband. I have concealed the truth of my situation to everyone else to protect him, but I don't owe him that anymore.*

*What I am about to tell you is personal, but I believe one's personal character is not really separated from his professional career. You may make your own choice as to how your business relationship could be affected.*

*I moved out of our home in late September after a year of suspicions. Several weeks earlier I'd found the evidence, proof of my feelings, locked in a file cabinet. My husband had set up a secret account to pay his filing clerk after he no longer employed her. He gave her substantial "loans" of our money with no strings attached. He took her to New York City and bought her expensive gifts in addition to other costly gifts, which he had hidden from me, but I discovered. He did all of this "under the table." Thousands of our dollars were directed to her. She accepted all of it and he calls her his "friend."*

*For 37 years I believed I had an honest husband and I trusted him completely. Our 38th year became a nightmare for me. I have no respect for the filing clerk and I have lost my trust in my husband. The strongest thing I can do for myself is to use the last weapon I have: To stand up and speak the truth. The kind of behavior exhibited by my husband and the filing clerk may be viewed as a messy love triangle, but knowing the facts may help you decide whether you can maintain a feeling of confidence with your financial affairs in the hands of these people.*

*I have been lied to, cheated on (emotionally, at least) and denied information that was my right to know. Writing this letter cannot surpass my humiliation and emotional pain. If I am to recover, however, I must be honest.*

*Alice*

**Later --**

When I read my "truth" letter to Debbie today, she said that putting my feelings on paper is a safe place to go. She encouraged me to express myself on paper in any way I wanted and to save my writing. She said in time I could decide if or how it could be used. I've decided for now not to send my "truth" letter.

Debbie asked me to really think about taking back my rightful place in the community -- have my husband move out and take his business with him. Let <u>him</u> find a place to live, be alone, have people ask him why he's moved out and let him suffer the consequences of his actions. She sees only me shouldering the burden so far. I have the emotional pain and he is merrily going about his business and whatever else and enjoying the comforts of home.

Debbie and I will meet again tomorrow to plan a strategy for when my husband comes to California. I explained that my first question would be to ask if he had seen or talked to the filing clerk. I also said I thought he would react negatively to that question. I can't welcome him if she's still in the picture, so I need to know. Tomorrow we'll talk about that.

Also, Debbie views my husband's relationship with the filing clerk as someone for him to rescue. Debbie referred to him as a "workaholic." She thinks his unwillingness to spontaneously agree to a suggestion like, let's take a walk or play tennis, is due to his need to control.

I like my counselor. She's very clear on my feelings and she definitely seems to "get it." I didn't cry last night and I didn't feel like calling my husband today. Jeffrey suggested praying daily for the people I resent. That's a tall order, but it has merit.

**November 11, 1994**

Again, I slept without crying. I had thoughts that were all over the place before I went to sleep, and when I awoke, I had one thought that squeezed tears to my eyes. The thought was that if I had some insignificant observation or funny story to share... who would I tell? Like if I stepped outside and noticed a fabulous moon, usually I would rush back into the house and say to my husband, "Come quick, the moon is magnificent!" And then we'd share the beauty of the night.

I have always shared everything with him and now I realize I can't trust him anymore with my private thoughts. That is one of my greatest losses and it really hurts.

**Later --**

My counseling session went well. Debbie encouraged me to hold "the question" (if he had spoken to the filing clerk since we talked) until our joint therapy session in Stockbridge. She agrees totally with me that there is absolutely no room for three in our marriage. She said I was one of the most mentally healthy people she's seen and that my understanding of my problem is totally on target. She also reminded me that I have been severely emotionally battered and to ever regain trust in my husband will be difficult. She said I would probably never have the same trust that I'd had before. We agreed that was a terrible loss.

I'll see Debbie again on Monday before I leave California. After that, we're going to plan to have sessions by telephone.

**November 12, 1994**

THE BABY IS COMING!!!

My son knocked on the camper truck door at 7 a.m. and announced the labor pains were four to six minutes apart. Starr is getting a massage from her mother to relax her for the coming event. I'll drive to the "Birth Place" in San Diego to see the baby born. Starr showed me where it was yesterday when we took the trolley tour of San Diego. We had a great day together and then she's been in labor all night. They are not rushing to get to the "Birth Place," so once we're there it probably won't take long.

**November 19, 1994**

I'm back in the cottage in Otis, Massachusetts. The birth of my grandson was a beautiful and emotional experience. His name is Justin. He is a perfect baby and they're off to a good start. After the baby was born, I drove back to the trailer park in Encinitas. I screamed and cried in agony all the way in the great pain I felt of having the first grandchild's birth surrounded by such marital stress.

When I got back to the trailer park, I decided I had to call my husband to share the excitement of the baby, but when I dialed I got an answering machine that he had put on our home phone since I'd left. I know he did it to screen out my calls. I was once again devastated. I called over and over until the pay phone on the street rejected my credit card number.

I packed an overnight bag and went to a nearby Holiday Inn motel and took a room at 2 a.m. There I continued to use the room phone to call him. Finally, just before 3 a.m., I called Molly and asked her to call her father. He called me at 6 a.m. He said the phone didn't ring. How could that be? My trust has diminished to the point of not knowing what to believe.

My next blow came when I knew he'd arrived in California to see the baby and he didn't make an effort to see me. My plane for Indiana left the next morning, so we crossed in California, but no communication was exchanged.

I spent one night in Indiana with my mother before driving home. I didn't really want to tell her about my marriage problem but once I was with her there was no choice.

"Oh no, it can't be. I always liked Garrick and it seemed you got along so well. After all these years, he still always kissed you. How could he do this to you?" my mother blurted out, as she seemed stabbed with horror.

Her next thought was to blame herself. She said she felt terribly guilty and that she must have been a bad mother in some way to have her child's marriage failing. Her notion that she had somehow failed was totally unexpected and it really jarred me. It hadn't occurred to me that my mother would feel embarrassed if I was divorced.

Two nights ago, on my drive back from Indiana, I stayed in a motel. I called my husband and left a message on his machine asking him to call me with his perceptions of the baby. He returned the call within an hour, but we only spoke for a few minutes. He said he would call me when I got back to my cottage in Otis.

Last night, Friday evening, I stopped at our neighbor's house for dinner. Pete and Ed had invited me to come by on my way back to Massachusetts. It was great to see them but it was the first time I had driven past our home in almost two months and I was very emotional. When I left Pete and Ed's place, I saw my husband wasn't home. I drove to my cottage, couldn't sleep and then decided to call my husband. He hadn't called me as he said he would. He knew I'd driven all the way from Indiana by myself. It was foggy and cold. When I got his answering machine again, I couldn't stand it.

At 1 a.m., I got in my car and drove through dense fog back to our home in Falls Town. I banged on the door until he woke up and let me in. I was desperate and crazy. I stood in the doorway and yelled, "The answering machine! The fucking whore! The lies, the cheating!" He said, "I don't want to talk to you." I marched passed him and went directly to the kitchen phone to remove the answering machine, but I discovered there wasn't one there. He said from somewhere behind me, "It's voice mail."

I went nuts and I went after him physically. I wanted to beat him up. I grabbed the front of the nightshirt he was wearing with both my fists and shook him until the shirt ripped. He wrenched away and turned his back and I grabbed his shirt from the back and shook him again. He broke away from me by thrusting his elbows back towards me and he jabbed me hard in the chest. In the last part of his movement I heard a "crack" sound and he collapsed and I went down with him. We were twisted together in a heap on the kitchen floor, both of us crying.

I knew he'd hurt his ankle. I said, "I think you broke your ankle. I can take you to the hospital." He didn't answer. We remained in a pile on the kitchen floor and sobbed.

Soon he got up and went upstairs. I went to the living room. We actually slept a couple of hours -- me on the couch and him in our bed. I stayed in my trench coat the whole time.

This morning, we resumed the fight. I ripped his work shirt using the same shaking-fists move again. When he fought me off, it felt good. The physical pain was such a relief from all my emotional pain.

After that, my husband showered and got dressed again and started to leave for his office, even though it's Saturday. It was an escape, another act of rejection. I couldn't really hurt him and I wanted him to hurt me.

I ran outside and lay down behind his car and said, "Go ahead and kill me." He got out of his car, took my hand and helped me up off the ground. He held my hand and led me back into the house like a little child. Then he left. A few minutes later, I drove back to Otis.

Today, I've been wrapping Christmas gifts. I talked with my friend Cathy and with Lilly and visited with my landlords. It is a beautiful Saturday and I feel overwhelming sad.

In my whole life, I can't recall violent anger. My emotional pain is so great; I have no idea what I'll do. I'm on the edge. It feels like my husband broke one of my ribs when he lunged back on me. It hurts when I breathe or move. My sister suggested getting medication for depression. My thoughts are all over the place -- good, bad, horrible.

Last night when we were on the kitchen floor crying, my husband said, "We're destroying each other." It's true. He has almost destroyed me and in response, I am destroying him. It is so weird that my emotional connection is extremely strong both in love and in anger. Not knowing where he is, how he is or what he's doing drives me into a frenzy.

We actually have an appointment for a counseling session on Wednesday in Stockbridge and it seems like years away. My husband made the appointment and told me about it during our phone conversation while I was in California. Each minute is critical. People are praying for me, but I can't pray for myself.

**November 21, 1994**

I am exhausted. My ribs hurt. On Saturday, the day after our "fight," my husband called me at my cottage to say his ankle is broken and in a temporary cast and that he is staying at Syd and Sheila's house. Sheila is a lawyer and client of his. He said he had called the cleaning girl to pick him up from the hospital.

I spent all of Saturday night thinking about my husband and his ankle and about what my responsibility is since I am still married to him. What do I do? I decided I should try to help him.

On Sunday morning, I got dressed for church and drove to Town. I went to the Syd and Sheila's house before church to visit my husband. It was extremely uncomfortable being there. Everyone treated me like I had leprosy. My husband was in the guest bathroom shaving and combing his hair and getting ready to go out. He looked terrible.

I told him that I wanted to help take care him despite our other problems. I suggested he stay at the Big House because it would be more comfortable and closer to his office. I said I was moving back into our home. I said I could drive him places, buy food, cook and help him live comfortably until he got better, especially with winter on the way. He said, "Don't bother. I've taken care of it." The message was I don't need you for anything.

I left and went to the store and bought a few groceries for him to have at the Big House. When I opened the refrigerator there, I discovered it was already full of all kinds of food. I stood there and stared at it all for a moment. Then I put the groceries that I'd bought in the refrigerator anyway so that then there were two cartons of eggs, two jugs of milk, two bottles of orange juice, two loaves of bread.

There were also two wine glasses in the dish drainer and a crayon under the coffee table in the living room. As I was leaving, I also noticed my husband had already moved his prized collection of CDs and his boom box from our home to the Big House. It appears he is already using the Big

House. He'd apparently started the process of moving in while I was away and before our big fight and his broken ankle.

Then I went to church. It was the first time I'd been to my church in months. It felt good to walk in the door and be in the familiar, comfortable place. I immediately decided that I would be "up front" with the news of my fight with my husband and I related the incident to the minister. I told him that I wanted to stand up in church and share my story with the congregation. He said, "Let me handle it. I'll ask for you to be held up in prayer." I felt relieved with his suggestion. I realized his way would be a better way to handle my very emotional state and need to communicate about it with my church community. And he did it very well. After the service, I received a lot of support from many of the congregation members.

I then drove to our home to find Syd and another friend, Cliff, removing my husband's clothing and personal belongings and putting them into a truck. It was a strange sight to come home to and very awkward.

I moved back into our home at that moment yesterday. My mind was on circuit-breaking overload. I felt total emotional trauma laced with flashes of the church, my friends, what might have been going on at the Big House, the change I was making, my uncertain life.

Syd and Cliff packed the last bits into the truck and drove away. As I watched them go I thought, once again, I am emotionally abused and shabbily treated. And my husband's getting away again, another escape. I am too tired to write anymore.

# DEVASTATION

**November 22, 1994**

Yesterday morning I called the lawyer, Tom, that I'd spoken with weeks ago and asked him if was still willing to represent me. He agreed to take my case and we arranged to meet in the afternoon.

The first visit to my lawyer's office was like my first visit to a liquor store – I felt uncomfortable and somehow like a bad person. Fortunately, Tom is very pleasant and very sharp. I updated him on my situation through occasional sobbing. He was understanding and patient.

**November 23, 1994**

I had a telephone appointment with my California counselor, Debbie. She went through some things to help me prepare for the first appointment with a marriage counselor with my husband today. She said we'd most likely be asked if we both agree to work on the marriage and to define our goals, which may be different. Debbie seemed to be preparing me for disconnected agendas. I'm trying to save the marriage and my husband may be trying to dissolve it. She understands that I am so accustomed to being on the same team as my husband.

Debbie said my situation is horrendous, but she also insisted that I can't be defined by this part of my life. I am a multidimensional person. She said I can mourn the negative and get on with the positive.

I read her my journal notes and she encouraged me to keep writing. It is good therapy; I pour out my emotions. Debbie suggested that one day I could write a book from my journal notes that would share my experience and might be used to help others in workshops or support groups.

Debbie also believes my anger is blocked. I need to let off steam, not explode. She said, "Anger turned inward becomes depression." She suggested I write a letter to the girlfriend, not to be sent, but to tell her off. She said my phrase, "Indian whore," is mild -- I can say anything I want.

I told Debbie that what I scream in my car lately is "fucking Indian whore," and that recently I've added "you bastard" for my husband.

It seems I need to let my feelings out to remain physically healthy. I've made it this far by crying, screaming, journaling and, as much as I'm able, communicating my agony to my husband.

Debbie said that I can't be a "good girl" anymore and not to worry about it. When I got off the phone and thought about that I cried so hard. My sadness came from realizing that all my life I've really tried to be a good girl. It has gotten me to this place and I can't stand it.

**Later --**

Thank God Debbie clued me in about the way the counseling session with my husband could go. When my husband and I sat before the counselor, he spoke first. He was emotional and somewhat rattled, but he said that we were destroying each other and that he refused to discuss the filing clerk as having anything to do with it. He said that he did not want to continue our marriage. He claimed he came to this conclusion after fearing for his life after our fight.

I wanted to explode with astonishment and disbelief and I wanted to set the record straight on my own behalf, but I was stoic. I looked at him speaking, crawling in his own skin, determined to have his fantasy, to lie, to pay the price and, in a way, even believing himself. He couldn't look at me. The counselor noted that he seemed full of fear.

When I spoke, I chose to tell about the incidents leading up to our fight, starting with my mother's party and following our story through to our fight. I felt I was pretty graphic in my description of our fight, but my husband wanted to clarify his version of it and he put forth a more violent and life-threatening scenario. He concluded that he feared for his life around me. I accepted his version as his version.

Our fight was never life threatening.

The counselor handled it all pretty well and said, "This is going to be very difficult." In the end she offered each of us separate help and then asked me if I would be willing to work again together with my husband. I said yes and that I would also continue with my California counselor. When the counselor asked my husband, he remained "on the fence" and would not commit to a joint appointment with me or consent to receive extra help on his own. We walked out to the parking lot like we were total strangers. I don't remember thinking. I just tried to make it home.

After a nap I had a talk with my daughter, Molly. I don't remember what was said. I think I shut down in shock.

I've been thinking about the way my husband related my behavior to the counselor. He depicted me as having a "mean sneer" during our fight when I asked him, "Who invited you to Thanksgiving?" I remember asking that question, but with feelings of crushing hurt as to why he would consider other invitations when Molly and I would be here.

When the counselor asked what we saw happening to us prior to the filing clerk, I said I saw distancing due to sexual failure. He only saw distancing.

**November 24, 1994**

Last night I had a 1 1/2 hour telephone appointment with Debbie. I read her yesterday's journal entry about the appointment with the Stockbridge counselor.

She said my husband was allowed to cast me as the "bad guy." Meanwhile, he can do the unthinkable -- have an affair, end the marriage -- and still be a "good guy," because he's "protecting" himself from me! He needs a reason to justify his behavior. Since his broken ankle, he now has a "cause" for divorcing me -- it makes it legitimate for him in his mind. Debbie believes he's been waiting for me to get more aggravated, more on the edge, to the brink of desperation – for his "timing." He has done everything to escalate the circumstances.

Debbie said that all of his actions have nothing to do with me. "Let go of the image of the husband you knew. He's changed," she said. "He will try to fulfill his fantasy. By the time he comes to his senses, you will feel differently. He has to run his course with this thing and he won't let go of it."

Debbie went on to say that my husband can't deal with what he's created. The problem is he got involved; it was wrong and a big mistake. He's self-centered and selfish and he has to have it his way.

I realized that in the past, I had simply accepted his strong need to have his way -- priority use of the bathroom, selecting the TV program, choosing the time to go to bed, selecting the route we traveled on vacation, in control of his career moves, his cars, his snacks, his music, etc.

Debbie advised me not to pretend my situation is temporary because my husband still has the same ingredients in him that made him do it this time. She said, "Consider planning a life separate from him. Start to let go."

She also asked me to question my feeling of wanting to be with my husband. She said I don't need to "make nice" anymore.

## November 25, 1994

It's my husband's 61st birthday, but I will ignore it. I couldn't find an appropriate card, so I'll do nothing. Yesterday was Thanksgiving and I had a really nice day with Molly. I went to her house and we took a walk in the woods, gathered some moss, had a fabulous vegetarian dinner and made topiary and Christmas things from our gatherings from the woods. Molly has been absolutely wonderful to both me and my husband. Now it's Friday and I'm home alone. I mailed Jeffrey and Starr their airline tickets to come here for an early Christmas celebration. I saw a friend in town and cried and then I came home ready to start making my house my home. The living room already looks great. I broke a lamp accidentally, so I'll take a lamp from the Big House. The Christmas topiaries and the little white pine I planted in a clay pot look great to me, too. My space feels good today.

**6 p.m.** My space now feels lonely and desolate. I was working on rearranging a few things and I began crying uncontrollably -- really wailing and hurting. My rib over my heart hurts when I move, lean over, breathe deeply or cry. I stretched out and turned on the TV but everything set me off into a deeper anguish. For most of my life I have found comfort with my husband.

## November 26, 1994

I woke up at intervals all through the night and cried. This morning I got up in the cold house and took care of the dogs, crying. When the phone rang, I hoped it would be my husband, but it was Nancy. She invited me to a movie tonight and I was very grateful. So, I'll take a bath, wash my hair and try to look as good as I can. My eyes are puff pillows, but recently I've been able to get a clearer face in a relatively short time.

One by one, the people in my town are embracing me and telling me they care. Basic emotional needs, according to my old nursing book, are categorized as love, trust, autonomy or self-control, self-esteem, identity and productivity. (I use my old nursing book like I use my dictionary. When I'm curious about a medical condition, usually for a friend, I'll look it up.)

A more detailed list in the book includes the desire for recognition, new experiences, security and response -- to give and receive personal appreciation, love and affection. Reading this section gave me somber pause. These are the things I've lost. The words came as wrenching validation of sanity and loss. Another thought I had: 40 years ago, my husband gave me his "all." He gave me his 45 r.p.m. record collection and record player. When we broke up during our engagement (he thought I was too dependent), he took back all of his records and his record player. Now, 40 years later, he packed all of his CDs and his boom box and moved them to the Big House as his only treasured possessions. An odd, but telling, recurring symbol.

I'm going to the cottage in Otis today to finish moving out. My landlord, Tony, wants to let his son use the cottage.

**November 29, 1994**

Recalling my trip to the Otis cottage to move a few days ago, my stomach still wrenches and turns over. While driving to Massachusetts, I couldn't stop crying. Then I was pulled over for speeding. Seeing my face full of tears, the officer asked me what was wrong. I said, "My husband wants to divorce me." He asked, "When did you find that out?" I said, "Wednesday." He said, "It's been two days. Get over it!" He didn't give me a ticket.

A friend called while I was at the cottage and still I couldn't stop crying. I felt lost. But I finally got all my stuff packed into my car and came home. Just as I was coming in the door, Nancy called to invite me to New York City to see "Madame Butterfly" at the Met. We made a plan to take the 8 a.m. train and on Monday morning we were off for a big day in the city.

I told Nancy all the "girlfriend details" of my story on the train ride. Then we saw a great performance. It was the dress rehearsal for the Metropolitan Opera, attended by the press and friends of the cast. Our friends, Marty and Kent, are tenors with the company and they arranged front row seats for us. It was grand.

Afterwards, we walked towards Grand Central Station, did a little window-shopping and passed by the Sea Grill at Rockefeller Center where my husband took the girlfriend for their $100 lunch. I said, "the bastard." Nancy said, "He is a bastard." We went to an early dinner in a cute little restaurant near Grand Central.

It felt good to sleep last night and then not so good to wake up this morning 6 a.m. crying. It's a strange phenomenon to wake up in the midst of crying. Until this all happened, I had never experienced or heard of this before.

I kept on crying while I had coffee, took care of the dogs and worked cleaning out my closet. Then I bathed, washed my hair, dressed in my new bib overalls and planned an outfit for this Sunday when I'll see most of the townspeople at the Christmas tree lighting. Phone calls from Molly and several friends helped to fill the time between cleaning the house and picking up a few pinecones. Molly is coming for dinner. We're planning chicken noodle soup.

I'm continuing to personalize my home, removing the things that I don't really like and adding a few new things. I went to the post office and chatted briefly with a few friends and acquaintances. Driving past my husband's office, I noted his car was there but I kept my head straight and I didn't cry.

I'm having a fairly good day and I've decided to call Debbie tonight to get help for the joint counseling session that is scheduled for tomorrow.

**Later --**

At 4 p.m., I laid down on the couch to rest and my mind drifted into a dream: I encounter the girlfriend on the street or in the video store. I faint when I see her. Then she comes toward me as I am lying there and that vision revives me and I scream out loud, "Don't touch me, go away, go away, go away."

I cried for a few minutes, breathing hard with my heart drumming and then I got up to wash my face. Shortly after, a friend called on the phone -- I sobbed. Then another friend called and I was OK.

I called Jeffrey to talk about the baby and I called Debbie in California asking her to return my call. She called at 10 p.m. and we just hung up. It's midnight.

**November 30, 1994**

My sister's call before 8 a.m. got me out of bed. I was still sort of dozing thinking I should get up and let the dogs out. Not crying and feeling rested and warm, I talked a few minutes with her and then thought about my day.

This morning I'm going to help Jean clean the church house and then she's treating me out to lunch. The big thing of my day is the 4 p.m. marriage counseling in Stockbridge. I'm not sure if my husband will keep the appointment. I have not seen or spoken to him all week. I plan to go ahead and see what happens.

Last night Debbie prepared me for the possible scenarios from him, including 1) variations of staying on the fence, 2) more brave and strong-willed about ending the marriage, 3) more cooperative. She observed that the more I fight, the more he backs away. She said I could say I want to work on the marriage, but if he chooses otherwise, I must accept that. Then it's out of my hands. She said I need to keep my individuality and yet extend the olive branch.

Debbie said my anger and other feelings are 100 percent valid, but my husband withdraws from a snapping turtle. She said his weakness is that he can't be comfortable with a full range of emotions.

Discussing my approach, Debbie suggested several ways: 1) If he wants out of the marriage, I can say, "I want the marriage, but OK," -- a friendlier approach. 2) If he wants to work on the marriage, then I can say, "I'm it, no other players, no room for the girlfriend." 3) If he is silent, I can profess, "I don't know, I'm confused." 4) Let him say what he wants to do and I can be on the fence for a change. I won't know what to do or say. I can ask him what he wants to do and how. 5) Ask my husband what he wants me to do.

If he says "all right" things, I'm still not sure what will happen. Debbie asked me if it's worth it to save the marriage. There are some unpleasant aspects about him. She seemed to want me to face the truth and be clear about the quality of our relationship.

Finally, Debbie said I could generously say to my husband, "Do what you want. How can I help you get out of this marriage?" And if I must open the talk at the meeting, I could say, "I hear my husband's desire to end the marriage, so, how can I help? What would you like for me to do?"

**9 p.m.**

The meeting was a disaster. My husband portrayed me as murderous, suicidal and dangerous to him. He recalled only the most negative things and said, flat out, that he wants to end the marriage.

I was ineffective. I was mentally blocked. I shut down. I was in total shock.

The counselor asked if I could give my husband "space" on the girlfriend issue and I said, "No, I can't."

When 50 minutes were up, we were done. The counselor offered to help us individually. I looked at my husband. He could not look at me. The counselor seemed sorry and helpless.

I walked to my car shaking with tears. Clenching the steering wheel, I screamed and wailed as I drove home. When I got home, I called my husband. I was hysterical. I also called Molly, although I could barely speak. I got both of their machines.

My husband's response to my call was to call my neighbors, Pete and Ed. They came over a few minutes later to find me crushed, helpless and out of control. Pete willingly gave her shoulder to cry on and Ed offered his arm as we walked up to their house. They were so kind to me and so understanding. I'm in their guest bedroom now. They insisted I sleep at their house tonight.

I know I can never count on my husband again.

**December 1, 1994**

Even though I barely slept, I left Pete and Ed's very early this morning and came home to take care of the dogs. After I let the dogs out, I called my husband and begged him to come to see me. I said I needed him and I couldn't stand it anymore. "I'm out of control, I'm confused. I can't think. I'm lost." My husband said he would come.

Some ideas I've had: Call Tom, my lawyer; call the Stockbridge counselor; call an ambulance; call my friend Nancy.

Molly called this morning and said she would call the counselor. She also said she'd put in a call to my doctor who knows nothing about my situation.

It's been half hour and I now realize that my husband has no intention of coming here alone. I bet he'll come with Molly. He says he fears for his life, but it's my life that's being destroyed. He's killing me. Tortuous emotional manipulation -- a thrashing and dangling, a killing by degrees, stripping me of my basic needs and leaving me like a prisoner in a cell. My sadness and loss feel overwhelming. So far, today, I can't cope.

I have an appointment to get my car tires aligned. I have an invitation to lunch and a walk with a friend. I have a scheduled telephone appointment with Debbie tonight. I'm up and dressed, but I can't predict myself. Can I make it or do I throw in the towel?

**Later --**

At 8:30 a.m., my husband and Molly arrived. Molly gave me a big hug. My husband sat in the side chair and Molly sat by me on the couch and held her arm around me. They stayed a couple of hours.

My husband was emotional about seeing the house. He said how nice it looked and started talking about the family Christmas. He said, "We're still family." Molly cut him off. She said, "We're not a family."

He cried when he said he was grateful that Pete and Ed had come to help me. Finally, he left to go to his office and Molly said she would stay all day. I took one of Molly's Benadryl pills and slept on the couch.

I can't describe how solid and clear-headed my daughter is. She shopped, prepared food and handled all the phone calls. I took naps and wept. Molly is going to spend the night.

I feel on the one hand I can't take it anymore, I can't go on, it's too much. On the other hand, maybe I'll get better, maybe I can cope with life and never be involved with my husband again. While I need and appreciate the help of my friends, I'm not comfortable relying on others for the support I've always received from my husband. That space in me is now hollow.

At 7 p.m. I called Debbie and read her all my notes. She made a point to remind me that I'm not a one-dimensional person. She said that the thread of hope I'd had was shredded and the horrendous death of the marriage is a brutal blow. She said falling out of control will reoccur but with less intensity. She said my husband needs to say bad stuff about me so that he has someone to blame. It protects him from his own guilt at my expense. Even if he comes over when I call, it's an empty response.

Debbie said that there will be days when I can't stop crying and that it's OK to stay in bed and cry. She said as horrible as it is, at least I am able to get my emotions out and it's better that I do. It will save me from breaking down completely. She acknowledged that without even a drop of encouragement from my husband any hope for the marriage is gone and I should limit putting myself "in the ring" with him. No more sparring, back off.

She suggested that I not go to a therapy session next week because it's too soon to plan the divorce and I need to get stronger first. She said if I'm notified of a therapy session appointment, I can say, "Maybe later for help with the divorce plans, but not now for me." She thought having a mediator for the divorce might be a good idea, but not right now. Time-out period first.

Debbie reminded me that divorce has not been my agenda, so I will need time to adjust and cope. She warned me that I might be served with papers from him and then I must deal with that.

She noted that when I am put in the position of defending myself, he escapes untouched. We discussed that my defensiveness occurs because I am thrown into shock by his dreadful behavior. I told Debbie that I wanted to say to him, "What about your girlfriend? Why do I feel suicidal? Why do I feel murderous? You have pushed me to feel these distressing and unwanted feelings. I have communicated my intense feelings to you, hoping you would understand my pain. My strongest physical actions have been to pull your hair, tear your shirt and lay down behind the wheel of your car. Every fiber in my body is screeching, "stop" or just finish me. I can't stand it anymore."

Debbie reminded me that my goal now is to take care of myself, to heal, to come to terms with the change and to start to accept that my husband is not the same person I remember. If my emotions are overwhelming, she said she could arrange for medication.

Debbie also said that I did right to say "no" to giving my husband "space" to resolve his "girlfriend issue." She said I need to come to grips with the fact that he's a person who has some ugly qualities. Let go of the old husband and accept the man he is today. She said I have been dealt a major blow and I'm in a personal crisis, but at least I'm well enough to ask for help.

**December 2, 1994**

I slept pretty well last night and Molly and I took the dogs on an early morning walk. I cursed my husband and his girlfriend several times out loud and I didn't break down.

Fortunately, I have things to do today. I'm going to have a part replaced in my car that's under warranty, then I'll meet some friends at the church house and make bows for Christmas decorations and then we'll go out to lunch.

**Later --**

We went to The Hub restaurant and everyone was especially warm and we had some laughs. One funny thing happened: At a nearby table, a woman my age that I didn't recognize asked if I was Mrs. Belt and I said, "Yes." She said she was a client of my husband's and that she had met me one time at the office. She thought at the time I was his daughter. She said she thought I looked even younger now. I told her she had no idea how she had just made my day. We all laughed.

Almost everyone comments on how good I look. I think they hear what I'm going through and are surprised to see me look fine. Even after my major upset yesterday, people are saying how good I look. Perhaps nature has a way of recovering when parts of the body are being overused -- like my eyes from crying. These days, even though I cry hard, long and frequently, my swollen, red eyes recover quickly.

After lunch, I came home and talked with my friend, Diane, about a tentative plan to go to Westchester tomorrow. Then I talked with Nancy and shared every detail for more than 90 minutes. Molly is coming for dinner and she's bringing ingredients to make Christmas cookies. She plans to spend the night even though she's going to Boston tomorrow.

Considering how utterly distraught I was yesterday, it amazes me that I'm dry-eyed writing all this down. At this moment, my husband is not important to me. I feel "together" and I'm comfortable. I'm being carried by Molly and my friends. Their words and actions are like soft warm cushions. I am becoming as open with my friends as I am with Debbie. In the past, this level of openness was only shared with my husband. He's out of it now.

**December 3, 1994**

I decided not to go to Westchester and I declined a dinner invitation. Earlier today, I did take a walk with Molly and the dogs and I cleaned the bedroom for Jeffrey, Starr and Justin's visit. I also removed all of my husband's clothes from the closet and his drawers. I bagged them and put them in the garage. I didn't put my things in his place. The closet is just empty and clean. Only a few tears during a few of the many phone calls that came in, but mostly I didn't lose it today.

At 9 p.m., Flora called from the church house and asked me to join her to finish the Christmas decorating. So I got up, got dressed and went to town to help her. Mostly I wanted her companionship.

**December 4, 1994**

I woke up at 7 a.m. thinking about what kind of soup to make for my kids. Deciding on potato soup, I put the dogs out, noted how warm the air was and started cooking potatoes. I plan to attend Falls Town's holiday tree lighting celebration at 5 p.m. and a dinner invitation at Nancy's after that.

The possibility of seeing the girlfriend at the tree lighting event is very great. I expressed my fear to Nancy saying that in previous months just seeing the girlfriend on the street caused a flood of emotions that turned my legs to rubber and made me feel faint. We decided I would go to Nancy's house first and then drive to town with her. She is going to stay with me and we'll leave if I can't handle it. Of course, none of it may happen, but at least I have a plan.

Molly and Michelle have decided it would be fun to have Christmas in Vermont. We can all go skiing and stay at Michelle and Pierre's home. This is terrific. I'm smiling and I feel so happy for this plan.

**December 6, 1994**

The tree lighting on Sunday night was great. Neither my husband nor the girlfriend came. Everyone welcomed me with hugs and comments about how good I look. Nancy invited the Falls Town Flowers group for a glass of wine at her house before her dinner party. It was wonderful to be with friends.

On Monday, I went to the airport to pick up my kids and grandson. The baby is perfectly beautiful. They have a schedule of plans while they are here. All of my kids will be at my house for an early Christmas.

My husband called this afternoon and acted like I should be happy to hear from him. Jeffrey spoke with him and gave him their schedule. I wondered how my husband felt to know our grandson would be here several days before he gets to see him. There will be family gatherings, dinner parties and showing off the baby to friends, and he will not be included.

Before I drove to the airport yesterday morning, I cried with a broken heart thinking about how sad it was to be alone for this special welcome to "Grandma's house."

This morning, Betty, a close friend from Iowa called and I told her everything. She was stunned. Her first thought was that I needed to protect myself financially. She is going to call her son who's a lawyer and ask him to call me regarding money matters.

I decided that I will call my lawyer, Tom, and discuss protection of finances with him, too.

Our friends in Iowa date back almost 30 years. However, they are insulated from other friends and wouldn't have heard about our problems because the grapevine would not reach them. I hadn't wanted to tell my story to my Iowa friends if there was any hope of saving the marriage, but without that and since Betty called, I told her all the dirt and asked her to pass it on.

Betty said my husband comes out a stinking rat. For the most part, our family and lifelong friends are now aware and there is no one there for my husband. My friend said everything my husband has, he got because I made it happen. She doesn't want to see me get screwed now. My husband has burned his bridges.

**December 8, 1994**

Jane, a friend from Chicago is coming to visit. Today, I'll make Christmas bows with Betsy, take a walk with Nancy, Molly is coming for dinner tonight and next week I'm having dinner with Pete and Ed. It's helpful to have engagements to look forward to.

Last night I woke up at 2 a.m. in tears and I wanted to call my husband to tell him about my anguish. I would have wanted him to respond by feeling my pain too, but I didn't call. I knew he couldn't feel any empathy. I put those hard feelings behind me before breakfast and made it through my day OK. I was ready to make some plans.

The living room is set for our Christmas and the house looks festive. The food shopping was completed yesterday and I'll make cookies and pies. I made more decorations for the church, had lunch with church friends and then had a good visit with yet another friend. My old friend from college called, she wants to come visit, too. Friends are great.

My short-range plans are mostly social. I'm trying to think ahead a little too. I need to get money from the Visa card and get a snowplowing service lined up.

I called Debbie at 7 p.m. I told her I thought my husband would be fair financially, but she wasn't so sure and I doubt him now, too. She suggested checking with my lawyer for financial advice.

Debbie said to redesign my life -- plan Christmas, deal with snowplowing, go about repairing my life and fill each need that was my husband's role with a substitute. If I'm overwhelmed, share with my friends. If I miss by husband's companionship, find another friend. She said when I reach out to my husband I get burned. She called him toxic. She encouraged me to turn away from him and turn to everyone else for everything I need in life.

This is a huge process because for most of my life I have turned to my husband for everything. I told Debbie about his phone call on Tuesday and my thoughts to call him in the middle of the night. She said my husband escapes validating my emotional wound by being light and not addressing the issue.

We scheduled another telephone session for next week.

**December 9, 1994**

I had a healthy breakfast and went to the church house to help with last minute preparations for the annual Christmas bazaar. Then as I left to come home to take a walk with Nancy, I passed my husband in his car on the street. He acknowledged me with a stupid grin and I nodded my head slightly. I shook with tears all the way home.

I feel so sad, but I can't change things. I want to lash out and say hurtful things but I bury that urge. I'd like to return the cheap ugly earrings he gave me for our 38th anniversary and say, "I don't want this crap."

Instead, I got on the phone to Tom, my lawyer, and made an appointment to see him next week to talk about our bank accounts and money matters.

Nancy and I did a three-mile walk in the cold day and then had coffee and fruitcake. At home, I made cookies and pies while I talked on the phone with Elinor. She invited me to a dinner party at her house after the Historical Society Christmas Open House the next week. So, my social calendar during the holidays is almost completely filled in.

Elinor asked me to be the community representative on the hospital planning session and the new board member when her term expires this spring. I told her that I'm too shaky emotionally to make such a commitment, but it felt good to be asked.

**5 p.m.**

Michelle called with some changes in their schedule. They'll arrive late Saturday night so they'll miss our "early Christmas Eve" dinner. Then, because Pierre has to work Monday, they will all go to see my husband on Sunday morning.

I feel angry that my day with the kids is going to be cut in half by my husband having them to the Big House for an early Christmas with him. He's getting his preferred times and he's in control again. I'm sobbing as I write this. I feel out of the loop and the memory of being a family together has struck raw nerves. In moments, I went from strength to vengeance to devastation.

I need to do some more grocery shopping but I feel scared to go to the store -- fear of seeing my husband, the girlfriend or people I know but haven't spoken to yet. I just want to stay in my house. Maybe I can go tomorrow.

## December 10, 1994

I wailed and writhed in agony much of the night. I had just dozed off this morning when it was time to get up. During the night I thought of making a list to take charge of the finances. I just got a bill for the safety deposit box. Maybe I should change boxes and put it in my name only. I could call Merrill Lynch and see if I could sell my bonds and open a new account somewhere else. I made a list for my husband of things I want from the Big House. I listed "current record of CMA and blank checks." Everything is to be left in my greenhouse where I can pick them up.

Another thought I had was to join the Chamber of Commerce and ask a friend to nominate me for president so that I could run against my husband. Then I had visions of myself standing in front of the church house door welcoming everyone to come in except the girlfriend when she appeared. Most of this is fantasy, but it kept my head spinning in frenzied directions all night.

At 8 a.m. I made lasagna. At 10 a.m. I went to the church bazaar and acted as a greeter to the guests. It was good for me. After lunch with a friend, I drove to the train station to pick up my son and his family. I was very glad to see them. They've been away visiting friends.

## December 11, 1994

We had a lasagna dinner with Molly, her fiancé, John, and my son's family last night. Even though Michelle and Pierre weren't present, it was a time for the other kids to talk and get to know each other better. We went to bed early since Starr was having some bleeding from doing too much too soon after the baby's birth and I was tired from too little sleep last night. I tried to keep my crying quiet and ended up sleeping pretty well.

Michelle and Pierre are going directly to the Big House with Molly after having spent the night at her place. Jeffrey and his family are meeting them there so that the kids can have their "early Christmas" with their father this morning. They are fixing a brunch at the Big House. I feel particularly dejected. It feels like I'm being robbed of my Big House, my kids and my life's efforts.

I did a huge renovation on the Big House a few years ago with much of my own sweat equity poured in and it is now all in my husband's hands. The Big House is well located, near the center of town and it adjoins the farm property we purchased after it had gone bankrupt. I worked with many tradespeople to remove dilapidated buildings, barns, silos and a greenhouse. We renovated the tenant farmhouse and we built a wonderful greenhouse. I also found a good farmer to rent some of the land. I supervised the restoration of 70 acres of beautiful land complete with two renewed buildings -- all of which had been an eyesore.

It hurts to add all of this to my loss. I don't know if I feel up to delivering the kids to my husband today. I feel like I'm doing all the accommodating for his visit with them. This has been my traditional family role so everyone is expecting me to do it. Dad gets his way and Mom makes it happen. This mode has to be unwound and the kids will have to adjust. But I need to buck up because the kids will back here by 2 p.m. and we'll have our "early Christmas" dinner and exchange gifts.

**Later --**

At 2:30 p.m. the kids weren't back and I lost it. I cried and screamed until 3 p.m. Then Molly called to say they were on their way. They had taken a walk on the hill and were late. Molly apologized and said they had lost track of the time and she called as soon as she could because she knew it would bother me.

After they came back, we ate smoked salmon and toast and had a turkey dinner. We played charades and opened gifts. We also passed the baby. It was very nice but it was tinged with sadness due to my husband's absence and the separate gatherings. Nothing was said about it.

When Molly and Michelle and Pierre were ready to leave, I came unglued, overwhelmed again with sorrow. I told the girls I thought their father was screwing me, taking the property, moving money away from me, spending it in ways unknown to me, pushing me out of the office, out of the Big House and leaving me dangling on all counts.

In the midst of all of this, I observed that my kids always seem to be several steps behind me. It's understandable. While I'm expressing devastation, they are in stunned disbelief. They seem to believe their father will be fair and that his role of handling family business is something they can count on. I disagree. I am distraught and perhaps irrational and they can't make sense of it.

After they left, I felt helpless and hopeless, but then, I started to feel angry and mean. I'd like to force him out of the Big House, serve him with divorce papers for emotional battering and mental cruelty, take half of our assets and leave him as shattered as he's left me. Tomorrow I want to take some action. I'll go to the bank. I'll call Merrill Lynch. I'll talk to my lawyer. I wish I knew a strategy. In my whole life, he has always been the one I turned to for help in handling tough situations. It's another reason I feel so lost now.

## December 12, 1994

I slept through the night without crying. It's cold out, but sunny. The Christmas gifts around the room represent such thoughtfulness from the givers. The kids were great to each other and to me.

Today's Action #1: I called the vet and scheduled the dogs and the cat for the kennel beginning on December 23 for an indefinite period of time with the bill to go to my husband. My plan is to go to North Carolina after I spend Christmas in Vermont with Michelle and Pierre. Jeffrey and Starr will be moving to Asheville so that Starr can continue her education. I offered to do the legwork of finding a house for them there since they're still in California and they have the baby. It seems like an appropriate project for me and I certainly have the time.

Action #2: I called my broker and asked for duplicate mailings of our CMA account and found out that I am entitled to 50% of that account. I told him the whole story. The broker will help me in every way he can. He said his heart goes out to me. I've known him for 15 years.

One thing came to light when I was talking to my broker. He said he suspected something when my husband stopped payment on a $50,000 check I wrote before I left in September. My husband told me that the check had bounced due to insufficient funds, so he lied about that. I had written the check when I left expecting to possibly have to cover myself for a long time.

Action #3: I called my lawyer Tom to confirm our appointment for tomorrow and I told him about my discussion with the broker. Tom said he was glad we were meeting in the morning and not later.

Action #4: Jeffrey announced he was having lunch with his father today and asked me to drive him there. I said, "No, your father will have to pick you up himself." Then Starr said she and her sister were going to join them for lunch and I said, "I want you girls and the baby to have lunch with me," and she agreed. So, I spoke up on my "wants" and they were granted!

## December 13, 1994

Even though I was worried about today's plans, I once again slept well. It is a luxury to sleep soundly.

It's bitter cold and I have my list of things to do. My kids plan to take it easy today; they leave tomorrow morning. Molly is coming for dinner so I need to shop for that. I see my lawyer at 10 a.m. and I have to shop for Christmas gifts for a needy family. I will also look to see if my husband placed the things I requested in the greenhouse. I had asked for bank account records, blank checks, my snow boots, lamps, etc.

My feelings fluctuate in my uncertainty; I'm angry and strong, willful and determined, then scared and faltering, vapid and somber. My survival instinct says, "Don't let him screw you," and my logic says, "No matter what you get, he still screws you." When I add it up, I'm screwed.

## Later --

I met with Tom at his office and told him about my financial concerns. After detailing as much as I knew about my husband's handling of our various accounts, Tom advised driving straight to Westchester and taking 50% of the joint account and putting it into an account of my own.

I came home and called my broker to say I was coming to take half of the money and he said my husband had just called and requested the sale of $55,000 of bonds to cover the loan against the account. My broker talked to the firm's lawyers and they decided to freeze the account immediately, with no further action on it. The broker said he would notify my husband that his requested sale would not happen and that the account was frozen.

The rest of my day was a bummer. I couldn't keep myself together. I desperately struggled to separate what was going on legally and emotionally with me while trying to have a happy visit with my son and his family on their last evening here and later when Molly arrived for dinner. I didn't talk about any of it, but a few times I just cried. It was a bad scene.

## December 14, 1994

At 8 a.m., I drove my kids to the airport. I was weepy several times, but I pulled myself together. Afterwards, I stopped at a bank in Albany and went to a teller to get $3,000 from my Visa card. I didn't think it would work because the Merrill Lynch freeze also stopped payment on the Visa charges. The teller had trouble clearing the request but she finally got it and I walked out with $3,000. Then I shopped for six kids in a needy family for our church's Christmas sharing. I used my Visa again. I also bought a video camera for my house-hunting trip to North Carolina and I'm going to practice using it.

Then I called Tom about the joint account freeze and he said he would call to get it in writing.

At 10 p.m., Jill, one of my kid's childhood friends, called and we talked until almost midnight. She had experienced some of the things I'm going through and it worked out OK for her. She and her husband actually managed to save their marriage. She depicted the struggle as a "dance," and said that I need to do a different step now. She said I could call her anytime day or night. She said she would pray for me and my husband.

When I stopped at the greenhouse yesterday the lamps and my snow boots were there. The CMA records that were joint or mine were there, too, but no blank checks (I figured). Also, there was no information about our other accounts, which are in my husband's name only.

The lamps look great in the house; I needed them. Tomorrow I get my tires aligned, have friends over for tea and talk to my counselor. I wonder what my husband's next action will be.

**December 15, 1994**

It's been four weeks since the "fight" with my husband and my rib over my heart still hurts, but not as much, just when I roll over in bed, when I breathe deeply or if I press on the spot. At 7 p.m., I spoke with Debbie about the early family Christmas and the Merrill Lynch problems. We also talked about the "pursuer-distancer cycle." She said, "Stop being the pursuer and the distancer will stop to see what's happened." I can shift the focus to me and simply have a life of my own.

She thought I had made incredible strides and had done all the right things this past week. She's encouraging me to make plans to move forward and start my new life, finding challenging and exciting things to do and being productive. After the phone conference, I met Flora at the church house and we wrapped the gifts for the six needy children.

Thinking about my conversation with Jill last night, she said my husband has a big hole in his heart and he's trying to fill it with the girlfriend who sucks up to him. I think the "hole" has to do with his age, impotency, self-esteem, loss of power over people, life in a small town, boredom, etc.

Jill said she had wanted to dance naked to get her husband's attention. I've actually done that sort of thing with my husband on several occasions. I think of the picnic I arranged on the hilltop when I stretched out naked in the sun on our blanket. I think of the time he was exercising alone in the basement and to get his attention, I got naked and started exercising along side him. I can still hear him say, with his benevolent tone of voice, "I pity you." Thinking of it still makes my head reel and my insides collapse. It was a crushing defeat.

Jill said she finally stopped showing her emotions to her husband and then <u>he</u> became emotional. I can see that, too. At times when I have been strong, my husband has been weak.

When I went to bed last night after Jill's phone call, I absorbed the comfort of the bed and said automatically and aloud, "God is good." I was surprised at myself and without thinking about it further I slept well all night.

**December 16, 1994**

Yesterday, I found myself tired of telling my story. I really want to move on and think about something else.

Directions I could go: Work with Flora to revitalize the church membership which would also be a fund-raising community activity, or take the hospital board seat and make something happen there, or become president of the Historical Society and make an active community preservation program to develop young people's interest in their community. Or I could grow my plants and develop a community food pantry source, but this idea calls for equipment -- a rototiller, a tractor and a wagon -- that I don't have.

A friend called and asked me to go to a gallery opening tonight, so I'll do that before another friend's dinner party at the church house.

**Later --**

Suddenly, at the dinner table this evening, the talk was about dancing. It struck a nerve. I thought, "I'll never dance again." I started to crumble, but I got it under control. I let go in my car and cried all the way home.

**December 17, 1994**

Today, I figured out how to consolidate some of my money in an interest bearing savings account -- my checking account, my B&B account, cash, etc. I'll do it Monday. I plan to meet my cousin, Ann, at Canyon Ranch Spa in Massachusetts where she works part time as a guest instructor. I feel lonely on this gray day. A call from my neighbor was welcomed.

**Later --**

I had a nice dinner in Lenox with Ann. I told her everything so now my list has grown and I can tell my story with only a few tears here and there. My network now includes about 30 people. They all have my permission to discuss whatever they are comfortable with to whomever they want. Others I have shared my story with, but to a lesser degree, include about 50 more people. And the entire town knows whatever through the grapevine.

I wrote this free-form poem after I came home and couldn't sleep.

*Gliding through the days and years*

*Happy times and sometimes tears*

*Trust and faith abide in me*

*Love embraces us as "we."*


*He lowered the dam*

*crashing forces upon the rocks*

*tossing her spirit to tortuous pain*

*battered, beaten,*

*washed to shore.*

# DAMAGE

**December 18, 1994**

Although my counselor, Debbie, used it during our very first meeting, "emotional battering" is not a phrase I'm comfortable with. I realize now that it is indeed applicable to my situation, but it's still startling to feel those words about myself.

It really began more than a year ago, from the onset of his "distancing." Then his deceptive behavior, further withdrawal from me and his need to control our situation were added to his arsenal. I was being yanked in every direction and my emotions flew like a yo-yo. I responded like a suffering victim. And still, I returned for more abuse after his proclamations of how he knew he really loved me "down deep," and "I'll always be your friend," and then later, when he said his "passion comes and goes." Even during my worst pain after he stated he no longer wanted our marriage, he said, "We're still family."

**December 19, 1994**

My strategy to pull through these days is straightforward. I keep journaling, writing poems, talking with friends, preparing for Christmas and mourning. Here are a few poems:

*Cry, scream, spew daggers*
*smash cups, slam phones*
*bare body and soul.*
*The blind do not see*
*The deaf do not hear*
*The dumb do not know.*

--------------------

*Liars hide their truths*

*in locked boxes.*

--------------------

*What have you done for Christmas?*

*Fractured our family*

*wounded our kids*

*using a tomahawk.*

*Left us hemorrhaging but not dead.*

*-- and you?*

--------------------

## December 20, 1994

At noon, I stopped at the post office before going to the bank to open a CD account from money in my savings account. I received a letter from Sheila, who apparently (and no surprise, really), will be my husband's lawyer. She asked for my lawyer's name so that she could contact him to resolve our marital problem in an amicable manner. I came home and called my lawyer, Tom, and I lost it several times, despite my efforts to hold myself together for whatever I have to do.

At 3 p.m., I called Sheila and told her Tom's name. Then I called Molly. She is a kind and excellent listener, but she doesn't say too much. I fear she is internalizing all these difficulties about her parents.

Finally, I called my counselor, Debbie, and read her my notes from the past few days. She said my poems "are an eloquent expression of my pain and striking pictures with words." She asked for a copy of the poems and said I should save them for a booklet. I told her I wanted to send them to my husband and she said it was OK to send them, knowing that it would not change things. I mailed him the poems.

**December 21, 1994**

Last night's dinner with my neighbors, Pete and Ed, was "tear-free" and pleasant. I didn't cry myself to sleep and I woke up early this morning and wrote some Christmas cards. I have written Christmas notes to 40 people. I plan to do about 15 more and let the rest slide until next year.

Later, thinking about how I am teetering on a shaky edge, I wrote this poem:

*Intuition stronger than thought*

*steps quickly*

*as scalding emotion*

*breaks into boil and then simmers.*

--------------------

I've also been remembering some of my husband's comments over the past few weeks and months and they make think about my finances. When he visited me at the Otis cottage, my husband admitted that our marriage problem is more his fault and thought that I deserved more than half. That's when he said, "I'll always be your friend."

While he may have said he wants to split our assets fairly, I don't trust him and I'm planning how to protect myself.

During lunch with friends, I learned that my husband's picture was in the newspaper because he has become the new president of the County Chamber of Commerce. The comments from friends about his picture included that he looked "old." He doesn't like "old."

I wonder who he'll take to the annual dance, maybe Molly? I haven't talked to him in almost a month. It feels bad to be without communication. Sometimes, I desperately want to call him and I wonder if he ever desperately wants to call me. I seriously doubt it.

**December 23, 1994**

I'm waiting for a call to set an appointment for the woodstove I bought to be installed in the fireplace. I'm also preparing to leave at 2 p.m. to pick up Molly and drive to Michelle's in Vermont for Christmas. This morning, I took the dogs and the cat to the vet's for boarding. I noted as I drove through town that my husband had closed his office for the day.

My periods of feeling strong are lasting longer. My bouts of tears are unpredictable, but shorter in duration. My car continues to serve as my safe place to explode and now driving results in fewer outbursts of anger and some are followed by a calm attitude of acceptance.

I've also seen the girlfriend in town twice as I driven through. Each time I looked, turned my head and drove on. I didn't lose it; I said "bitch."

When I'm in my car or at home, the radio is often my companion. Public radio is my source of information and music. Classical music is better than the popular love songs usually played on the other stations.

**Later --**

I picked up Molly and we drove to Vermont. She said she had dinner with her Dad recently and he'd said how young he feels and that he was doing fine. The recent Chamber newsletter got mixed into my mail and his photo was in it twice -- in one, he's flanked by the very young board members and the other was a headshot taken while he spoke about his past business experience. He did look good in both of those photos.

When we arrived at Michelle's, we had a wonderful fondue but we didn't ski due to rain.

**December 24, 1994**

It's still raining today so we looked around an antique shop and then went to Burlington for lunch. That's when the next bomb fell. Suddenly, my credit card didn't work and the waitress said she could not return it to me. I took it out of her hand and said I would not give her my card and that I would pay in cash.

Later, back at Michelle's house, I called Visa and learned that yesterday my husband had reported our Visa cards <u>lost</u> and had closed the account. What a lie! As a result, I no longer have a credit card and no access to funds in an emergency. I can't believe it even though it had occurred to me he might do it. I have used the credit card for my basic needs and to maintain a modest lifestyle, certainly less excessive than his. His cancellation of the credit card without my knowledge is more emotional battering and I feel helpless to protect myself. I'll try to call my lawyer on Monday.

I'm confused about the next step. If my husband sues me for divorce, he doesn't have the grounds. He may try to set up the idea that I'm dangerous. Or he might drag his feet. Right now, our joint account is frozen. The interest on a loan against the stocks and bonds in the joint account is eroding that account by hundreds of dollars every month. I have no credit card and now my only access to money is to draw on my own savings, which diminishes the only thing I have for the future, particularly since he's likely already tapping the assets that should be equally divided between us. So a "do-nothing" scenario seems to have a monstrous financial downside.

If I take action and sue <u>him</u> for divorce, my grounds are infidelity and emotional abuse. My only "proof" of infidelity, however, is his alienation of me, his lack of affection or sexual relationship with me and his inappropriate behavior with his filing clerk. My lawyer said we could subpoena the filing clerk girlfriend on these charges. Emotional abuse is also hard to prove.

We should split our assets but I wonder how to protect myself. How can I get control of my half of our assets? My husband is in the driver's seat. He knows everything about finances and a lot about the law. What reasons do I have to imagine that he'll be "fair" to me? My kids say if he screws me, they will have nothing more to do with him. I wonder if they've told him that. They don't believe he'll screw me. I think he already has. And now he's lied about the credit card. So, I'm on my own with this concern.

Since he seems to believe he's so young and cocky, I believe he'll continue to screw me without remorse, without guilt, and with keen instincts for this game he knows much more about than I do and that he is determined not to lose. I think the money has little to do with it for him -- it's the maneuvering, the control, the winning. He will not be on my side as he has always been in the past and that changes the picture completely. As an opponent, he must win -- it has always been his way.

I feel so sad and angry. I want to strike back in ways that won't help me – like, I want to embarrass him by joining the Chamber of Commerce and ' going to the dance, telling the Chamber people the truth about him, going to the girlfriend and demanding the money back that I believe he's been giving her and showing her how distraught I am. I know these actions wouldn't be useful to me, but I still want to do them.

Christmas Eve was pretty good. My son-in-law, Pierre, prepared a fabulous meal -- quail, wild rice, braised endive -- and we went to a little country church nearby. The service was so out-of-control we had to laugh. There were tons of little kids running wild. We'd never seen anything like it. When the young minister served communion, the kids rushed to the front of the church, grabbing at the bread and pushing to be first. Later, back at Michelle's, we played the video I had taken during our dinner earlier. That was fun.

## December 25, 1994

Michelle planned great walks for the day; one through a mountain pass along a stream leading to a lake. Her dog came with us and the walk in the snowy woods with fresh cool air was wonderful. After lunch, we did a shorter walk on a snowmobile trail closer to her home. We played a game of Clue, watched a movie video and talked a little about my problems. Michelle was adamant that my husband has already destroyed his life and that if he screws me financially, the kids will cut him off. Molly called her credit card company and ordered a card for me on her account. She'll have the card in seven days. It will give me an emergency back up. My daughters agreed that my husband is not the man I married and that maybe I would have to divorce him in order to separate our finances.

Pierre cut wood for me to take home tomorrow for my new woodstove. I wonder if my husband will try to stop the delivery on that.

## December 26, 1994

Today I plan to call my lawyer and talk about finances as a priority.

My lawyer's office is closed.

## December 27, 1994

I talked to my lawyer, Tom. He said my husband wants to sell the bonds in our joint account. My husband claims he will divide everything 50-50. My lawyer asked him to put something to that effect in writing. Since the Visa is canceled, Tom said he would call my husband's lawyer, Sheila, with more urgency to settle the split in finances quickly.

I told Tom I had worked out my ideal scenario for splitting up our assets, but I didn't believe my husband would agree. Tom and I both thought that my husband's "Trust me" is absolutely worthless.

It's 10:30 a.m. and I am waiting for the delivery of the woodstove and for the plumber to come and drain the pipes in the guest cottage. While I wait, I'll work on a condensed version of my story (so far) that I'd begun a few weeks ago. I believe it might help me see my path more clearly.

*May 12, 1956 - Promise to love, honor and cherish until death do us part. That was then.*

*Through the years - "I love you with all my heart," he said. We were sustained by trust, love and admiration. That was then.*

*1993 - Where is the love? Where is the warm embrace? Where is the loving sex? Where is the honesty? It's directed at a 30-year-old filing clerk. A girl who blatantly sucks up and he sucks back.*

*1994 - Through this year, I acted out my feelings. I cried and screamed. Occasionally, I was hysterical. I talked to him, I wrote, I demanded, I begged. I was humiliated, depressed and angry. I was scared. I felt suicidal and murderous and I felt hatred and anguish. I was suspicious and lost my self-esteem. I had diarrhea, stomach cramps, high blood pressure, fainting spells and a loss of my ability to carry on an intelligent conversation. I couldn't sleep and sometimes couldn't eat.*

*August 1994 - After a terrible summer of emotional agony and confusion, I found the hidden key to a locked file cabinet in my husband's office. There I found evidence of my suspicions. I found a $400 dollar Indian painting intended to be a gift for her and three books about divorce issues. There was a note for an appointment to see her marriage counselor along with his handwritten criticisms about our marriage. There was a* *record of payments made secretly to her all summer long. Credit card records revealed that he had taken her to New York City and bought her clothes at a Trump Tower boutique and a $100 lunch at the Sea Grill. It also appeared that he had lent her $10,000. After I confronted him, he admitted to their New York City spending spree.*

*He refused to allow me to use his counselor (he met with her once) so I sought my own. I found the Option Institute in Massachusetts. From August to September, it was a rocky ride.*

*The Ups: his 11th hour decision to join me at the Option Institute, his decision to build the front porch on our house, his initial commitment to work on our marriage and sex life.*

*The Downs: his waffling on the whereabouts of his passion, his need for "space," his ambivalence over if he loved me or her, his excessive phone calls to her discovered only because the phone company contacted me concerned that our phone credit card might have been stolen, my call to her demanding the return of the clothes he bought her and the money he had loaned her, her return of the clothes to his office and his cutting them up and throwing them on the floor of our home.*

*September 25, 1994 - I moved out to give him his "space." I made my second phone call to her as I left. I read my prepared written message to her and hung up. She called my husband.*

*September 26 - October 26, 1994 - I lived in a rental cottage in Massachusetts. I started rebuilding my life with friends. I had repeated bouts of anguish and I reached out to my husband for help. He responded by coming over and focusing on his feelings, refusing to talk about his filing clerk or anything in the "past." He was willing to go on as if nothing had happened, willing to enjoy sex, small talk and camaraderie with me.*

*Choosing to stay on the fence, he was noncommittal to me. I had periods of coping, walking, seeing friends, entertaining, talking on the phone, as well as major crying jags, depression, horrible emotional pain and a death wish. My husband said, "Deep down, I know I love you." He didn't get my emotional pain. He said he had emotional "drain."*

*When I ask the question, "Are you still talking to her?" he reacted by cutting me off at deeper and deeper levels.*

*November 1994 - While in California, I met my counselor, Debbie. I asked my husband "the question" over the phone. Then put voice mail on our home phone and eliminated my ability to call him. He is determined to retain all control. I couldn't even call about the birth of our first grandchild.*

*November 18, 1994 - I left California and drove home from Indiana. I left messages at his office and repeatedly at our home on the voice mail with no return calls. That was it; I'd had enough. At 1 a.m., after I returned to my Massachusetts cottage, I drove back to our home, determined to remove what I thought was a dastardly answering machine on our phone. After all, it's my home, too. Once there, I discovered it was voice mail from the phone company and not a machine. In a rage, I grabbed hold of my husband, pulling and shaking and when he pushed away from me he fell and broke his ankle. Later, he found a way to use this "fight" to depict me as life threatening and he showed an unusual amount of emotion relating the fight to the Option Institute counselor. I believe he knew full well that he had effectively resisted me by jabbing me in the ribs. I had no weapon, only my bare hands and much less strength than he, so he needed to greatly exaggerate the "fight" to build a legal case for himself in a divorce. He had nothing to warrant a divorce up to that point.*

*November 30, 1994 - He said he wanted to end the marriage. I lost it. I'm not able to speak or be coherent. I called him in my greatest moment of need and he sent my neighbors over. They took me to their house. Later, he came with my daughter, Molly. It was a hollow visit and the last bridge he burned. During that visit, he was emotional. He liked the way the house looked and he wanted to be together for Christmas. Molly said, "We are not a family. We (the kids) will see you separately."*

*December 15, 1994 - All communication stopped. We have lawyers and our joint account is frozen. Financial problems set in. I no longer keep my feelings between my husband and me. I opened myself to our kids, then to my closest friends and family, then to more friends, my broker, my lawyer and even total strangers, and of course, my good counselor, Debbie.*

*I returned to our home and my husband moved to our Big House. My life is filled with phone calls, support, lunches and dinners and activities that aren't stressful. I'm OK sometimes and sometimes I'm not.*

*December 23, 1994 – Telling another lie, he canceled my "lost" Visa, leaving me without a credit card. According to his lawyer, he wants to divide everything in half and we can trust him. I told my lawyer that I've heard the word "trust" before and have then seen his actions. I don't trust him at all.*

**Later --**

The woodstove is now installed. What a relief. While sleepless last night I thought: When we were OK, I liked his sense of humor, his embrace, his honest character, the way I always knew I was his woman and he was my man. I liked the way he helped people in his work and then set them free to advance.

I always said, "Between the two of us, we cover the bases." He was the aggressor and breadwinner. I was the homemaker, supportive partner and mother. I worked hard to create a happy home and to smooth the way for my husband's career. While placing him on a pedestal for family and friends, I trusted him completely and I felt loved. With love and trust, it worked.

And yet, when we were OK, there were some things that bothered me, too. I see them now like bright headlights in the rear view mirror. Characteristics that he may have thought served him in the business world, but that I found unkind.

He treated people in labor or "blue-collar" positions in an unfriendly and disrespectful manner, like waitresses, janitors, clerks, toll collectors and taxi drivers. In the early days, he would also litter.

He was often a rude driver and I was uncomfortable with his outbursts of anger. In a traffic jam, he would hit the steering wheel, yell loudly and give "the finger." He often displayed poor sportsmanship in competitive games like tennis. If he made a bad shot or didn't win the game, he would throw his racquet and fume. He also occasionally initiated and persisted with argumentative discussions with friends. His need to win and his criticism of others would put me in the "peace maker" role.

Sometimes I felt controlled by his judgments. He thought the church people were either too old or were jerks, the Lions were duds, etc. Our social plans had to fit his mood -- the movie of his choice, the food of his choice, the activity of his choice.

He <u>was</u> controlling, he set his time and space and I had to adjust to him.

Even as I look at this list today, though, I realize the things I didn't like were trivial in comparison to the good qualities he once possessed.

Good news: My sister, Lilly, plans to join me in Asheville when I go to look for a house for my son and his family.

**December 31, 1994**

New Year's Eve day in Asheville. Molly called. I didn't ask her about my husband's New Year's Eve plan. She and I agreed that 1994 was the worst and things had to get better.

Today, I'll drive through neighborhoods to house hunt. A poem I wrote in a motel en route to North Carolina:

> *Glimpses of wholeness*
> *emerge in the sight*
> *of a mind that gathers it's pieces*
> *from its shattered world.*

--------------------

**Later --**

While I was working on the house-hunting project, I felt OK. But when I came back to the motel room, I broke down miserably and longed to call my husband. I ate a piece of cheesecake, watched a TV movie and went to sleep.

**New Year's Day - January 1, 1995**

I woke up thinking about my house-hunting project and how I'd managed to make it through the night while wondering what my husband did last night. I have feelings of loving him and some of "let it go." I am glad that Lilly is coming tomorrow. I plan to go to church today and keep looking at houses.

At the church, I spotted a lady with a good haircut and I asked her for the name of her hairdresser.

**January 2, 1995**

I met with a real estate agent today and we looked at a couple of houses. I like him. Lilly and her husband, Neal, arrived and we went out to dinner.

**January 4, 1995**

No houses today. We did some sightseeing and got haircuts. We had invitations from the motel manager to the "corporate" cocktail party and buffet in the lounge so we decided to go. It was a good ego-builder for me. I managed to attract several men in my age group -- a retired air force colonel and a recently widowed telephone executive. I declined the invitation to go to the colonel's room and I didn't show up for the dancing later, but it still felt good to be notice by attractive, intelligent men. Lilly and Neal are leaving in the morning. They said they were glad to have found me coping well and looking ahead. We've had some good laughs.

**January 5, 1995**

Remembering last night, I wrote this little poem:

*Standing alone among friendly strangers*
*dipping her toe in the water,*
*was noticed*
*and rescued for dinner and asked to dance,*
*shed only a tear to clear the air*
*and moved on to laughter.*

--------------------

## January 6, 1995

I'm waiting for a call back from my lawyer, Tom, and I'm feeling shaky, I don't know what the issue is. I think it's finances, so I'm trying to get clear about my responses.

The message from Tom was that Sheila wants to send a summons for divorce. I'm to assemble my monthly "maintenance" costs and send it to Tom. I faxed a list of monthly maintenance costs; my total was $6,000, plus legal fees.

Even though I looked at houses for my son today, I'm distracted and nervous and really angry at my husband. I'm not crying, I'm saying " you bastard."

Some of Starr's family live nearby and they treated me to dinner. I really dumped on my husband to them. They understood my "venting" and we had a good time.

## January 7, 1995

Still at the hotel in Asheville, I found a place to copy the video of the best house I've found so far so I can send it to Jeffrey and Starr. I talked to friends on the phone, watched public TV and made a menu plan and guest list for my 60th birthday on January 20th.

Awake at 3 a.m., with random thoughts: Tears filled with memories recall the knife now withdrawn; I am beaten awake with a mallet pounding my body and brain.

Sleeping has been easier, I'm crying much less, but the fears hang in.

## January 8, 1995

Newt Gingrich was on C-SPAN at 8 a.m., in his first day as Speaker of the House. He sounded optimistic. I went to the Baptist Church and felt inspired. The sermon topic was "underliving life" -- the downfalls of no risk-taking and not living life to the fullest. I felt some courage to try something new, to be bold -- maybe I'm not afraid to go back into my greenhouse and continue helping my community, reclaiming my stake in my town, even if I lead a different existence.

Also, I'm thinking of the furniture in the Big House. Should I remove what I know I want or should I move everything into storage in my barn? I'll talk to someone about that.

**January 9, 1995**

It's 4 a.m. and I'm awake, not crying, but feeling shaky about the divorce summons and what is to come. My fantasy this morning was to send an invitation with a RSVP to my husband for dinner at my house. If he came, I would wear a see-through lace blouse, have a fire in the wood stove, a candlelight dinner and sex. Only as I write this does it make me cry.

Today, I'll put $500 down as "earnest money" on the house I found for Jeffrey and his family and get a contract.

**January 10, 1995**

During the night, I wept a little and felt adrift in confusion. But I woke up this morning ready to go on. Jeffrey and Starr like the house on the video. I made a $40,000 offer on the house.

I had a telephone appointment with my California counselor, Debbie, and she said to call my lawyer about issuing a divorce summons myself and ask him about the Big House furniture.

I went to the church gym and did an exercise class. It was good.

**January 11, 1995**

I read a little of the Divorce Recovery Workbook that Lilly gave me. I'm thinking of going to the weekly "corporate" party again tonight at my motel.

The house offer of $40,000 was countered with a $48,000 asking price -- back to the drawing board. My husband has not said yes or no to my son's request for a loan for half of the money for the house.

**January 12, 1995**

I'm wondering about whether to "up" the house offer and where to get the money. I looked at another house. At least I'm not crying or focusing on my husband.

I did go to the corporate party last night and the men did take notice. The retired colonel came looking for me and invited me to dance. Another man also asked me to join him. I went to the lounge to dance with the colonel. He was a smooth dancer and was clearly interested in pursuing a friendship -- a different hotel, dinner, calling me, etc. I think I'll have to fend him off. He says a good woman is hard to find. While he was in the bathroom, other men stepped up for the next dance. One guy said, "You don't leave a good looking woman standing alone in place like this."

Other than having my ego boosted a bit, I was uncomfortable in the setting. Even though the colonel was decent, intelligent and somewhat attractive, being in the arms of a man other than my husband didn't feel right. I may not be ready for this, but already I do see that if I look out, men look back. I also see I can move ahead as a single person.

Jeffrey is calling my husband for the extra $5,000 they need to make the offer on the house. With it or without it, I think I'll make the offer.

Jeffrey just called to say my husband agreed and the lawyers are working on it. My lawyer, Tom, called to say my husband wants the money to come out of our joint account. I said, "OK, if 100 percent of it is paid back to me." I made the offer and the agent thinks it will be accepted.

In my conversation with Tom, I learned the divorce summons coming from my husband charges me with being "cruel and inhuman." I broke down thinking about it, but only for a minute. My lawyer said it is one of several "causes" for divorce available in New York. He says we will counter with "infidelity and emotional battering" and that he is looking into an accountant for me if my husband does not come up with a fair settlement in a week.

**6 p.m.** - We got the house! It will close on February 28th. I called all of the kids.

**January 13, 1995**

I started home today. It was a nice warm day and as I drove, I was able to listen to music with lyrics without crying.

**4 a.m.** - I woke up in my hotel room after dreaming that I was being embraced and the sexual chemistry was there and flaring, but that I didn't know who it was with me.

I have some apprehension about receiving the divorce summons.

**January 15, 1995**

Driving home yesterday brought up a lot of anger and hurt. When I got home, I called my daughters, a friend and Debbie, since I was having trouble resisting calling my husband. After talking to Debbie, I realized to call my husband would be setting myself up for rejection again, so I didn't.

Today, I put our wedding picture back up on the wall. (I had put it in a bag.) Only as I write this does a tear come to my eye.

I'm cooking, going to church and later, to a movie with Nancy. I want to invite my husband to lunch. I think I want him to see what he's missing and somehow regret it, but I'm probably wrong.

Well, I did it. I put a message on his machine. I said, "If you'd like to come for lunch, pick up a sandwich and I'll be home at 1 p.m." At 1 p.m., I started baking cookies and at 2 p.m. he called to say that he didn't get the message on time and that he'd already had lunch. I believe that was a lie since I saw his car there at 10:45 a.m. and at 12:15 p.m. So, I just spoke politely with yes, no and OKs.

He also said he had taken our dog, Tootsie, from the vet's while I was away and was keeping her at the Big House. I guess this is his "division" of our pets. Even though I would rather keep only one dog and the cat, it was hurtful to think that, once again, I'm out of the loop. He's taken his action, I am not asked or consulted, he's already done it, he's in control and I'm the last to know.

**Later --**

This afternoon, on my way to the vet's to pick up our other dog, Spooky, and the cat, Chicken Feet, and deliver some cookies to friends, I saw my husband walking Tootsie on the driveway at the Big House. I drove up behind the barn and got out of my car. With my car and about 25 feet between us, he said, "Your hair has grown." I said, "I can't afford to get it cut." He said, "That'll change."

Tootsie trotted over to me and as I started to walk toward my husband, he turned and ran! I walked faster to catch up and he acted like I was going to clobber him. It was unbelievable. Finally, I stopped and said, "<u>What</u> are you doing?" He stopped and I said, "I'm not 'cruel and inhuman,' I am kind and human. I never broke your ankle -- you injured me!"

I restated my 40 years of loyalty and said I didn't know how he could live with himself. I was never closer than 10 feet from him. He looked haggard. I left.

After I picked up Spooky and Chicken Feet, I saw he was still walking Tootsie. I drove back behind the office and walked Spooky on the farmland and visited the neighbor and her new baby. Then I came home.

As I look back on today, I think I was wrong to call my husband and also to confront him and try to talk to him about what he's doing to me. Emotionally it brought up all the anxiety and pain. My feelings were not about loving him (although if he hadn't run away, I was going to kiss him), but instead, about how he continues to abuse and hurt me through his actions. I want to retaliate, but I can't. One of my books says the best revenge is getting yourself together. Mostly, I'm together, but the edge is close.

On the other hand, I was glad I expressed my feelings and asked him how he could live with himself. Sometimes I think I will recover and sometimes I think I will never be able to bear the divorce, separate lives and him going on. It's like, "How dare he go on and have a good life, he doesn't deserve it." I'm not crying, but I'm wallowing in anger.

On the driveway earlier, he denied referring to me as "cruel and inhuman." He claimed he didn't know what his lawyer said. I don't believe that, it's another lie.

**January 17, 1995**

I played tennis with some friends. It was really fun. Again today, I was overwhelmed with wanting to call my husband, but instead I called Molly. She talked me out of it.

At 7 p.m. I had my telephone conference with Debbie. She said my long marriage was too significant for me to get over losing it in a short time, but that I am getting clearer. I admitted to her that I often want to call my husband and see him, she said, "The price of hope is to go into the lion's den." What Debbie says feels right. I know she's on target and I value what she says.

She asked if my husband might be competitive with me since I have a strong, positive image in the community. She may be right here too. He is competitive; I just hadn't thought he would be competitive with me.

I read Debbie a list I had made about our marriage and she thought it was something I could share with my husband.

|      | YOU | ME |
|------|------|------|
| 1955 | friend | friend |
|      | trusted | trusted |
|      | passionate | passionate |
|      |      |      |
| 1956 | love | love |
|      | loyal | loyal |
|      |      |      |
| 1993 | impotent | uncertain |
|      | secretive | curious |
|      | controlling | judgmental |
|      | philandering | jealous |
|      |      |      |
| 1994 | dishonest | emotional |
|      | unfaithful | hysterical |

|                     |            |
|---------------------|------------|
| rejecting/waffling  | humiliated |
| total rejection     | devastated |

|      |                   |            |
|------|-------------------|------------|
| 1995 | noncommunicative  | angry      |
|      | selfish           | acceptance |
|      | emotionally off   | pity him   |

Today as I go on, I still cry, but I <u>do</u> pity him. I remember how it feels to be pitied, so I'm sorry for him. I wrote this:

*"When He Ran From Her"*
*Pipe dreams vanish*
*when she steps forward*
*to embrace the mate*
*locked in her memory,*
*now a cold, old man.*

----------------------

**January 18, 1995**

The latest word describing my husband was "neurotic," coming from Debbie. Others have suggested "Alzheimer's," "brain tumor," "mental illness," and "disease." He looks terrible.

I visited Russ at the pharmacy, spoke with other friends, cleaned the church house, sent a fax to the Realtor in Asheville, had the storm door fixed (again), made vegetarian soup for my birthday party on Friday, went shopping, sent birthday cards to the little kids I know who have birthdays the same day as mine and sent my husband the list of "YOU and ME," along with some tax information.

Tomorrow, Molly, Michelle and Pierre are coming here for a "Birthday-Eve dinner" that they planned for me. They will stop by the Big House where my husband is living and get some party things I need for the party I'm hosting on Friday.

## January 19, 1995

My former minister's wife called last night; it was the last night before they were to leave for their mission in Haiti. She invited me to come to Haiti with them. A man from my church called and said I was an "endangered species," because good women like me are hard to find. Another male friend said I was a "national treasure." Still another male friend said he refers to my husband as "Alice's husband." Another man stopped by and suggested I start seeing other men.

Some people think I'm out of money. Some people are passing judgment on me and my situation and they haven't even met me. It's a hot topic.

With my 60th birthday tomorrow, the flowers are arriving. My daughters prepared the most loving and wonderful Birthday-Eve dinner tonight. We ate brie and crackers, Greek olives, baked salmon, julienne vegetables, rice pilaf, mixed greens salad and chocolate soufflé. They gave me gifts of flowers and a sweater and Molly read a special toast:

*Happy Birthday, Mom!*

*How proud we are of you and everything you've done. You've always been honest, caring and loving. A nurturer, a supporter someone to lean on, someone who can be counted on, a leader, a motivator, someone who is creative and can get things done. Intelligent and wise, spiritual and spirited, you touch and inspire. You are a woman of beauty, a woman of strength. These things you are -- these things carry you forward. Sixty is a number. Every year you've been here is a reason to celebrate.*

*Love you,*

*Molly*

## January 20, 1995

I woke up to my 60th birthday, cried hard and then did laundry and started preparing for my party. My husband gave my daughters the wrong plates; I need the large ones. So I called my husband's office answering machine at 8 a.m. and let what used to be "our song," "Unchained Melody," play into it. Then I had to call back to leave my message because the machine cut off before I had a chance to say anything. I asked him to leave the large plates in the greenhouse for me.

Last night, Molly brought me my earliest journal notes dating from Summer 1993 and my photocopied information from my husband's locked file cabinet which she has kept stashed in the trunk of her car for safekeeping all this time. Looking at it all made me so sad. My feelings today are intense and mixed-up. My first birthday in 40 years without my husband. I feel lonely and angry. I want to call Debbie or ask someone to come over while I wait for this evening when my guests will arrive. I want to march into my husband's office and cry so he'll see my pain.

Instead, I think about what I'm going to do -- laundry, prepare salad, make the salmon spread, bathe, wash my hair, organize the kitchen and set the table. I called Nancy and told her my feelings. She agreed to stop by the greenhouse and pick up the plates. I feel too emotional to go there.

## January 21, 1995

The party was great. Twelve people including me -- ages 33 to 65. We played charades and Pictionary. We laughed, danced to music from the 70s and had a wonderful time. It was a very successful party. I didn't think they knew it was my birthday, but they all did and they brought little gifts and two big cakes. It was fun to see the men really get into the interactive games they normally wouldn't play. I thought that if my husband had been present, he would have discouraged my plan to play games and we probably wouldn't have played any. But since the "birthday girl" wanted games at her party, all of my guests happily cooperated and we had real fun. Today I'm helping with a lunch at the church house.

## January 22, 1995

Another overwhelming desire to call my husband last night resulted in trying to call Molly and then calling Nancy. She suggested a movie, so we did that and had a pizza.

This morning I woke up crying and I called my husband. I suggested coffee and toast and he said he was going to church in Berryville. He sounded weak and almost crying. He said he wanted to go alone and he couldn't see me yet. In his benevolent way, he turned me down again. It's the "lion's den" thing, I think.

Yesterday, I received an invitation to visit friends in Connecticut and a lovely note from friends in Iowa. My Iowa friend, Gert, said that tears well up in her eyes when she sees a glowing sunset or a pretty home decorated with lights and greenery because they make her think of me. Her description made me cry.

For some reason, mostly from how my husband sounded on the phone, I think he's in a new level of his confusion and maybe having second thoughts. I notice his hours at the office are limited and that he is at the Big House most of the time. In the phone conversation when he said, "I'm going to church," I said, "I'll meet you there." I know my suggestion pressed him to say, "I want to go alone." Instead, I could have said, "That's nice," or nothing at all, but I used my suggestion to press him for his position. I don't know what that is in me.

At church this morning it was announced that Nancy, the friend I went to the movie with last night, had had a fire in her house. I was shocked. I went directly to her house after church. Apparently, while we were at the movie, an arsonist broke a window, unlocked a door, entered her house and ignited a fire in a closet in a part of her house that she uses for storage. At 11 p.m. she woke up smelling smoke. The smoke detectors in her house had not sounded. Nancy escaped with her cat. A big section of her house was destroyed.

**January 23, 1995**

I stopped to see Nancy again. She is doing what she has to do with insurance, fire marshals, builders, cleaners, etc. The incredible violation to her life is striking and awful and has hit her hard.

I decided to make a positive move on my greenhouse plans. I called the man who has supplied me with plant plugs and he said he would do it again. He barely knows me but he had heard about my marital problem. Then I told the Falls Town Flowers group that I would grow the town's flowers and hanging baskets as I've done in years passed. Also, I called a couple of people from the church and told them I thought raising plants and flowers in the greenhouse could be a fund-raiser for the church this year.

While at the greenhouse, I will rely on volunteer help and keep myself surrounded by friends so I won't have to look at my husband's office just across the field. Additionally, I ordered a seed catalog and looked through my supply catalog. Even if the divorce summons comes, the divorce won't be sudden, so I might as well plan a season in the greenhouse.

**January 29, 1995**

A good old friend from Chicago came on Tuesday and will be flying back today. Jane lost her husband seven years ago. She is a thoughtful, intelligent conversationalist and a great listener. She certainly listened. It took five days to tell her everything.

In some ways, it was good to hear myself relating all the details of what's happened. I can realize now how I was shut out of my husband's life over a period of time. It happened gradually, but consistently. Incident after incident, and with and without the filing clerk's presence. I was pushed out by his newspapers, his work, his videos, his meetings, his lunches, his dinners out, his finances, his tractor, his music, his clients, his seminars, his medical appointments and recently, even his whereabouts -- told to me only on a "need to know" basis.

I talked a lot to Jane, maybe too much. We had good laughs -- many of them from dumping on my husband. We did some interesting activity each day of her visit including a meeting at the local hospital. We were able to make a big point for Falls Town that was entered into the goal list for the hospital's community planning.

Even though I hadn't seen Jane in many years, the quality of friendship was just like those early days when we were both having our first kids.

Tomorrow, I have an appointment with my lawyer, Tom, about my finances. Just the thought stirs my stomach. I have no idea what my husband might be proposing and I don't know how I'll react to it.

**January 30, 1995**

Once again my instincts are correct. My husband submitted a plan for "equal" distribution of assets. The plan may have seemed equal and organized to an untrained eye, but when I analyzed it, line by line, I discovered that my husband's plan was to keep the farm and the Big House for himself and to allocate all the unsalable property to me! Furthermore, he overvalued that property, claiming that the eight acres for me are worth an unbelievable $8,000 per acre.

The farm, on the other hand, which he stated to be worth $225,000 actually underline includes a $200,000 office, according to what we've put into it; a $50,000 greenhouse; a $25,000 barn; and 62 acres of prime land. Even if the 62 acres were valued at $8,000 per acre, as he suggested for my eight unsalable acres, his "cut" would have a real value of $771,000 not $225,000. His numbers are totally bogus and fraudulent.

He also failed to mention several bank accounts, as well as what I believe to be a substantial IRA. He's covered up a half million dollars and I believe even more. It was a bad day.

**January 31, 1995**

I called Lilly's husband, Neal, at 6 a.m. with all the numbers in my husband's proposal and we talked through what I should do. Neal is an engineer but he is particularly good with finances.

Then I called my lawyer, Tom, but he wasn't in. He has 1:30 p.m. appointment scheduled with my husband and his lawyer, Sheila. They are to discuss fair settlement and Tom did not want me to attend. I think he sees me as too emotional. I called Tom's secretary and gave her point by point the flaws I saw in my husband's financial assessment. Since I'd been able to thoroughly review it, I wanted to be sure Tom had all the accurate information. And I cited explicit instructions for Tom about the frozen joint account.

My plan is to stay near the phone today. I skipped tennis and Molly plans to come here for dinner. I told Molly about her dad trying to screw me financially. She sees it but she loves her dad. It's such a difficult position to be in.

I feel angry and emotional. The embers of any reconciliation are dying. At the moment, I feel like fighting him for my financial rights even if I go bankrupt trying. Everyone says he's a "gay blade" around town and they comment on his good looks.

Yesterday, I received a strange phone call. An elderly neighbor called to ask how I was doing and to say how sorry she was about the gossip. I told her I was OK with the gossip, it's just one of the things in a small town and the good things outweigh that sort of thing. She then asked if I had received the letter of apology from the "other woman." I said I had not received any letter and I asked her who the "other woman" is. She said it was a client of my husband's. She told me she had also called my husband on this same subject and had asked him if he had received a letter and he said it was all straightened out. I don't know anything about any of it. It's hard to know who or what to believe. It was just odd. I told Tom about it.

I remind myself that Debbie said there would be days that wouldn't be good for me. Today and yesterday are days like that.    I am anxious for 7 p.m. so I can call her. I'm trying to motivate myself to make my seeds and plants plan. I can see that going to the greenhouse will be a major hurdle. I feel shaky, sad and tired.

**February 1, 1995**

After waiting all afternoon yesterday for Tom to call me with the outcome of the meeting he had with my husband and his lawyer, I felt discouraged by the end of the day. I ended up just having dinner at home with Molly and having my telephone appointment with Debbie. She is my lifeline. She encouraged me not to sign anything, to fight and to get a new lawyer if I find mine to be "too nice." She said to write when I'm upset, to go ahead and cry and to get my maintenance payments from my husband by court order, if necessary.

**February 3, 1995**

Yesterday was lousy. It began with a two and a half hour meeting with Tom looking at finances. He said he would propose that we go 50/50 on a payment to my son for the house loan. I would take my half out of my funds and my husband would take his half out of his funds.

At his meeting with my husband and Sheila a couple of days ago, Tom did use a very clever tactic. He suggested to them that since my husband says his proposal is an "equal" division of assets and property, that I could then take his part and he could take what he's delegated to me -- a fair and "equal" swap, 50/50. My husband and Sheila balked immediately with no consent. They never agreed to the "50/50 switch" plan.

So we're back to trying to work on a fair settlement with my husband. Tom suggested we could subpoena financial records, if necessary. I said I could hunt for more evidence of his relationship with the filing clerk and for hidden finances.

After the meeting with Tom in Hudson, I drove to Westchester to have lunch with Gerry. Then I drove back home for the soup supper I had planned for Nancy. In my mail was a form letter from the telephone company. It had been issued by my husband and was to give me responsibility for all existing bills as well as ongoing responsibility for my telephone. I didn't sign it. I ignored it.

At the soup supper party for Nancy, I was very shaky and I broke down several times. My friends told me that people had seen the filing clerk's car at my husband's place at night and his car in her driveway some mornings. He had also been seen eating out with her and shopping with her. I came home and tried to call Tom at home but I didn't know his number and I called the wrong number. I called Molly and Debbie but I didn't reach either of them. Out of the blue, my nephew, Dave, called to give me advice. He's been through a divorce and he said I should be careful not to let business and financial matters slip through the cracks.

At about 1 a.m., Debbie called back. I told my kids that I now hate my husband. I took my wedding ring off in the middle of the night.

**February 3, 1995**

The forecast this morning predicts a major snowstorm is on the way. Since I'm the only person on my road right now and it's one mile to the next road in either direction, I need to carry in wood and shop for some essentials. I called Tom and asked him to hire a private detective immediately and he agreed completely. I sent a $1,500 retainer to the private detective who said he would come next week after the forecasted snowstorm tonight. I'll be paying him $45 per hour plus mileage and film. He said the more information I can gather about the patterns of their lives and when they might be together the better. Also, he said if I can "catch anything" this weekend, he would write it into his notes.

So tonight I had dinner at Nancy's and then drove past the filing clerk's house and by my husband's. It appeared they were both in their homes at 8:30 p.m. I could see the filing clerk's daughter in her house and my husband's TV was on at his house. I plan to go back around 9:30 p.m. and see if anything has changed. My friends are also going to keep an eye out. It's hard for me to believe I'm in this position.

My spy-notes say: My husband left his office at 5:45 p.m. and went straight to the Big House. At 6 p.m. he had the east porch lights on, which is unusual, and the back floodlights. At 9:30 p.m., with his car in the driveway, the lights went off in the TV room and the lights went on in his bedroom. At 3:30 a.m., with his car in the same spot, the lights are off in his bedroom and the light is on in his bathroom.

At 9:30 p.m., the filing clerk seemed to be home. At 3:30 a.m., her house was dark.

I'm glad I didn't pay a private detective for this night. I physically shake when I think about or execute the spying activities. I'm not comfortable in this role.

**February 4, 1995**

I called a friend at the hospital and asked if I could get a chest x-ray without a doctor's order and she said I could go to the emergency room. My rib still aches in the spot where I got jabbed in our fight.

At 11:30 a.m. in a snowstorm, I drove to town to get my mail. I saw car tracks in my husband's driveway, slightly drifted, and I saw no evidence of car tracks at the filing clerk's house. When I circled back through town, I saw my husband's car at the post office approaching from the Big House direction. I'm making a calendar chart to fill in what I see and what my friends see.

The storm is bad -- high winds and drifting snow. I feel isolated and lost.

Since it's Saturday, I don't like to call people and it's also a time that friends don't call. Molly did call and invited me to dinner at her house, but it would not be smart to even try to go out in this storm. I am very tired since I've had very little sleep over the past few nights, so I think I'll just go to bed. I feel depressed and lonely -- not suicidal, not murderous, not angry, just overwhelmingly sad. I keep crying. Molly and one of her friends plan to come here tomorrow morning.

**February 5, 1995**

When I spoke with Michelle last night I was pretty upset. I told her I felt like my mind was shutting down. I couldn't remember if I ate and I couldn't remember how I got my husband's new phone number. I can't hold simple ideas in my head from one room to the next. I wander around the house trying to remember what I'm doing. I wish for someone to call me and talk. My cousin, Ann, called and I talked too much.

When the man came to plow the driveway and asked if he should send someone to shovel the walk, I broke down and said I didn't think I should have any service that I might not be able to pay for. I told him I was having big trouble with my finances and he said he would plow for nothing if my husband wouldn't pay. He also encouraged me by saying the whole town is behind me and to hang in and fight. He said that people in town can't believe I'm able to keep my life going with what I'm going through, but as he could see, sometimes I'm not able to keep going. It's not as bad as the worst times, but it's bad.

Michelle said my husband plans to drive up to see her in a week or so. I'll find out the exact date because that will be an opportunity for me to search his office.

Besides having a cold, I feel sick anyway. I just want to collapse and cry. But then, Debbie's many words of encouragement brim forth from the back of my brain and make me think... maybe I'll do a hot bath, wash my hair, look as good as I can for Molly and her friend, and I'll shovel some snow.

I really hope my neighbors call me today. Ann plans to come next weekend and take me out. I don't know what to do about my greenhouse. It'll take about $1,000 to get it started and I can't spend that much money. It seems I'm back to lost and confused, powerless and tired. Church was canceled due to the snow. I took a bath, washed my hair, did laundry and I see myself looking haggard in the mirror.

I remember something Michelle said pertaining to my husband's call to her and his plan to visit her. Michelle told me, "Dad should leave town. It's not fair to you that he's in your face." I hope he does leave town. When I drift into speculating what he'll do, I realize it's a waste. I need to concentrate on what I'll do.

For now, I'll get a chest x-ray to hopefully prove that I did receive a broken rib from his blows to me during our fight in November. I'll also expand my efforts to fight for my rights. I'll spend whatever it takes to be sure that he doesn't walk away with everything, even if I lose money doing it.

A friend called and gave me an interesting comment that her husband had heard from my husband -- my husband is having a hard time sleeping at night. He should be.

**February 6, 1995**

Last night I took a look at the filing clerk's house on my way to dinner at Nancy's and my husband's car was in her driveway. I went straight to Nancy and asked her to go look to document what I saw. She and her sister went and took their camera. They took a photo as they drove by. At 6:30 p.m. I saw his car back at the Big House. This morning, I called my lawyer and the private detective with this information.

Then I went to the emergency room and got a chest x-ray. The doctor will report a domestic tussle on November 18, 1994, which resulted in a deliberate injury to my chest. He could not claim a broken rib, but he did claim a definite injury to the location.

Receiving my mail has taken on new meaning, never knowing what will be in it. Today, I had a form from Spiegel saying they regret to cancel my order of January 31, 1995, due to my Visa card not being approved. I have never ordered from Spiegel. I called them and found out the order had been a mock sweater, leggings and a T-shirt, all in adult women sizes. They also told me of other purchases made during the fall of 1994 -- some had been made by Michelle and Molly on the Visa card as gifts from my husband while other purchases, in much larger sizes, were not for my daughters.

I then called Visa and said my "lost" Visa had been used illegally on October 29, 1994, and had been tried again on January 31, 1995. Visa told me that on January 24, 1995, two orders had been returned and that on December 24, 1994, two "fast cards" had been sent to my husband after he'd reported the Visa cards "lost." They said those cards would be canceled immediately and two new cards issued.

It would be amazing if we could nail the filing clerk on credit card fraud. I laugh aloud thinking about it. It seems too good to be true and maybe there's some other reason for it. But it's a new intrigue that is interesting. She does appear to have use of <u>our</u> credit card account, however, half of which is mine.

If the credit cards happen to come to me, I wonder if I should withdraw the limit in cash to keep myself going. First I'll see if they get put in my mailbox, then I'll ask my lawyer.

A friend suggested that I get an accountant to evaluate what my husband's business is worth in order to get half and to estimate the amount of money the filing clerk has been given from him because half of it is mine.

**February 7, 1995**

My call with Debbie tonight was good. She complimented my recent positive actions. I read her my husband's notes to himself (dated August 8, 1994) that were part of my findings in the locked file cabinet. She said they revealed that he'd projected his feelings of hating to grow old and hating not having enough attention, as well as his low self-esteem, <u>all</u> onto our marriage. Debbie said that dumping all of his problems in a heap of blame on his marriage will only give him a hollow victory.

Now that Debbie has explained it, it seems so clear and I believe she's exactly right. If she were to counsel him, she could help him to see it too. Debbie advised me to make copies of all my original "evidence" and secure them under lock and key. She wants me to be super-protected because she doesn't trust what could happen. I think she's right. I'll make copies tomorrow so I have two full sets.

**February 8, 1995**

This morning I took my bag of important papers and notes with me. I copied the Spiegel letter at the Falls Town pharmacy. Russ, the pharmacist and owner, told me he had no animosity towards my husband and that he goes in there every day to buy his newspaper. I knew that was OK, but it stung anyway.

Then, there were no Visa cards in the mail and I felt dashed in the hope that the cards would land in my mailbox. I talked to the private detective and he said he'd try to establish a paper trail between my husband and his girlfriend. He asked me to get a sample of her handwriting and to keep a log of bank accounts and charges.

Feeling really down, I wondered if I should bother going to the church meeting, but I cried hard, washed my face and went. While there I learned our names were taken off the prayer list a couple of weeks ago and that it was my husband who had asked them to be removed. I wailed in my car coming home from the church meeting. I feel so lost, so ineffective, so worthless and helpless.

The private investigation is starting and I can't talk to my kids. The elderly neighbor told me the gossip is horrible. I can't reach out to other people today, even though I know some people who are going through tough times themselves. I just came home and cried. There seems to be such a fine line between coping and falling apart.

I called my mother. I attempted to appear strong for her sake. I wanted to sound like I was coping. She saw through it immediately. Her way to get a grip on my situation is to search for solutions. She wondered if maybe I was being hasty or maybe I could ignore what I know is going on and act as if I don't care. If he dies, there's his pension, she says. At least I could be financially secure if I could just look the other way.

Mom doesn't get it. I have become clear on what I want and I want it all. I cannot live in a marriage without trust and love. I will find a way to take care of myself. I'll fight legally for my rights. My mother supported me in her way -- coming from 80-year-old, Midwestern, rural values -- she gave me all the advice and emotional support she could.

It's 4 p.m. and I'm just very sad. I know I'm supposed to think about myself, get myself going, let go of my husband and the girlfriend, plan positive things and realize I'm OK; but today, even very small things hurt me substantially. I feel really tired and stupid and very much alone. I need a piece of good news. At the church meeting today, I suggested to my friend, Betsy, that with the abundance of bad news around town that we should "manufacture" some good news. That's about the most positive thing I did today.

**February 9, 1995**

Gosh, yesterday was a bummer. Last night, however, I had a long talk with Nancy and then another long talk with Jane in Chicago. They both called me and they both know everything so they were really great to talk to.

At 10 a.m. this morning, I had a meeting with my "nice" lawyer, Tom, and with my new "tough" litigation lawyer, Victor. They're partners in the same law firm. They suggested appraisers for the real estate. I asked if I could bring a friend to our legal meetings and they said, "Sure." I explained that two heads are better than one and I thought it would help to have another person listen and ask questions objectively. I'm not used to hearing all the legal talk. I'll bring Nancy; she has a good head.

The strategy will be to serve divorce papers on my husband in about two weeks. I need to come up with $7,000 to get the lawyers started.

**February 11, 1995**

In my bundle of mail, there was a statement from the U.S. Federation of Small Businesses and I learn from it that my husband buys dental insurance for the girlfriend. She hasn't worked in his office for months. There was also Visa bill, which showed a charge on New Year's Eve at a nearby Inn. I called the Inn and learned that the amount charged was probably a dinner for two. This information is daggers through my skin. Any money my husband spends on anything is half mine and it sickens me to realize what he's spending on his girlfriend.

I ordered my greenhouse supplies to be delivered March 2. It's a beautiful day today, but I'm trembling.

I called my mother for her birthday. I kept the call short and I was strong and positive to minimize her pain. I plan to see my cousin, Ann, this evening. I called Neal, Lilly's husband, to run by him my idea of taking a lien on the Big House as a guarantee for payment of my legal fees. I'll suggest it to my lawyers.

Three days ago with the knowledge of his forthcoming divorce summons issue still fresh and stinging like nettle, I wrote this letter (not sent) to my husband:

*Someday when you face yourself, you'll see the ugly truth of your selfishness that actually began when we married. You controlled me to accomplish your own goals. My counselor suggests that you more than contributed to our son's problems by not allowing for his self-esteem because you were always grabbing your own. You were not there for him when he needed you.*

*I covered up for you all the time, making sure you were viewed as the wonderful father the kids still believe you were. And now, through your final act of selfishness, I will be free to be who I really am. I only wish you had found an Indian-whore twenty years ago. Maybe then a wonderful boy might have been saved from growing up under the cloud of alcohol and drugs he used to use to make himself feel better. Luckily for our son, he has forgiven us and his life is set straight. I have forgiven myself and I did it by saying, "I'll never bury my feelings again."*

*When you sue me for divorce on the grounds of "cruel and inhuman," put a mirror to your face. You will be looking at a cruel, inhuman, selfish and pathetic life. I pity you.*

*Alice*

**February 12, 1995**

The weekend neighbors came to visit me and I shared quite a bit with them. Then I went to the Canyon Ranch Spa in Massachusetts to pick up my cousin Ann after she finished work. We stopped by to visit friends in Stockbridge and asked them to join us for dinner at the Red Lion Inn. We had a good time.

Emotionally, I'm hovering. Back to back, I think of how unfairly I've been treated and then I think how lucky I might be to have my life for myself. I try to motivate myself to prepare my case -- the finances, the sequential notes of what's happened. I try to carve out a little time each day to enjoy the outdoors and play with Spooky. My legs are shaky, my stomach is nervous, sometimes I want to go to sleep and escape all of it.

Today, my mindset is to spend whatever it takes to assure my rights in the divorce. Tomorrow, I'll call my lawyer, Victor, with comments on a few issues: 1) the Big House furnishings have been promised to our kids, 2) the Merrill Lynch mix-up over the loan to our son, 3) the dental insurance for the girl and 4) the payment of legal fees by a lien on the Big House.

We are waiting for my husband to respond to our request for maintenance money, his income tax records and his calculation of his net worth. We don't expect any cooperation.

## February 13, 1995

I dreamed last night that someone from the private investigator's office mistakenly called my husband and told him the details of what they were doing. I woke up scared and shaking. At 8 a.m. I was still shaking.

Molly came to visit yesterday while Ann was here. She brought a cute "black dog" hat for my Valentine's gift. Again, she is so thoughtful.

Just before it was time to go exercise with Flora, my broker called. My husband wants to sell the bonds in the frozen account. So I called my lawyer, then called my broker back, then back to my lawyer and after all day, it was decided to sell $52,000 of bonds to pay the interest debt created by a loan that was made against the securities in the account.

Later, a friend told me that my husband's car was seen at the girl's house on Christmas day. After that I just broke down.

Then my friend Catherine from Chicago called and we talked for an hour. She said she understood my feeling of my husband being "taken" by a younger woman -- a fear many people identify with. I was really glad she called when she did. I needed to talk to someone.

Tomorrow is Valentine's Day and I'm dreading it. I figure my husband will do something spectacular for the girl. I just hope the private investigator sees it.

**February 14, 1995**

An appraiser called to say my husband's lawyer had contacted him to appraise our properties, including the house where I'm living. He is coming here tomorrow at 11:30 a.m. I called my lawyer, Tom, to tell him. Then I slammed down the phone and standing alone in my kitchen, I screamed aloud, "I hate you, you bastard, I hate you."

It's his Valentine's present to me. I knew there would be something. Where is that "friend" he said he would always be?

I've ordered the plant plugs for the greenhouse flowers and I've ordered the other supplies. I have a plan to clean the greenhouse on March 1st and start the plants later that week. I'm committing $1,000 to get the greenhouse started. My lawyers think it's a good idea.

I'm halfheartedly washing the walls to clean my house for this weekend. My landlords from Otis are coming to visit. I made chili. Later I called Starr's family to be sure the closing on the house in Asheville was moving along. At 6 p.m., I had my telephone session with Debbie. She was happy to hear that I had told two people today that my husband is "a goddamned fucking bastard."

**February 15, 1995**

The appraiser and my husband's lawyer came to appraise my house. He immediately commented on how nice the house is -- great view, warm feeling, private, peaceful. I said it's small, but he said size didn't matter. I told him I wanted the farm and the farmhouse.

**February 16, 1995**

Nancy went with me to meet with my lawyers. We went over finances and the ideas of splitting the joint account into our separate accounts, getting a value on my husband's business, on his CPA degree and on his earning power. I came home and started to put together the exact costs that went into the renovation of the Big House. On top of paying $222,000 for the house, I already have receipts for another $200,000 and I'm not finished -- decorating, furniture and all the lumber bills aren't included yet. Then I met Nancy and Molly at the pizza place in Massachusetts and we went to see the movie, "Little Women." It was good.

NOTE: I didn't cry at all today.

**February 17, 1995**

I woke up with thoughts to exercise, prepare for guests, finish the costs of the Big House and clean my house a little -- no crying. I made a couple of statements aloud like, "You fucking bastard" and "Liar and Cheat," but nothing that kept me from my activities. I'll get on with my life, but first I'll fight for my rights in the divorce. I feel tougher. I believe my friends and Debbie are giving me a new charge of courage, and so is Victor.

At Debbie's persuasion, I continue to follow my instincts about my lawyer. Victor is sharp, professional, well-dressed, fit and intense. He's a gentleman with a dry sense of humor and eyes that seem to look for lies. When he asks, "How are you?" I feel a genuine concern in his greeting. His "Ivy League" appearance is compatible with his quiet awareness of everything going on. He's constantly absorbing information with an incredible memory for detail. His comments are precise and his questions are astute. He suggests strategies and options and I feel respected. He is truly supportive of me.

After one particularly difficult session in which we were hashing out how to protect myself and get a fair settlement from my husband, Victor's eyes narrowed and he looked straight through me and said, "We'll paint him Lucifer." That comment sealed my trust in Victor.

When I think about Debbie and what it is about counseling that feels so essential, I realize she points out my honesty and the progress I've made. She shows me where I have been and where I may be going. Through her expertise, she helps me see my situation as created by my husband's choices. He is not the person I was married to or would want to remain married to. Debbie helps me realize that I have a variety of roles in life other than just being his wife, and that many other people can fill the void created by the loss of my husband. Debbie shows me the light at the end of tunnel. Together, we are a team in recall, evaluation, analysis, strategy and action.

Sometimes I can set my emotional side apart and really work on my business side as if this is a project and I'm the chairman.

**February 19, 1995**

Tony and Bev, my young landlords from my rental cottage in Otis, came over yesterday for lunch. We did a little walk around my property and took a ride around Falls Town. We stopped at the greenhouse and since it looked like my husband wasn't around, I tested my key on the office door. It worked! So my plan for next Saturday is on. I believe he'll be visiting Michelle then, so I'll get my video camera ready to go. My plan is to search the office for anything that could help my case and remove the items that belong to me from the Big House. It makes me shake with nerves, but I need to do it for my case and to protect myself and our kids financially.

I haven't cried in several days and I'm thinking more in terms of my own activities and at least allowing the idea of another man in my life. I have no prospects but I would like to have fun with someone.

When I woke up this morning, I was dreaming that the young man accountant, Brett, at my husband's office had quit and the girl had come back. I wanted to prevent it, but there was nothing I could do. It was a helpless feeling of bearing the hurt and humiliation and struggling to go on in the face of it.

Today, I'll take Spooky on a walk in the fields; it's such a nice day. And I'll go to a friend's 65th birthday party; he has terminal cancer.

Saturday and Sunday are lonelier days because they seem to be everyone else's special days. I think I need to make more fulfilling plans for my weekends. The weekdays are busier, but they have the underlying fears of the divorce, the summons, legal actions, etc.

**February 21, 1995**

Yesterday, I did a long walk in the fields with Spooky and my two energetic friends, Anna and George. We took our lunch and sat on a log. Later, we lay down on a grassy bank with patches of snow dotted all around us and relaxed in the warm sun and talked. Then I drove to their house and spent a couple of hours photocopying my emotional journal notes so that I have a second set. I read a couple of my poems to them and for a minute I thought I could make it without crying, but the feelings welled up and I broke down a little.

Today, I did another field walk with Spooky. Molly came for dinner and I had my counseling call with Debbie. I read Debbie another letter I had written (not sent) to my husband and she thought it was wonderful. She thinks I'm a good writer. She also said that someday I could show my husband this letter. It seems pretty vile to me but Debbie said, "Oh no, not at all."

The letter:

*Husband -*

*As we approach the countdown to the divorce, I am beginning to feel liberated. I see myself as a sexual, beautiful woman with much to give and to receive. I have become this person even under your gripping control and selfish, deviant behavior. Even though you have lied, cheated, scorned and tried to destroy me emotionally for your own sexual youth fantasies, I am emerging with the power I should have taken long ago. By taking my free will, I can see I have a positive effect on our kids and my many friends. I am proud to say you have not dragged me into the gutter with you and you haven't been able to drag our kids into your slum.*

*Since I pretty much raised the kids by myself, I'm very pleased to see them strong and moral. Your devotion to your career left them with an absent, selfish, ego-centered, power-hungry father, who did nothing to promote their individual self-esteems. But now your horrible behavior is setting us all free.*

*Our kids know the father that their mother mistakenly put on pedestal all those years. But at last you are revealing yourself and it's not a pretty picture. The admiration, respect and trust are gone. The father our children still love is a foolish, old man -- fallen from respect from every friend and family member of his life. You are winning a hollow victory for the sake of fucking a whore. You have destroyed our family and ruined our financial stability.*

*The good news is that it's worth it. I have paid an enormous price to be free of you.*

*As you rot in hell, you have my pity. I can call you a bastard to everyone I know and I can forgive you for your ignoramus behavior. I am as clear now as I was when you refused to get counseling to save our marriage. I want it all -- love, sex and trust. I'm worth it. I have never deviated from honesty, loyalty and commitment. Only you have had the privilege of the depths of my emotions. I was saved by my honesty.*

*Alice*

**February 22, 1995**

Plans are in place to go skiing tomorrow with friends. We are going to Otis, Massachusetts, where I have a ski pass.

**February 24, 1995**

Yesterday was great. I took a beginner's lesson and we all had a great time. The weather was mild and it snowed a little. Today is my final day of preparation for the search in my husband's office and the removal of my things from the Big House. A friend plans to meet me at 10 a.m. to help me photocopy any "evidence" we may find in the office. I wrote these poems in anticipation:

*Butter on my toast today*
*caressing a fear,*
*will tomorrow's reality*
*be today's expectation?*

--------------------

*Body tense*
*stomach queasy*
*key to the office*
*Damning evidence?*

--------------------

*Why should I fear*
*to enter my house,*
*remove my things?*
*Now my "rights" surpass my esteem,*
*Tomorrow may my self-esteem*
*equal my "rights."*

--------------------

## February 25, 1995

I woke up at 3 a.m., trying to think of the possible scenarios. Should I call his house at 8:15 a.m. to see if he's home? Should I drive right up the driveway and hope for the best? What if the girlfriend is there? What if he's still there? I could bring my grant-writing book and say I was dropping it off for him to take to Michelle. Yes, that seems to be the best idea in case I run into him.

I woke again at 6 a.m. As soon as I have cognizant thought, my tormented anger bursts out of me. In my nightgown, lying in bed with my head barely up off the pillow, I screamed into my bedroom, "You fucking bastard! You whore!" Then I sobbed. Then a queasy feeling, diarrhea and unswerving nervousness set in. But I got up, bathed, ate my oatmeal and banana breakfast, took care of Spooky, cleaned the bathroom, got the fire going in my wood burning stove and contemplated calling Lilly for moral support, but ended up using my last minutes to write all of this in my journal.

Just looking at the wood stove brings on a rush of sensations -- the uncertainty and angst I felt wondering if it would be delivered as well as the companionship of the chimney sweep. After the wood stove was installed, I asked our chimney sweep to stop by to check and clean the chimney. While working here he asked, "How's Garrick?" Of course, I had to tell him about the marriage problem and I read him part of my journal. He said, "If you do make it a book, sign me up. I want a copy." He identified exactly with what I was sharing with him. Turns out, he, too, is going through a divorce and his wife has taken up with another man.

So I've organized my video camera, my notes, etc., I'm ready to go but I feel confused. The "what ifs" seem unlimited. I feel like aborting the plan, but I need evidence to support my case. If God is leaving it up to me, I am praying for strength to do what I think I must.

**8 a.m.** -- To the bathroom one more time and I'm on my way. What I'm doing is totally foreign to me. I hope I can stand it.

**Later --**

At 8:25 a.m., I drove past the Big House and saw my husband getting ready to leave. The trunk of his car was open. I drove to the church house and waited. He went past and I went to the Big House. He had changed the locks at the Big House so I had to find another way in.

It was still my house, after all. I had supervised the renovation and I knew many of the quirky details about the old house. The basement window was usually ajar, but was also very small. The window to the pantry next to the dining room had a faulty latch and the door to the basement had glass panes and a lock on the inside that I could reach if necessary. I decided to go for the pantry window, but I would need something to stand on to reach it from the ground outside.

I checked inside the garage and found one of the sturdy Adirondack chairs. I dragged it across the yard, being grateful there wasn't snow on the ground, and put it under the window. I stood on the armrest, jimmied up the window and with more physical strength than I thought I had, pulled myself up and through the window above me. I came in head first and with a bit of a crash, but I was in. Standing in my own house, shaking, I willed myself to be swift, smart and thorough. My heart was pumping and I was totally wired with adrenaline; it's the only way I could have pulled myself through that window.

I chose to use the west porch for loading because the access to the driveway is good and that door can be locked from the inside without a key. I can pull it closed when my mission is complete and it will stay locked.

With furtive glances, like a robber leaving the bank and almost wheezing for breath, I unlocked the door and went outside to pull the Adirondack chair out from under the window. I checked for marks on the ground from the chair, but it was OK.

Back in the house, armed with my new video camera, I held it shaking against my eye. I braced myself to move through the house filming. The camera has a built-in microphone so I made comments along the way to further explain and document what I was seeing. I videotaped all the rooms. My quivering voice and erratic breathing revealed my nerves.

In my determined race through each room of the house, filming and providing my own soundtrack of information, I made myself stop and laugh out loud when in the kitchen doing a 180-degree pan, I automatically recited, "This is the refrigerator."

There were several new books about American Indians lying around. There was also a large bottle of Kalua, which must be her drink because my husband never drank it before.

I stopped cold when I came across the Valentine's Day card and a Valentine's Day gift she'd given to him -- a gift certificate for a catered dinner-for-two. The card was jarring. My stomach seemed to roll up into my throat as I read it and my legs wanted to collapse beneath me. I knew my lawyers would be thrilled, but I couldn't spend time dealing with it then. I had a lot to do under a time limit. I was making split-second decisions with everything I found and I had to just keep going. I decided to take the card and gift certificate with me and call my lawyers for advice.

I called my friend and he arrived in minutes with his truck. We removed and loaded several pieces of my furniture into his truck and I carried out to my car a few of my mother's quilts, the card and the gift certificate. I left a note for my husband listing what I had taken. There was nothing valuable but strictly personal things that are mine and meaningful to me, like gifts from friends to me. My friend drove the furniture to my home.

This transfer of articles did not take long and once it was done I called another friend and we met at my husband's office At least my key to the office door still worked.

In the office, we found my husband's records of paying his girlfriend on the payroll as if she still worked for him. I found his file on me, labeled "AL." In it was my list of "You" and "Me" characteristics and my poems and letters that I'd sent him. I did some videotaping in the office, still shaking. I filmed the souvenir Indian coffee mug with the thank you note from the girlfriend's mother. Apparently my husband had made a "generous donation" to an Indian charity. There was also a receipt for a gold ring in the mug. I assumed the ring was a gift for the girlfriend.

I didn't reach my lawyers on the phone so I decided to photocopy the Valentine's Day card and gift certificate and replace them to the Big House.

The Valentine's Day card read:

*It started out as just*

*a little small talk*

*two people sitting together,*

*passing the time away.*

*But as they talked,*

*she noticed how intense*

*his eyes grew*

*when he was deep in thought,*

*and how his voice made her feel*

*all shivery and alive.*

*And he realized that her laugh*

*sounded a little like bells,*

*calling him closer,*

*and that her hair caught the sunlight*

*like a painting*

*he'd seen once in a museum.*

*It started out as small talk*

*to pass the time away*

*but <u>below the spoken words</u>*

*<u>two hearts were already whispering</u>*

*<u>in a language all their own</u>.*

She had underlined the last portion of the printed verse and then added in her own handwriting,

*"In a big way, this story reminds me of our beginning. Love, Natalie."*

My friend and I photocopied every other piece of paper we thought might be helpful to my case. My friend noticed a real estate news clipping about a house for sale. We thought maybe he has plans to buy a house.

I decided to retrieve the papers from the folder marked "AL" and I took them with me. It's sadly ironic to realize he's been keeping them as "evidence" against me since I had sent them hoping he would understand my feelings and come to his senses. And yet, it was instantly clear to me -- he hadn't kept them because he cared, he'd kept them because he was going to use them to "prove" that I'm overly emotional or irrational. Debbie had warned me that he might use my letters to him against me. I had sent them as a hopeful gesture.

When I got home, I called Tom at his home and set an appointment to see him and Victor on Monday. I also had a short call with Debbie. She advised me to change all the locks at my house ASAP. So I called a locksmith, said it was an emergency and within an hour, he'd changed all the locks.

At 6 p.m., I went to Betsy's house for dinner. I didn't talk about my day. She knows I'm in a traumatic time. I told her I was totally exhausted and left early.

Now that I've made it through this day and written it all down, my energy is depleted and I can barely hold this pen up.

**February 26, 1995**

Even though I had concern for what my husband would do when he came home from Michelle's and discovered I had been in the house, I went ahead with my plan to pick up Ann and her parents at the train station and take them up through Connecticut, have lunch at the White Hart Inn and then have them come to my house. When I took them back to the train later in the day and came home again around 7 p.m., I could see that my husband was home. Nothing happened.

While at the office yesterday, I noticed on my husband's calendar that he had marked the date last November when we had our brawl with "AL attack - broken ankle." This is clearly his case and his perception of the "fight." If he's talking about his "fear" of me, the "cruel and inhuman" one, I think we could look at his numerous "fears," in general, as part of my case.

I believe he would acknowledge he has an unusual fear of high places. He's afraid to ride a ski chair lift, he becomes faint when he drives over high bridges and he breaks out in a cold sweat and turns pale in the balcony seating of a theater if he's not seated on the aisle. He fears death, old age, hospitals, surgery, loss of love and failure.

He does not fear me; he fears what he's doing to destroy our marriage. He sat on the fence for a long time and he knows he can't have it both ways. He's fearful because he's taking a huge risk with only the hope that he's made the right choice. He fears his own moves to change his life.

Yet, he has done it. So he only has the "marriage" or "AL" to dump on. When he dumps his fears on me, he can have a girlfriend half his age and he can pretend to be young -- it's justified in his head. He has used me for 40 years and this ultimate "use" at his whipping post is so that I can be the scapegoat for his ruinous behavior. He parrots his lawyer and is influenced by everything the girlfriend does or says. He admires the qualities he believes she has. He said before that he thinks they're on the same wavelength. He's confused, misdirected and destructive.

# ANGER

**February 27, 1995**

Shaking with fear that today is the day that the shit hits the fan, I'm walking on wobbly legs. I decided to listen to the CD I removed from my husband's office during my search there a few days ago. It's called "The Colour of My Love," by Celine Dion. But I discovered that I had taken an empty case -- the disk is in his office stereo! I broke down in frustration. It really bothered me that I picked up an empty CD case. I had also brought an old clock of mine from the Big House and discovered it wasn't working. These incidents feel like "losing."

I called an electrician and asked him to make sure the electric was operating well in the greenhouse for starting it up. I asked him to send the bill to my husband and I also came right out and asked him to support me in this difficult time. The electrician said the whole town is behind me.

It's snowing big flakes. My plans today include an exercise class, copying my video, photocopying my journal notes up-to-date and dropping off information to Victor.

**Later --**

At 8:45 a.m. I was on my way to Nancy's and I saw my husband's car at my greenhouse. He was between the car and the greenhouse. Russ said he also saw him there earlier this morning. I decided to come back home, lock my doors and cancel my plans. I can get my video and notes copied later.

I am frightened of my husband. I am asking my friends point-blank to support me. Even though Russ had told me before that he has no animosity toward my husband, I asked him today if he could muster up some animosity. He said he was on my side. Another friend called to make a

plan for dinner. Then I wrote a few poems and tried to relax with Spooky
by the wood stove.

*Anger swells within*
*my thumping heart --*
*pushing words that vent*
*a peephole for pity.*

--------------------

*Smoldering anger*
*erupts into flames*
*and extinguishes itself*
*hosed down from the dam of tears.*

--------------------

*Looking into my own closed eyes*
*the mind pictures*
*thoughts of what the day delivers.*
*Will it be the divorce summons?*

--------------------

*Spooky, my dog,*
*diffuses anger*
*with unconditional love.*

--------------------

*It's as easy to say*
*"you fucking bastard"*
*as it is to say*
*"have a nice day."*

--------------------

*Skinny dipping lets me feel the world,*
*Dancing naked lets the world feel me.*

--------------------

## February 28, 1995

Later yesterday, I went to Anna and George's to copy my video. The quality of my filming was poor, but I think I still captured a lot. Then I helped Cathy and Debbie create some posters for Falls Town Flowers and was told my husband was spearheading a committee to organize activities for youth in our area. I say it's bringing activities to the girlfriend's daughter and more clients for himself. Debbie said she refused to serve on his committee and Cathy said she had refused to speak to him when she saw him in the store. I felt grateful for their support.

Today the forecast is calling for freezing rain. It's the closing date on Jeffrey and Starr's house, Molly plans to come for dinner and my tennis game will probably be canceled.

It's 6:30 a.m. and I need to talk to someone. I'm scared and shaky. My telephone appointment with Debbie is hours away. I wonder what will happen today. Later this morning, I'll call Victor about dropping off my notes and video. Then I'll bathe and try to look as good as I can. People say I look great as if they can't understand it.

**12 noon** -- Victor called to plan a meeting. We are ready to start litigation. I'll take my notes over at 2 p.m. today. And my son's Asheville lawyer called to say the house had closed.

**March 2, 1995**

The greenhouse is cleaned up and the supply company delivered the soil mix and pots. The little plugs of begonias, impatiens and petunias will be delivered on Saturday. So I'm set to grow.

I have another meeting with Victor this afternoon to work on finances and a dinner plan with friends, so my day is solid. I'm going to Vermont on Sunday to visit Michelle and hear her concert. She plays oboe with the Vermont Philharmonic. There's enough good news going on that I haven't spent much time on my own bad news.

**Later --**

Victor said at our meeting that the divorce summons would be ready for my signature on Monday. My husband will simultaneously receive a state Supreme Court order for a $6,000 a month maintenance payment for me and a divorce summons charging him with "cruel and inhuman" and infidelity. He'll also be charged with my legal expenses.

I was ticked-off when I learned that the private detective watched for my husband and the girl all last weekend when I'd said my husband would be in Vermont with Michelle! It was a mishap of miscommunication between me, my lawyer, Tom, and the PD. The detective will stake them out again this weekend, but it will cost me more. I agreed to this weekend and I think that will be the last of it. I have given them their best evidence so far and it may be enough. Also my husband's lawyer sent a fax to Tom about me entering the Big House and taking my things. She suggested they might get a court order against me.

At dinner with Marilyn and Bob I ended up spilling my guts and crying a little. Re-thinking some of the painful stuff really stirred up my emotions.

## March 6, 1995

On Saturday I got the greenhouse started and took in the little plants. I spent Sunday at Michelle's and then called Victor from her house this morning to confirm our appointment to sign the divorce summons I will be issuing. Then I tumbled into emotional upheaval. I cried at Michelle's and most of the drive back. Michelle asked me not to destroy Dad. I said if he's destroyed, he'll do it to himself. I went to Victor's office at 4 p.m. and signed the summons. It will be delivered to my husband tomorrow.

Before I went to Victor's office I stopped at the greenhouse. I happened to see the young accountant from my husband's office, Brett. He told me I would be better off without my husband. He said my husband is very controlling and all they do is work. Another young woman named Kim comes in occasionally to file. I was glad to hear from Brett that no one else is employed so the fact the girlfriend is on "the payroll" without having to ever show up at the office is a strike against my husband.

At 6 p.m., a man came to my door with the divorce summons from my husband. I'm depicted as cruel and inhuman -- a raving maniac. I called Flora, Lilly and Neal, Michelle, Jane in Chicago and Debbie. At the same time, I cooked split pea soup. I've invited Marty and Kent for lunch later this week. I've also decided to play tennis tomorrow after I go to Victor's for an appointment to review the property appraisals.

## March 7, 1995

Today the shit really hit the fan. My husband was issued my divorce summons along with the legal request for maintenance payments. His reaction came through his lawyer who called Victor immediately demanding that the joint account be unfrozen and threatening to shut off my phone and electricity by week's end. My husband has paid for the utilities until now, but there's no other money coming in at all. My house without electricity means no heat, no water, no stove or refrigerator. I said, "Go ahead, I'll manage." I will get some wood from my neighbors, I'll store up some water in jugs, I have candles from a friend -- I'll camp in my house. I spread the word about his actions and by tomorrow the whole town will be buzzing about it.

It's weird, but I'm beginning to feel sorry for my husband. Why would he never get help? Why couldn't he let go of her? Why did he lie and hide things? Why did he become incurably infatuated? Why would he never see my pain? Why did he deny his relationship with her existed? Why was he willing to destroy our family for her? Why couldn't I stop it?

Now I need to stick by my guns and see it through and then let it go. My lawyers will do what they have to do. My husband will really be upset when they have his business evaluated. I sort of wonder if he can stand it. He always had me for his support, and if the girlfriend doesn't give him support, he'll be on his own. I have many friends. The greenhouse is up and going. I'm OK.

When I feel stronger than my husband, I feel sorry for him.

**March 10, 1995**

It's 4:15 p.m. and I still have telephone and electric. I called my mother and friends to notify them that the phone might be cut off. I am prepared but I wonder if it was an empty threat. Tonight is the Chamber of Commerce party so I'm wondering what will happen there. Overall, however, I'm sleeping OK and I'm not crying. In fact, I have some periods of happiness and joy.

Flora and I are planning to launch a Saturday morning gourmet "coffee house" at the church house. The coffee sales rep called today and it seems like it will come together. We're going to scope out some other coffee houses in our area next week.

The greenhouse is about one-third planted. The geraniums, begonias, pansies and petunias look wonderful.

Molly will return from her trip to Greece on Monday. It's been a long week with her gone. Nancy's trip to Turkey feels incredibly long, too. However, my young friend, Judy, is coming Sunday and Diane is coming Monday to stay all week.

I signed up for a writing course at the junior college. The course is supposed to offer information for learning how to publish one's writing. I want to explore the possibilities of publishing my story. Flora signed up for guitar lessons at the same time so we can car pool.

I called Kathy, my friend in Illinois, at 6 p.m. She is recovering from a broken leg, but her bad news was that her husband just found out he has prostate cancer. We talked for one and a half hours. Thank goodness my phone still works.

The outfit I ordered from Talbot's to wear at the court date was delivered to my husband. He deposited it in the greenhouse (which is considered mutual neutral territory) and left a note saying, "The plants look great -- as usual." I thought it ironic that he chose to communicate just as he has threatened to cut off my telephone and electric.

People have told me the girlfriend is dumpy and not at all pretty and that she has nothing to offer. They say her cooking and household habits are poor, she's a pushy parent and her child is unappealing. People wonder what he sees in her. It has also been rumored that he's having an affair with his lawyer.

## March 15, 1995

Yesterday, I received a letter from Victor about a renewed threat to disconnect my phone but with an apparent backing off of shutting off the electricity. It's 7 a.m. and so far my phone is still working. The whole town is talking about it. No one can believe that he would deny the basic utilities of my home plus not give me one penny of maintenance.

I wrote this poem about the townspeople:

*Wagging tongues*
*Spying eyes and*
*Straining ears*
*fertilize the grapevine of*
*disbelief and judgment*
*growing mutant*
*among the community that*
*harbors the characters*
*on their stage -- Church Street.*

--------------------

I had a good meeting with Victor yesterday. He is willful, strong, smart and decent. He seems to have a side that's sensitive and understanding, too, but he doesn't let his emotions get in the way of his legal mind. Sheila, my husband's lawyer petitioned to dismiss my case. We are proceeding with intent to deny all of my husband's charges that I'm "cruel and inhuman." My husband has to answer the summons for maintenance payments to me by March 21st. We have our first court date on April 4th. I completely trust Victor.

Diane came up for the week and we played tennis outside today. It was a beautiful day. Then I went to my writing course at the college. It's great.

My ideas are considered very marketable and the course will supply me with the information I need to try to publish my work. I'm passing the word around about my writing course so my husband will know there's more to come -- the written truth.

**March 19, 1995**

Life is keeping me busy. I'm not crying and obscenities are less frequent. Feeling sorry for my husband is a more prevalent emotion and everyone advises me to put that feeling aside until it's all over.

Victor's recent list of "demands" issued to my husband's lawyer bothered me a little because I think they're serious enough to put a lot of pressure on my husband. He must come up with all kinds of financial data about the last five years and also for his Viacom payout. It seems to be a lot of work for him to do in 20 days especially since this is the most intense time of tax season.

My telephone and electric are still on but I wonder what he'll do in retaliation for the "demands." He'll figure out we plan to have expert witnesses and subpoena people to testify. I'm not totally convinced my case is a winner but I'm not nervous about adverse reactions. I can't make predictions anyway.

**March 20, 1995**

After having a really nice brunch yesterday with my cousin, Ann, and Marty and Kent, we all looked around the greenhouse and took a walk. Then I drove Ann to the train station. I climbed into bed early and turned on the TV to a movie. It was about a businessman having affair with his wife's friend's daughter. Much of the scenario was the same as mine. In the end, he came to his senses. I cried hard for the first time in days.

The movie and my pain over it made me realize the intensity of a completely opposite feeling a few days ago. While walking with Spooky up the hill behind the greenhouse, I experienced a joyful freedom that was magnificent. I felt an awareness and a oneness with nature that made my spirits soar -- feeling the fresh air, seeing the beautiful view to the mountains and overlooking the town, smelling the damp earth with spring emerging underfoot, enjoying the power of my healthy body with no aches or pains and Spooky bounding along beside me. It was enough. I don't need more. I have all I need for complete joy.

After I thought about this astounding sensation, I decided that if I had not experienced total devastation, perhaps I could not have been open to total joy. As I write this, I recall another time of amazing joy walking in a field with my husband. At a point of exhilaration in the beauty of nature, I went into his arms in an embrace that made our friend, Ed, who was walking with us ask, "Should I leave you guys alone?" But the other day, alone with Spooky, I captured as great a joy that feels even more lasting and it can be renewed, maybe even shared.

It's been a week since the divorce papers crossed. I cried on that day and then had a week of few tears. I wept just now as I read what I wrote about the joy I felt with my husband in that field. Since it's Monday, I figure there will be legal developments and that scares me. My husband has a court date tomorrow. I have an eye exam -- the first in seven years.

**March 21, 1995**

I've paid almost $3,000 to the private detective for the very poor job he's done investigating my husband's actions with the girlfriend. He did get him going to her house and going in, but the local police made him move his car. Then my husband was gone and the PD lost track of him. It's mostly been a waste.

The cash in my wallet has diminished to $30 and my checking account is under $600. I need gas in my car and to have it serviced. I need a haircut and groceries. I looked through the want ads for jobs. If the maintenance money doesn't come through, I'll need a job within the next 2 weeks. I have no available money. My bonds and CDs are my life savings and I should not allow erosion to that nest egg for current expenses that my husband's earnings have always covered before. When I paid for my tennis court time and lesson today, I said I couldn't afford to come back. I almost cried but I pulled it together and the instructor treated me to a bagel.

My house is cold today since I don't have my wood stove going, but there's no danger of freezing. It's raining and cool and the cupboards are pretty bare. I don't want to borrow money so I must find a way to stretch my checking account or find a source of income, other than emptying the piggy bank. I suddenly understand the urge to buy a lottery ticket.

It's Flora's turn to drive to our classes tonight and I'm looking forward to my second class. Debbie said she hopes I'll keep writing in my journal with publishing in mind. She envisions a self-help type book. The possibility of helping others motivates me to work toward a goal of publishing. My "journaling" certainly helps me. It enables me to view my daily situation, express my entire range of feelings freely, plan strategies and hopefully in the future, witness my progress.

**March 24, 1995**

My mail made me weep today. Friends in Connecticut sent me a check for $1,000. They sent it as a gift to help me. I sent a thank you note saying

I would return the money to them if my financial situation became resolved.

Besides my car maintenance, I have received the car insurance bill from my husband through the lawyers. Ironically, when I came out of the insurance office, I stopped to chat with a neighbor and I looked up and saw my husband getting out of his car across the street. I turned my head, but I got a good look. He looked terrible -- fallen face, long hair, slumped shoulders -- not at all attractive.

**March 25, 1995**

It's 1 a.m. and I'm awake, seething with anger. I don't know exactly why. I want to give my husband the "divorce countdown" message. I want to tell him what an asshole he is. When I saw him in town yesterday, I withdrew with a kind of fear. It was good to have my dog in my car, she's used to hearing my riling and obscenities. When I imagine a conversation with him I begin with, "If you're still fucking the whore, don't talk to me." And with my financial concerns, my first demand to him would be "Get my money back from the whore."

Obviously, it's best to stick with my lawyer for communication. I explode verbally and on paper in my journal. The culprit target for months was the girlfriend and now the bull's-eye is shifting to include my husband. My anger-language is strong enough to be offensive and free enough to be vile. Friends seem to accept my ongoing metamorphosis as I shed a lifetime of beliefs. This process is exposing the bitch in me that is no longer willing to be a victim. I don't have any physical anger; I think it's tempered because I don't restrain my anger verbally. It's wild to feel anger dominating my emotional scale while a whole range of moods mix randomly on my bare surface.

I do wonder what's in my husband's head. What does he think when he sees me? Extricating himself from this long marriage is a process he's been working on for a long while. He's masterminded it all over a period of time. Still, I have been difficult to discard and I sense that as we proceed, it will not be pleasant.

One observation: When I was crying and weak, Molly felt sorry for me. Now that I'm stronger and even angry, she's siding with my husband, kind of protecting him. I think this is her way to "help."

**Later --**

Chris came over today to fix the brick that came off the stoop. I was in the hardware store buying concrete mix to fix it myself and he just came over after work and did it. I feel the support of many friends. I also feel the division from people who have sided with my husband. Nancy, the caterer, supports my husband but she also likes me. She can't understand it. When she and I were having dinner at a restaurant, the cleaning girl from the Big House came over and said how glad she was to see me. She said she had called and left a message in December with my son. I didn't get the message. The cleaning girl is in an awkward situation. She continues to clean for my husband and she picked him up from the hospital after he broke his ankle. She's not to blame but I can't be nice to her.

**April 3, 1995**

Life has been OK for me -- friends, dinners, laughs, a trip to Vermont, the greenhouse, spring, etc. The threats of telephone and electric cut offs have been renewed and more bills have come my way. Out of nowhere, my husband left a check for $600 in the greenhouse. The court order for maintenance payments has been stalled by legal maneuverings, so I guess the check was his version of what I deserve to pay the bills.

I am faced with a court date tomorrow. Victor and I will meet with my husband and Sheila about his maintenance payments and his motion to have my divorce summons dismissed.

A local lawn service man told me he had been asked by my husband to mow the lawn at the Big House and at the office but not to mow in front of the greenhouse. It made me so angry. He knows he's left me with a lawn, no mowing equipment and no money. I said my husband is a "Goddamned fucking bastard." The lawn service man also told me that the girlfriend's husband had accused her of something going on before Christmas.

All of that plus the unknown of tomorrow's legal meeting made me cry in frustration and anger. My close friend Nancy called and we talked as we ate dinner in our own homes. I'm thinking of calling Debbie tonight. I put a message on Molly's machine earlier. I'm going to bed early to try to look good.

**April 4, 1995**

It's cloudy and rainy and the temperature has been dropping all day. I wore a dress and a sweater with my Burberry raincoat to the meeting and I carried an umbrella. So much for looking good. Victor and I walked to the courthouse from Victor's office and we immediately spotted my husband across the park standing by the stairs leading to the courthouse doors. It gave me time to focus straight ahead and walk past him as if he were a lamppost.

Victor stayed downstairs and I sat on a bench in the hallway. I saw Sheila come in and I didn't look at her. She and Victor went into the courtroom with a judge. While I was waiting, a group of potential jurors passed through and I knew two of them. One, my friend Sue, who knows what's going on, said to me, "You know, cream rises to the top and you are cream." Only words, but they magnified into powerful encouragement at a time when I needed desperately to be OK.

After an hour, Victor re-appeared to say we would go to his office to look over an affidavit from my husband that Sheila just issued to us. We walked past my husband again. I didn't look.

Back at his office, Victor said that my divorce summons issued to my husband would stand. The maintenance issue will be gone over in still more detail. It seems "stalling" is the entrenched strategy used by my husband and Sheila in order to avoid maintenance payments.

We looked over the affidavit and, once again, my husband's statements are mostly lies. Fortunately I have proof to back up my statements and to prove his wrong.

It appears my husband is unaware that I've been in his office and doesn't know what I found there. His lies in the affidavit can be directly addressed with my proof, which, for the most part, came right out of his office. It will ruin his day when we respond. And, as he tends to react to his bad days with attacks on me, I think I'll brace myself for repercussions, like my telephone and electric being cut off.

He will also not be happy to know that my divorce summons will be treated equally with his. Victor said my husband will have to answer our list of demands and we'll hire a CPA/lawyer to go over his business records.

Some of his "inaccuracies" in his affidavit and my corresponding proof are: He claims that his business makes no money and that he "retired" in Falls Town. Yet, together we spent huge sums of money for renovations to the Big House and to the farmhouse so they could function as his offices, and he has used both spaces for his CPA practice. He also spent large amounts of money on sophisticated computers and other equipment related to his business and, in fact, on his 1993 federal income tax returns he shows an expense of over $7,000 spent on software alone. Of course, he also hired both full-time and part-time staff over the years, and in his recommendation letter for the girlfriend's resume, which I found in his office, he said she was hired because of a "burgeoning" client load. Not bad for a business that supposedly doesn't turn a profit.

He denies a "romantic relationship" with the filing clerk and states that it's my obsession with that idea that soured our marriage. Yet, I have copies of his handwritten notes to himself about divorcing me with her initials in the notes, as well as his books about divorce, his gifts to the filing clerk and records of payments to her from his ATM card, etc., all of which I found in his locked filing cabinet when I discovered the hidden key. There are also the records of their clandestine New York City shopping and dining spree, other shopping expenditures and dining outings including New Year's Eve and copies of her love letter and romantic gift to him for Valentine's Day.

He says the filing clerk was fired in June 1994 and has never been on his payroll when she didn't work for him. Yet, I have copies of payrolls from January 1995 and the current payroll and she is on them and he pays for her dental insurance. He claims he cannot afford to support me and yet, clearly, he has the wherewithal to support his girlfriend.

It goes on and on. The affidavit is so vicious; it's hard for me to believe he signed it. But he did and I'm not feeling sorry for him now.

When I got back to Falls Town, I stopped at the insurance office to find out if I was covered for the lawn service man, who is uninsured, since my husband has hired him to mow the lawn at the Big House, which is still at least half my house. I'm not. So I called Victor and was advised to ask the insurance company to notify my husband of this insurance need.

Then I saw a local lawyer, who happens to be the girlfriend's husband's lawyer. He said her husband had told him that my husband had broken up their marriage. The local lawyer and I had a few laughs at the expense of my husband and Sheila. He said he hated her guts. I said, "I'll join you in that."

## April 9, 1995

Molly came over last night and we talked about her day and her engagement to her fiancé, John. I've been typing up my journal notes on my old 1940's typewriter and I shared some of them with her.

She said she had dinner with my husband on Thursday and he was unhappy. He told her he thought I looked thin and he asked her if I was seeing anyone. At first, I thought he'd asked because he had feelings for me, but later I realized he'd asked to get ammunition against me if I was being "unfaithful." He told Molly that he hadn't seen the girlfriend in a month and admitted he'd been infatuated with her. He also said she'd done some tax work for him. I think he was trying to cover his tracks because of my charge of her being on his payroll while she's not working for him. Molly wanted me to drop the CPA investigation into his business and I said I've already gone ahead with it. She said, "Dad isn't hiding anything." I said, "He's lied about everything else, why in the world would I trust him about finances?"

Rereading what I've just written made me cry a lot. Today my eyes are red and puffy. I don't think I'll go to church. I'll call my mother and write her a letter on my old typewriter.

**Later --**

I did my homework for my writing class. It's a query letter regarding my writing, <u>Emotional Survival in the Wilderness of Divorce</u>. Then I boxed my wedding rings and wrote an angry note to my husband. I don't know if or when I'll give it to him.

For some reason I have hit a renewed sadness and sentimentality. Looking at my wedding ring and diamond ring lying there in the cardboard box tore my heart apart. I plan to give them back to him along with the crappy flower earrings he gave me for our 38th anniversary. Although I've felt happy and confident for several days, the old feelings came boiling up.

**April 11, 1995**

Even though I'd written the wrathful note to return with the rings, I only mailed him the rings in the little box and the crappy flower earrings, all together in an envelope for 87 cents. I cleaned my diamond before I sent it. I have no idea why.

The rings represent 39 years of a marriage turned into lies, deceit and cruel behavior from my husband. I would never give such cursed jewelry to anyone, nor would I sell it to have tainted money.

The telephone bill I received today was addressed to me instead of to my husband, which shows he's trying to push that bill off on me. I am sending it back to the telephone company to have them resend it to him.

Overall, it was a sad and emotional day for me. The bright spot was decorating the church house with Flora for the new coffee house. It is going to be so cute with a grapevine around the archway and white twinkling lights, blue and white checked tablecloths and hanging flower baskets.

A friend dropped by with the tennis schedule and I have an appointment to get my car serviced for a problem, which is, fortunately, under warranty. The greenhouse is going well and I'm anxious to go to my writing class.

This is a wedding ring poem, which I did not send:

*Return to original owner*
*used rings in a box*
*87 cents postage*
*Tarnished with deceit*
*after 39 years on her finger*
*Fool's gold!*

--------------------

**April 12, 1995**

Yesterday, Victor called to tell me that my phone would be cut off on Friday. He advised me to put new phone service in my name. I said, "I'll go without a phone." No maintenance payments means no money to pay bills, so I won't take responsibility for more than has already been pushed on me. I wrote:

*Brutal allegations crush me*
*with threats and lies.*
*Responding to daily battering to pay his bills,*
*I feel stalked by a beast that wants to kill me.*

--------------------

Since my husband's phone at the Big House is in my name, I asked my lawyer if I should cut off his phone. He said, "Yes!" I called the phone company and ordered it disconnected immediately.

# April 17, 1995

As promised, my telephone was dead on Friday. My husband made good on his threat. I broke down crying and called him a bastard.

I decided last week to start selling off my retirement savings. I'm not comfortable borrowing money from friends and family. The money I spent on the private detective came from my sister and my mother has offered me money too, but so far I haven't taken any from her.

Victor is always asking about and checking on my financial status and he's a bit concerned about my plan. In the end, however, he believes it will work in favor of my case -- that it's necessary for me to get money to live on through such drastic measures. So I sold my U.S. Savings Bond and my life insurance policy and arrived at Victor's office with the $7,000 first payment I owe them. Then Victor gave me my husband's most recent affidavit of terrible lies and I really lost it. It's unbelievable. My husband signed the lies.

He said in the affidavit that I purchased the Big House for the purpose of a Bed and Breakfast Inn, which is a lie. Then he suggested that I should live on the third floor and operate a full-time B&B to earn income. It's his ridiculous scenario to show I don't need anything from him.

He said his employee, Brett, was part time and that he had re-hired the girlfriend in January. He said my attitude toward the girlfriend had soured our marriage and that there was nothing romantic to their relationship. He said he wouldn't pay me any maintenance money and asked for a court order against me.

The effect of all these lies is to further stall the maintenance payments issue by piling up other stuff to be dealt with. It just goes on and on.

His wretched lies burned through me like red-hot daggers and I cried hard over and over again. I wanted to confront him verbally and tell him off, but instead I just spread the word of his despicable behavior to more people.

Yesterday, my neighbors by the greenhouse, Jim and Rako, invited me over for a drink. I filled them in on my bastard husband. Then I dressed to the nines in my best pants suit and went to a funeral viewing of a friend who died recently. A lot of people were there but my husband wasn't. I spoke to some friends and several said how great I looked. Men, particularly, commented on my appearance. As I was in the parking lot ready to leave, my husband drove up. I saw him walk into the funeral home. He looked terrible to me, heavy and old.

Then I stopped to see some friends and from their house I saw the girlfriend and her child go into her husband's house across the street. Her husband was at the funeral home greeting people since he's the director. When I'd seen him there earlier I'd said hello. Later, a friend told me that when my husband entered the funeral home, the girlfriend's husband turned away and went upstairs.

Today, my anger is mixed with hurt and a renewed drive to fight. I'm an emotional yo-yo. Within a few hours, I felt angry, then the knife went in and twisted and I felt like giving up. Then I talked to friends and pulled myself up to forge ahead again.

I wrote an article about my cousin, Ann, and her training major league baseball players. It's my homework for class and hopefully the local newspaper will publish it.

One positive note about not having a phone: when I take a bath, I don't have to get out of the tub to answer it.

**Later --**

It's now 11 p.m. and my day is finished. I'm not as sad as I was 10 hours ago. I don't love my husband anymore, but he still makes me feel battered. I think I'll write him a letter (which I probably won't send) to tell him what a fool he is and ask him "Why?"

**April 19, 1995**

Using Pete and Ed's phone to call my counselor, Debbie, I told her about my disconnected phone and the latest affidavit suggesting I live on the third floor and run a B&B out of the Big House. I told Debbie that a close friend had visited my husband and shared with him her personal experience of an affair that occurred in her marriage. She was pulling out all the stops to try and help me save my marriage. She hoped a light bulb might go on in his head. I mentioned, too, that another friend had seen my husband and the girlfriend and her daughter eating together in Wal-mart.

Debbie said I should call Victor tomorrow to go over my responses to the affidavit. She applauded me for recognizing I should not turn my back on my divorce plans nor allow my resolve to wane, even though I'm feeling battered. Unless he gets help, he won't be different. Debbie suggested our kids might be able to encourage him to seek help.

The gossip around town is hot and heavy and it seems everyone is checking in for their information "fix."

**April 26, 1995**

It had to happen. All at the very same time, my husband left the Big House, the girlfriend drove up from town and I left the greenhouse to go pick up Nancy. So we all ended up one behind the other on the same two-lane road. My husband was first with the girlfriend right behind him and then me. I saw absolute red as my husband led this procession and I acted on instinct. As he turned to enter the garbage and recycling station, I laid on the horn at the girlfriend in front of me and I continued on the horn following her to a T-junction down the road. At that point, she went on and I turned around and drove back to go pick up Nancy. My husband was racing up from the other direction, undoubtedly having heard my honking. I pulled part way into his lane, crowding him towards the shoulder of the road. He stopped and shouted, "What are you doing?" I yelled, "Go ahead and fuck the whore. Tell your goddamned lawyer I'm crazy -- you bastard!" Then I drove away.

I picked up Nancy to go to our tennis game and I told her what I had just done and how angry I was. I said, "I only honked my horn but I wanted to run her out of town." I mentioned that my husband looked horrible and that I believe he followed after the girlfriend when I left.

My tennis game was great. Everyone there noticed I was hitting with real fury.

It's now 1 p.m. and I'm still shaking and wondering what my husband will do next. Call his lawyer? Get a court order against me? Finally get depressed himself? Strike out against me in some other way?

I'm not proud of my behavior today and yet I couldn't stop it. I want to vent my feelings on my husband and the girlfriend until I dissolve from exhaustion into a pool of jelly. I don't want to touch them; I just want to scream until I can't let out another breath of agony. My heart is pounding.

I told some friends that I don't think I can make it. The girlfriend in my face has been a vicious rip in my wounds and the latest affidavit set me back emotionally.

As I was writing this, trying to think of words to describe how awful life is for me at this moment, I started to cry and Spooky came over and licked my tears.

If I can get myself together, I'll go to my greenhouse and work; maybe mow the grass if the old mower I found in the barn has been fixed and returned. Its tires were flat and it wouldn't start, but the local mower repairman was very helpful and understood my situation.

I'm also thinking I should call Victor and tell him about the horn honking, but I guess I'll let it play out.

The horn-honking episode makes me feel like the "bad guy." I like to be "good." Being "bad" scares me. Why doesn't he come clean and be honest, finally? What does he have to lose? The marriage is over; nothing needs to be hidden from me. Just scream at me, tell me why he did it to me. Listen to my anguish. Allow me my feelings -- not on a deaf ear, but with understanding, and not pity, but with sorrow.

**Later --**

Encased in my torture chamber, there's no way out. I feel isolated, alone, unloved and helpless to change anything. I noticed my husband's car at his lawyer's office for a long time today. I believe he is trying to bring serious legal action against me. It's possible he is there to review his deposition information, but the timing seems more like a repercussion from this morning's horn-honking scene.

Seeing his car and the girlfriend's car turn the corner together, heading in the same direction as me at the very same time, sent off a searing flare in me. Unfortunately, his wretched affidavit was still stinging, along with all the other burning wounds, and I wasn't able to keep my anger on paper and in legal actions. Even though I have a right to my feelings, it is so out of my character to publicly display poor behavior or to speak coarsely. It is so demeaning to myself. I am guilty of unleashing honest emotions that are expected to be suppressed, or at least controlled.

It's so hard to keep getting up and on my feet. I welcome the fatal blow and it will come from my husband. He alone has beaten me to a weakness that is so severe, I really wish I could die. Today I don't have the courage to fight the battle.

I called Molly for help and left a message on her machine, but what is she to do? There is nothing she can do and I shouldn't even drag her into my emotional quagmire. She deserves a life free of this turmoil. It's a happy time for her and it is being marred by her parents' bizarre behavior.

I wish for that friend I relied on for 40 years. He has turned into a traitor. Fending for myself is hard enough, but to live with his whore flaunted in my face, lies on legal affidavits and "cruel and inhuman" from my husband is all more than I can stand today.

Getting through these hours will be an accomplishment. If I can go to sleep, I will see a new day. Perhaps it will be better.

**April 27, 1995**

Spooky got me up at 6 a.m. I'm still tired but I have thoughts of getting my day going. On my mind -- where's Molly? Has she contacted my husband? Will I meet with Flora for a walk? Will the police come and arrest me for honking my horn? Will the lawn mower be repaired so I can mow at the greenhouse? Will my article be in the newspaper? If I end up with any money, should I give a trust to the church? Maybe I'll clean the garage later today. Who should I write letters to and what can I say?

How does it feel to wake up happy? I forget. Listening to news on public radio seems a little in touch, though the focus continues to be on the

Oklahoma City bombing and the O.J. Simpson murder trial. At least the news gives me a perspective check. My life could certainly be worse -- as it is for all the people involved in those tragedies.

**April 28, 1995**

Before 5 a.m. I woke up in the realization that there's been a change in my attitude toward the girlfriend. A year ago, I had diarrhea when I saw her. Six months ago I had rubber legs and a queasy stomach whenever I heard about her. Now, I'm willing to take out after her and blow my horn until she's out of town. I don't know what that means.

Yesterday, Molly called my husband, my neighbors, Pete and Ed, and my counselor, Debbie, too. I'd left a message telling her about the honking incident and that I feared what my husband might do.

Then she called me and told me that my husband was not going to take legal action against me and that he didn't want to hurt me. He also told Molly that it was his lawyer's idea that I should run the Big House B&B. Yeah, sure. As if he doesn't know or have any control over what his lawyer does. He signs all the papers. He told her that "the girlfriend" was scared from the horn honking.

He can be as generous about me to Molly as he wants, but my reality is in the hands of the judge, and what my husband says and signs off on in his affidavits is what the judge rules by.

Molly is going to talk to Debbie today because she wants to help me get a handle on my anger. I think she's heard different versions of the honking incident, knows her father will do what he wants and thinks I might need more accessible counseling, locally. She knows how angry I am and she's heard my language, which probably surprises her. Frankly,

I'm glad Molly will have an opportunity to speak to Debbie. Debbie will most likely find a way to help Molly cope with her situation.

It's 11 p.m. and I've had a decent day. I worked at the greenhouse and had lunch there with friends. Then I worked in the garden, went to the church house to help Flora and went to Marty and Kent's house for a dinner party. They are singers with the New York Metropolitan Opera and they gave us a beautiful concert of show songs. I appreciated the wonderful music they shared but I felt very sad. On the way home, I broke down in tears in my car.

**April 29, 1995**

Here it is 7 p.m. already after a busy day. My young friend, Tricia, helped me with transplanting at the greenhouse. I baked cookies with friends at the church house, sold some plants to benefit the church and the choir, visited friends, got together with Molly and John and saw my husband across town from afar. I'm off shortly to pick up Ann at the train station. Tomorrow, we're going to help Molly clean her new apartment.

My anger continues. I am more aggressive in my attitude towards my husband and the girlfriend. Rather than turn my head and look the other away, I now turn my face toward them and stare. What does that mean?

**May 1, 1995**

I calculate it will take me at least seven hours to mow my lawn at home and another four hours to mow the lawn near the greenhouse. It's almost more than I can handle along with my greenhouse and garden work, taking care of my house, plus trying to have a social life. If I am denied maintenance payments, I'm not sure how I'll take it -- not lying down, I'm afraid.

**May 3, 1995**

I woke up angry. But, it's a beautiful day and after I open the greenhouse, I have a tennis game. Then I'll clean the church house, vote on the new school bond, do some transplanting at the greenhouse, sell a few plants, talk with Debbie and have dinner with Nancy. As I write this, I'm testing a corn muffin recipe for the coffee house and doing my laundry. There is more time in my days recently because there are no phone calls. My communication system is a network of dozens of friends who relay messages by visits and notes and have offered their phones, if I need one. It's interesting that my support network has grown more powerful as a result of strong-arming from my husband.

My husband is in his office alone. I noticed he walked down from the Big House so it looked like no one was there. Tomorrow I'm going to Albany airport to pick up my sister.

**May 4, 1995**

Lilly is here. I picked her up at the airport and then we went shopping. We stopped at the greenhouse, watered the plants and then Molly joined us for dinner. Sisters and daughters together made for a great visit.

**May 6, 1995**

Time flies when you're having fun. My sister and I have worked in the greenhouse, the garden and the lawn and have gone out with Nancy. We are going to dinner with Diane and Stu in Stockbridge tonight and we have a full day planned for tomorrow, too.

**May 8, 1995**

My day started out OK, although Lilly left yesterday and I miss her already. I went to the greenhouse to do my work. Spooky came with me and watched me mow the grass. My husband's lawn service was doing his lawn at the same time next door. A friend is meeting me for lunch at the greenhouse so I dashed off to pick up my mail and the newspaper to see if my article about Ann was in it, yet.

There were two pieces of mail from Victor's office so I sat in my car and opened them. One was a bill and the other was a notice of the deposition for my husband on the 15th and a note to call Victor. Just then a police car pulled in front of me and the officer came to my window. He said, "I have some bad news for you. You should come to the station and I'll give you some papers. I'm sorry to have to do this, Mrs. Belt."

The girlfriend had issued a reckless driving complaint against me. I cried as I told the young officer how awful my husband was treating me and he acknowledged that my husband had given the girlfriend the information to use against me -- my full name, date of birth, license plate number, etc. He said none of the officers wanted to come to me to issue the complaint and he was sorry that he had to do it. I told him I knew he was just doing his job.

My court date is next Monday at 7 p.m. in Falls Town. I called Victor from the police station and he said to bring the papers to him.

After I left the police station, I went to Nancy's house. She understands how my outburst happened and she has such a good head, she helped me to think clearly. I suggested that her son-in-law who is a movie producer in Los Angeles, write a script for my story and come to Falls Town to film it. It could be a low budget film and it has all the ingredients of a good movie -- including a car chase! We even laughed about the ridiculous situation.

Later, I went to Victor's office and he said it might make sense to take it to trial since he could cross-examine the girlfriend pertaining to her "work." In her charge against me, she claims to be a full-time student, no mention of a job. My husband stated in one of his affidavits that she is employed by him. Someone isn't telling the truth. And Victor believes it may be an opportunity.

Today, I let go of my husband a lot more. I am OK about doing legal battle and I have much less need to protect him. He has pulled out every possible stop to <u>not</u> protect me -- no emotional support, no financial support and no consideration in any way with no phone, no lawn mower, no communication. Now he's putting me in harm's way, abetting his girlfriend in charging me with criminal action that is not true. I was <u>not</u> reckless. I blew my horn. I don't know what he'll do next.

It's now 10 p.m. and I'm OK. I'm grateful for Spooky and Nancy and Victor. The police were really nice and I was able to do some mowing, enjoy the beauty of the lawn and flowers and I wrote a letter to my son, Jeffrey. I still have electricity and I am content after I cried for only a few minutes. Spooky gets up and licks my face when she hears me cry. What a good dog.

**May 9, 1995**

Victor says he will be with me for my May 15 court date. I'm all right about the events of yesterday. I'm not crying and I have a rather tame anger going and a strong resolve to see it all through. We'll see if I hold up or crumble. This incident could be an exciting chapter in my book.

It's 8 p.m. and I'm ready to take a bath and get in bed. Victor called to say that we are postponing the deposition of my husband as a tactic to punish him for abetting the girlfriend to file charges against me.

I'm pretty mellow and I have little anger and no fear right now. I think Victor gave me confidence. Brett, the accountant from my husband's office, came to the greenhouse today and we had a little talk. I gave him some plants. He said my husband was really ticked when his phone was cut off. He didn't know I did it. He thought the phone company did it by mistake when he ordered mine off. I said, "Good."

I now stop and stare at my husband from afar every time I see him. He sees me but looks away.

**May 10, 1995**

I woke up thinking about "the movie" idea. Nancy's son-in-law, Jonny, has wanted to film a movie here in Falls Town but didn't have a script. I'm thinking that not only would he have the script, but all the scenes -- Church Street, my house, the greenhouse, the Big House, the Center Hill Road car honking scene and plenty of extras. It seemed like a good idea. With this scheme in my head, all the real-life terrible things serve to enhance the plot.

Today we'll get the church house ready for the trial opening of the coffee house. My weekly telephone conference with Debbie is at 6 p.m. I'll call her from Nancy's house and then stay for dinner. Nancy is the "best supporting actress!"

**May 12, 1995**

I almost automatically wrote May 12, 1956 -- our wedding date 39 years ago. It's 7 a.m. and so far I'm not crying. My day will be spent with my wonderful friends. I'm thrilled Molly and John will be here on Sunday for Mother's Day. John's coming from Boston, he'll be moving in with Molly next week, and with their wedding plans underway, they're very busy. They're so happy with each other and he has been an understanding support for me and for Molly. It's pleasant to think about their happy engagement on my ex-anniversary.

**May 15, 1995**

On Thursday, May 11, Molly's fiancé, John, committed suicide. Molly was notified at work on Friday, May 12. It was 4 p.m. that afternoon before I was able to connect with her. With no phone, the message was given to Michelle in Vermont and then to my neighbors, Pete and Ed, who came to find me at my greenhouse. By the time I tracked Molly down at John's parents home in Stockbridge, Massachusetts, several hours had lapsed for her in agony. She was sitting alone in their kitchen when I arrived. John's father, who is very elderly, was in a different room. His mother was still in California on a business trip and his sisters hadn't arrived from Boston yet.

I stayed with Molly until the sisters came and then I went to another room to give them some privacy. After that I brought Molly home. On the way I asked her if she wanted to see her father and she said, "Yes."

I drove up the driveway of the Big House but he wasn't there. As we were going down the driveway he returned to the house. I stayed in the car while he held Molly and she cried. He returned with her to the car and he reached in to touch me. I withdrew my arm and leaned over the steering wheel and cried hard. Then we left.

It was a tough night. We went to Pete and Ed's to use the phone so Molly could speak to Debbie. We slept very little, if at all.

The next day Michelle came from Vermont. It was a godsend to have her here. I called the telephone company to get emergency phone service and within two hours we had it. The phone has been in constant use ever since. My daughters and I went to Molly's apartment to get clothes. We made phone calls and bought vegetables to make soup.

Yesterday, Molly went with John's mother and his sisters to view his body before the cremation. Michelle and I waited outside and then we all came home. Molly said it was a healing thing to do to see his body. They realized he was gone.

Michelle went home a little while ago, feeling we were under control, coping fairly well and with soup to eat. Molly has spoken with Debbie several times and it has been enormously helpful. She also spent some time with her father.

The horn honking court date scheduled for today has been postponed indefinitely.

**May 16, 1995**

Molly has become capable of thinking clearly. She's helping John's family with decisions, working in their yard for the funeral service and planting flowers for them. She took a walk with a close friend and is starting to eat a little. She's been making essential plans, talking, crying, sleeping a bit and receiving many cards and flowers.

I am standing by. I haven't talked about my husband and our situation. I'm trying to be here for Molly without adding any other concerns.

**May 17, 1995**

Time is a blur. Molly is being flooded with her spiritual side. She is questioning, pondering, looking for meaning, writing her feelings and talking. This morning she prepared her own cream of wheat and walked Spooky. She's taking naps and taking care of herself. I am concerned for her when she drives alone to his family's house but I understand her need to do it. Now that I have a phone and it rings, I stay near it to protect her from it. It's a mixed blessing. We definitely need it but it is a shackle.

Molly said my husband has offered to pay some of the phone bill. I said I can pay all of the bills but it is his responsibility to pay the bills, and in doing so, then I have, in effect, paid for my half of the bills. I said when I get maintenance payments from him then I will pay all of my bills myself. Until then, it's his responsibility.

Molly and I both "ruffled" over the issue until she understood my point. Debbie has told me that the natural progression of emotions for Molly will be to find someone to vent anger on and that will most likely be me. She will need to do it and have a place to put it. She will start to say things that hurt. I am grateful to Debbie to tell me in advance this may happen and I can see signs of it beginning. I need to understand and be there for these feelings to leave Molly. I think it will be very hard.

**May 18, 1995**

It is a day of quiet. Molly is resting. She does not sleep well and gets up in the middle of the night with thoughts and then writes. I've asked Nancy to come over for a couple of hours to answer the phone while I do some greenhouse responsibilities and errands.

We're anticipating a very difficult call from John's friend who may have been the last person he talked to. There are other men in John's family who have also committed suicide and Molly is learning more information about John's manic-depressive illness and its role in his suicide.

Molly has an appointment to talk with Debbie later today. I am cooking vegetable soup with the hope that it will appeal to Molly -- she's picky.

**May 23, 1995**

Life is not normal even though it's May and the weather is beautiful. We do the usual stuff -- clean, cook, plant and talk. The pleasant things surround us -- good friends, chirping birds and wonderful Spooky. Underneath it all is utter sadness. Sad for Molly and sad for me.

Michelle and Pierre and my cousin Ann were all here for the weekend. The funeral service for John on the afternoon of May 20 was beautiful. It could have been a scene in a tragic love story movie. The parents' home, stately, comfortable elegance, set along the golf course with magnificent views to the Berkshires. An idyllic day, beautiful family and friends gathered. Molly spoke the most eloquently and deeply. Not a dry eye as hearts ached for her. In the next days, she's continued to make an amazing recovery. She's tapping into all the good resources -- Debbie, friends, spirituality, family and peaceful surroundings.

I conquered an important issue for me. I stood up to my husband. I demanded a bedroom set that I had promised to my son and his wife. I said, "That set is mine. I've given to Jeffrey and I will take it or I'll break your door down and get it." He said, "OK," and within two hours it was delivered to my barn.

My next victory was driving to Albany airport and going to the American Airlines ticket counter and asking them to reproduce the ticket that my husband was holding ransom. Old friends of mine in Illinois had invited me to a reunion of neighbors and I used our frequent flier miles to order a ticket to go. Unfortunately, the ticket was put in my husband's mail and he gave it to his lawyer. I told the American Airlines people at the airport that I never received the ticket so they voided the old and printed me a new one! It felt good to do it, whether I ever use it or not. For this day, I feel strong and in control, with only a touch of anger.

The town flowers are being planted by the Falls Town Flowers group and my greenhouse is nearly empty.

## June 27, 1995

I've been busy and time goes by whether you're having fun or not. Victor called to say the trial has been set for the horn honking incident: July 19 at 2 p.m. I have to prepare to be cross-examined. The girlfriend will have to prove beyond a reasonable doubt that she is correct. The idea is to cross-examine her about her "work." I am uneasy, but I'm willing to go through with this.

Earlier this month we received a ruling from the judge saying that my husband must pay me monthly maintenance, retroactive to March 7, 1995, and that it must be paid on or before the 7th day of each month beginning in July. He was also ordered to pay a chunk of my legal bills by the end of July. We'll see if he does it this time.

Molly is back at work, having returned gradually and with her fellow employees as wonderful support. John's family has shared the healing process with Molly, which has been very meaningful and helpful to her. Her friends have also kept her busy with tennis and meals together. She's coming here on Thursday. We'll do a good walk with Spooky and have dinner.

I hoed in my garden today but the weeds are getting out of hand. I am thinking of tennis, maybe calling someone to come over. It's such a nice evening.

There is a certain amount of stress related to these court dates and legal things. I guess I'm OK, just tense. I should bake cookies for the coffee house, but I don't like baking that much and it's pretty hot in the house.

## June 29, 1995

An article I wrote about a young man from Falls Town who does environmental protection work in Rwanda came out in the local paper.

He's doing a talk and slide show at the church about his work. The article got a tagline on the front page, "Africa Comes To Falls Town," and then on page two, a big article by Alice Belt. I was really excited about it, but other parts of the day irritated me.

The young accountant, Brett, spoke to me at the greenhouse and told me that my husband is now yelling at his lawyer over the phone. He tells her what to say.

Brett said the people at the Chamber of Commerce, where Garrick is president, think he's wonderful. I was told he was elected treasurer of the youth activities project he helped to spearhead and there's some big money and fund-raisers behind it. Brett also said my husband is childish and not fun to work for. He said there's hardly any work in the summer and that he did almost all the taxes by himself. I think he'll quit.

I received another affidavit from my husband. He once again signed off on some ugly accusations and lies and he continues to demand that the joint account be unfrozen. Victor responded with an affidavit and stated that the account should not be disturbed until our other remaining assets are equitably distributed. He stated that the greater portion of those assets are in my husband's name, including his IRA and his pension accounts and thus it's likely that I will receive a greater portion of the joint account in the final distribution of assets.

The only improvement for me was none of it made me cry. I just got angry.

**July 1, 1995**

I woke up feeling blue. I had the responsibility of the coffee house this morning and even though it went well, I felt sad. I came home for an hour between the coffee house and the Falls Town Flowers table at Community

Day that I helped with and I cried for the whole hour... just very sad. I saw my husband's car at Community Day and I braced up to walk alone into the festivities. By the time I got to the area he was in (the youth activities project table) he was gone. I guess he saw me coming. I continued to feel sad as I visited with people and felt "out of place." One of the youth activities project volunteers asked me to buy a raffle ticket and I said an emphatic, "No."

My husband put up a new CPA sign at his office and he is clearly digging in his heels to stay in Falls Town. I cried hard as I drove home and now at 7 p.m., I think I'll go to bed.

Well, there's a bright spot. I just spoke with Michelle and I refrained from mentioning my husband or my feelings. Life is going well for her.

**July 2, 1995**

I woke up at 3:30 a.m. and was busy all day. I went to church this morning for the new minister's first day. It seems she will be very good. She plans to be at the coffee house each Saturday to socialize with the community. I hoed my garden, had new neighbors over to see my house and picked up Ann at Canyon Ranch. We went out to dinner at the Hillsdale House, one of my favorite restaurants.

**July 3, 1995**

Last night, Ann told me about a "letting go" sermon she'd heard at her church. We agreed it totally made sense but doing it was the hard part.

I have glimpses of "letting go" and just yesterday I was trying to frame my situation differently in mind. I was saying to myself: Look at it this way, a few years ago I was frustrated with all the "care taking" I had to do to keep his ego bolstered and I sometimes thought I couldn't keep it up for the rest of my life. "Divorce" is now my own solution, too. It is my choice to be free -- to have a new life unencumbered by control and demands. So if I choose this freedom I am happy to feel it, to fight for it, to have it. I am in control of myself and I don't have to consume myself with my husband.

And yet "letting go" isn't a constant for me yet, it comes and goes.

## July 4, 1995

A gorgeous 4th of July, warm, sunny, with a gentle breeze. I'm having about 20 people over for tennis, barbecue and music. Marty and Kent will bring their singing talents and their electric piano.

I was thinking about my finances. I have already cashed in my U.S. Savings Bond plus I sold my life insurance, but that was pretty small. I also cashed in a CD account. Maintenance payments are supposed to start on July 7, according to the order from the judge, and I hope they do because my oven has just gone out. The water heater also conked out this week and I had to pay in full for my eye exam because of the high deductible. On top of it all, Spooky got very sick by eating rat poison at the neighbors house by mistake a couple of days ago and I now have big vet bills. Fortunately, I'm having a cheap party -- hot dogs and pasta salad and everyone's bringing other food and beer.

## July 5, 1995

My party was terrific. Everyone had a good time and raved about it. We played tennis, ate good food and sang songs. It was a terrific mix of people -- young and old and loads of talent. The only bad part was racing Ann to the train station and arriving just as the train was pulling away. I honked the horn and she jumped out and the train stopped to let her on, luckily.

Today, I played tennis and straightened up some of the party mess. I'm thinking of taking a nap. I am anxious to call Debbie at 6 p.m., feeling good.

**July 6, 1995**

A poem:

*Skin*

*Sensational skin tenaciously*

*holds me together*

*drawn by raw nerves and*

*clenched with taut muscle*

*it divulges my feelings even*

*while it seeks to hide me.*

*Penetrated with abrasive words,*

*mental images and memories*

*my skin erupts*

*as a picture of pain.*

*It speaks for all to see*

*listen with eyes*

*through my sensational skin is me.*

--------------------

After lunch with friends, I went to Anna and George's swimming pool. I shared some of my recent writing with them as an update on my story. They were touched by it. Debbie also liked it when I read some to her over the phone. I still cry a little when I share my story with friends.

I saw the girlfriend's car at my husband's office today and I bummed out.

**July 7, 1995**

Today is the deadline for the maintenance payment. I wonder if I'll get it.

**1:30 p.m.** - I called my Victor's office to say I had not received any maintenance payment and his secretary said a check came today to Victor made out to me. My husband had divided the back pay into three separate payments and deducted the $600 he left in the greenhouse a few months ago. He also sent a bunch of bills including one from the counselor's office in Stockbridge we'd visited together. His gall never ends. He's atrocious.

**July 8, 1995**

What do you do when the going gets rough and you have already leaned on your family and friends for almost a year? They're all moving on, they're all getting over it and you're being slapped with ugly affidavits and atrocious bills. My tears feel trite and conversations seem to rehash what a bastard we already know he is.

Crying on the phone to my son-in-law, Pierre, he says, "We feel bad too, but there's nothing we can do."

With all the small town connections, even my good friends have connections to my husband's activities. His youth activities project is attracting everyone in one way or another with fund-raising or social functions. Today he sent, through Victor, about $15,000 of bills to me. I am so sad I can't stop crying. I've placed a call to Debbie.

For the first time in months, my thoughts are suicidal. I can't stand what he's doing to me. The girlfriend has been at his office for several afternoons and it gets me totally down. The fun I've had in past days is obliterated by my depression today.

At 2 a.m. last night I wrote:

*Night Poem*

*A memory wafts across my mind*
*and hot tears push against my closed eyelids.*

226

*It's 2 a.m. Sleep avoids me*
*as acrobatic thoughts leap*
*aimlessly without a safety net.*
*The clock ticks a quick rhythm that*
*frustrates the wish to drift.*
*Beating out its quick ultimatum,*
*the clock dominates in darkness*
*until thoughts are forfeited and*
*sleep returns.*

--------------------

It's 4:30 p.m. and I am consumed by the nightmare I'm living. I wish for Victor's advice, Debbie's encouragement and Nancy's loyalty. On a Saturday afternoon, all of that seems missing. Molly is soothing her own grief with John's family. Michelle is pursuing her ambitions in music and writing, performance and education. My friends have lives and I will see them in a couple of hours at the Rwanda program. I have reason to feel terrible but I also have reason to let go and enjoy the evening. Will I be able to put on a happy face and greet everyone as a perfect hostess?

**11 p.m.** - I guess I did it. I made it through. It was a good program and I came home and cried. Then I wrote this letter (not sent) to my husband.

*Now I see that your word is as worthless as your character. Your immoral behavior makes me so ashamed of my choice in marrying you. I am repulsed by your name and I am so sorry my children are fathered by you. I feel tarnished and abused and overwhelmed by your horrible treatment of me. I have lived my whole life to be honest and decent and have always been treated with respect. Now, to have the man I was married to for 39 years treat me like a rabid dog is more than I can stand. I have bounced back abuse after abuse -- the emotional battering has been devastating. You have nearly destroyed me, but I keep fighting. I will either make it or I will kill myself. It's a fine line between believing in myself and giving in to your vicious attacks on me.*

*Never in my life did I believe you would stoop to such inhuman behavior toward me. I'm completely drained of respect for you. You have kicked me in the stomach, shot me in the back and run over me with a truck until I was ground into the pavement. Then you spit and shit on me. With tears in my mutilated eyes, you can't kill me more -- you've done it.*

*Even as I write this, my resolve returns to fight you until the end. I can scrape myself off the pavement. I can tell my lawyer, "Do what ever it takes to do the bastard in."*

## July 9, 1995

Re-reading yesterday's thoughts, I broke down in a flood of tears again. I even entertained sending these thoughts, but wrote them to myself instead:

*Dear husband -- Something must be terribly wrong. How can it be that two people who loved each other all their lives are now on a path of destruction? Why would you, in your right mind, treat me so horrendously? Forgive my right to defend myself; you have left me with nothing else.*

Today I have plans, as usual. We desperately need rain, but it's a beautiful sunny day.

## July 16, 1995

A storm came through and the electricity went off for four hours. My houseguests, who are attending the Winterhawk music festival, went without water or a real breakfast. And the heat is almost 100 degrees. They had leftover bagels in their car from which we managed to make a breakfast and we had fun talking. Later, I went to a friend's party. It was wonderful; about 100 people of all ages, great food, volley ball, horseshoes and a play area for the kids. I played volleyball and loved it. I related my stuff briefly to a friend when she asked, but otherwise the party was pure fun.

Victor is back from his vacation to Europe and tomorrow we meet to prepare for the trial of the horn-honking incident. I have a feeling my husband might be at the trial as a witness for the "girlfriend." That will be a major bummer but I'm bracing myself for whatever happens.

When my mind drifts over my husband's behavior and the things he's done to me, I am renewed in pain but also in resolve. I almost need his continued battering to be reminded that I'm dealing with a snake.

## July 20, 1995

The trial for the reckless driving charge that the girlfriend filed against me took place at 2 p.m. yesterday at the Town Hall with the local judge, the county DA, a stenographer, Victor, me, the girlfriend and my husband.

I had prepared myself for it. I was nervous ahead of time and my heart was thumping. To calm myself, I talked to Debbie in my head, I stopped at Nancy's house and spent a few minutes with her carpenters (she wasn't home) and then I went into the police station to chat with them, but they weren't around. Another friend was there cleaning so I talked to her for a few minutes.

When the judge arrived I went into the room. Shortly after, Victor arrived and soon I saw my husband's car come up. The girlfriend drove in at the same time. The best thing that happened for me was when they came in I just looked at them and had no emotion -- no anger, no hatred, no jealousy. My husband looked ugly to me and she looked like a streetwalker.

The girlfriend testified first. She was emotional and confused and looked sleazy. She was wearing tight white leggings that showed her fat butt and her underwear. She sat in a very unlady-like position -- pulling her thick leg across her knee. When she was asked if she was having an affair with my husband, she look at my husband and then at the DA who said, "I object."

She did answer questions relating to her "work" since she'd said she was a full-time student. She said she did a little "part-time" for someone. Then she finally admitted she did a little work for my husband; taxes from her home, if there were any to be done.

My husband testified against me just as I suspected he would. He said he saw me driving fast and close to her car and he was worried because of the things I had said about her in the past six months.

I testified that I honked my horn, did not exceed the speed limit and stayed a safe distance behind. I said my horn was a "voice." When asked what the "voice" said, I said, "I am not happy with you."

Later Victor said I was "excellent" on the stand and that he'd seen enough to move for trial in our divorce case. The girlfriend was "great" in that she was stupid. My husband was "great" in that he appeared to be crawling under his own skin. I was good even by my own perception. I looked neat, I was composed, I had no emotion and I was honest. It was satisfying.

Later the stenographer said, "It's amazing what old men will do; he's lost his good taste in women." The DA, Victor, the stenographer and I all had a laugh.

The trial itself worked out well for me. The charge was reduced to a minor infraction and I paid a fine of $50 and a $25 court fee. The judge said he hoped I wasn't mad at him.

All in all, it seems like a major turning point for me. I'm OK with me and my husband and girlfriend have lost their control over me. It's as if tremendous shackles have been taken off my body.

My husband's testifying against me was very positive for my case. Victor is pulling out the last reserve and plans to go for a divorce trial. He'll subpoena the girlfriend and Brett, the accountant in my husband's office. He'll get expert testimony on my husband's business and finances from the top CPA/lawyer in New York. Victor's already low opinion of my husband dropped even farther down and my husband made it easy for us to move ahead legally.

My husband's actions against me have also allowed me to be free of him emotionally. As he danced merrily away from me, I have a feeling, finally, of dancing merrily away from him.

Even as I write this today, feeling good, I know there will be more hard times. Hopefully, I'm now better prepared for them.

**July 25, 1995**

More hard times came on Saturday, July 22. I went to the post office and two of the employees there told me my husband was seen removing a legal size letter from my box that day. They said they would change my lock and hold my mail until that was done. I immediately called Victor at home.

I cannot believe the sordid tactics my husband is resorting to. I have no idea what he removed from my box or if he has been taking my mail all along. I referred to him as "that bastard" to the post office employees and continued on with my weekend to Lake George as guests of my good friends, the Carlin family.

These days, the girlfriend's car is at my husband's office for longer periods of time. Brett left and moved to a CPA office in Hudson to get some auditing experience. So when I see her car by my husband's, I know they are in the office alone together. The other day she wore her bathing suit with a short skirt. It makes me depressed.

I'm tired and lonely today. I've had to push myself to get motivated to write this and I'm going to type up an older piece of writing that I had written last summer or spring. It isn't dated but I described my feelings at the time, which was before I'd discovered the locked file cabinet.

Tonight I have my word processing course and I plan to go early to practice. I'm doing well with it even though no one could be more inexperienced with computers than me. This is my third class and I think I'm finally getting it. Nancy and I go together to classes -- she's learning clock repair!

**July 31, 1995**

At 2 p.m. today, I return to Sheila's office for the continuing deposition process, which may take all week. It started last Friday morning at Victor's office with Victor asking questions of my husband until 1:30 p.m. when Sheila had to leave so it ended.

The questioning began with "When were you born?" and proceeded with details of my husband's career from the beginning up through his current work. I sat across the table from my husband. He tried to look strong, but he wasn't. He never made eye contact with me. He was stoic and displayed no reactions. I looked at him while he spoke, trying to look through him and understand what's in him; what is he thinking, what is he doing and why?

He seemed to enjoy recounting his career and the sequence of beginning his practice in Falls Town. His testimony clearly depicted the Big House as his office and not as a B&B, as his affidavits have stated.

If I had something to say to Victor or if it got difficult for me emotionally, Victor and I would leave the room for a moment and regroup before going back in.

Victor says he will subpoena the girlfriend and Brett, too. Today, my husband will be asked about the filing clerk/girlfriend's work.

**August 1, 1995**

I wrote this perception of my husband during his deposition yesterday:

*I know you. You are sitting there crawling in your own skin, trying to be smart and clever. You're a little cocky and a lot vulnerable.*

*I know you. In control, you think, but spiraling out. A naughty child in an old man's body.*

*I know you. Acting out your fantasy even though you ruined your family of 39 years.*

*I know you. You're self-centered, strategic and manipulative, always careful to get your way. You play by rules that suit you and protect you. You've been willing to destroy our marriage, our family, our home, our finances and security. You have lowered yourself to lying, deception, infidelity and unthinkable acts of cruelty. The pain you have caused our family is unforgivable. I have suffered enormously.*

*When you testified against me, it was the turning point. The shackles came off me as you sat next to your whore and I saw you were willing to stop at nothing. I am everything I've always been and more. I am a free woman. I dance naked. I have retained every lifelong friend but one -- you. Looking at you across the deposition table doesn't hurt me. I would not choose you if I were to do it over again, because now I know you.*

## August 4, 1995

Yesterday's deposition is sinking in. The sickening pain is back as the battering goes on in ways I could not have comprehended.

He testified he gave the girlfriend his bank card and PIN number to use and she had access to his (our) account for a year. She removed thousands of dollars from our account. He also admitted he filed tax returns for himself as "single" and took my charitable flower contributions as his deductions. He also didn't bother to tell me that he left me delinquent with the IRS because I thought he'd filed our taxes jointly. He also sold $50,000 of bonds, without consulting me, to eliminate a high interest debt in our joint account. I'm concerned he'll leave me with half the capital gains tax on that sale but none of the money earned.

I needed to vent some anger so I visited Nancy and called Pete and Ed. I tried to call Debbie but couldn't reach her.

When I related the deposition to a few friends after our tennis game today, I managed to choke back my tears. I know "the truck" has rolled back over me again, but it's not too bad. I must be getting tough. Right now, I believe I can stand the onslaught and keep going with my legal battle.

Victor told me today that the judge granted the restraining order that prevents me from entering the office or the Big House; however, the judge denied my husband's demand to unfreeze our joint account. My husband and Sheila had filed papers asking the judge to grant both.

I'm stunned with my husband's persistent obsession about unfreezing the joint account. It seems the wise action taken by our Merrill Lynch account advisor to freeze the account when he thought something strange was happening really threw a wrench in my husband's agenda. It must have greatly upset his devious financial plans. Most of all, I know how much my husband despises not being in control and not "winning."

According to his sworn testimony yesterday, my husband has already given the filing clerk thousands of dollars, half of which were mine and, of course, I was never informed. It must be what the records I found in the filing cabinet of daily $200 withdrawals from an ATM were about. He probably had intentions to siphon off thousands more from the joint account to her or elsewhere, where he and only he, could get access to it. He alone has always handled our finances, I would have never known. Then, when the division of property eventually happened in the divorce that he alone was already contemplating, the funds in our joint account would be tiny since he would have walked off with the lion's share much earlier before.

It's staggering. For months, he spent our money in whatever ways he wanted, including on his girlfriend, and now he wants to spend money that is 50 percent mine already to pay maintenance to me and to pay his bills with! No wonder he is so obsessed with unfreezing our joint account.

My daughters are coming over for dinner tonight. I'm really anxious to see them. I would like to share the events of the past few days with them, but I think it's best to keep my husband out of our conversation. Instead we can focus on the stuff going on in their lives and my upcoming trip to Indiana and Iowa for a wedding and to visit family and friends.

The trip is part of my effort to take care of myself (advice from Debbie) and to live in the manner I was accustomed to in order to establish my "needs" (advice from Victor). Although I was loath to do so, I guess cashing in my "nest egg" savings over the past few weeks has been an investment in me and my case. Eventually, I just hope to have my rightful share of the assets.

**Later --**

Victor called to ask directions to the girlfriend's house. A messenger from his office is delivering a subpoena to her. He'll also deliver one to Brett. Shit will hit the fan when my husband finds out. Fortunately, I'm leaving town. I have a little rush of excitement as the plot thickens and my husband gets to sit in an uncomfortable position for a while -- at least that's what seems to be happening.

**August 6, 1995**

It's 3 a.m. Sunday morning and I can't sleep. I want to sleep since I'll be starting in a couple of hours on my drive to Indiana. But the events of yesterday keep going through my mind.

By an odd chance, I came home around 2 p.m. to change my clothes. I'd decided I would go on the Historical Society house tour after all and start my trip to Indiana on Sunday morning. The phone was ringing when I walked in and the caller asked for my husband. I asked who was calling and he said "Islander Pools." Then I identified myself as Mrs. Belt and asked what the call pertained to and he said, "The 15 by 30 foot pool that your husband ordered is ready to be installed." I said, "Where?" He became hesitant and said the order said "Church Street." A pool for the Big House! I was flabbergasted and told the caller to reach my husband at his office.

I immediately tried to call Victor, but couldn't reach him. I called his secretary and she suggested driving to Victor's house. I went to Pete and Ed's for a little while, vented on them and then tried to reach Victor again. I got him and he was stunned about the pool, too. I told him my friend had seen newspaper clippings of a house for sale in Columbia County taped above my husband's desk in February when we went through his office.

Could it be my husband purchased a swimming pool to go with a house he bought? Or did he buy the pool for the youth group project since he's treasurer? Or did he request the lawn mower, the pickup truck, his stereo and pin ball machine all be given to him because he is moving into a new house? Did his comment in his deposition that he was living "temporarily" in the Big House mean just that -- he's about to leave?

When I put two and two together, it seems he bought a house, is putting in a pool, will have his "toys," will cut the lawn and possibly has moved some of his stuff there already. If this is the case, what will I do with the Big House -- especially this winter?

Meanwhile, he's balking on making maintenance payments to me and continues to push to get the joint account opened. Victor says his buying the pool works for my case because it proves he has plenty of money. He claims he's running out, that he's had to cash in marital assets "in order to survive," and that he is on "the brink of insolvency;" which I guess he could be if he just bought a house, a pool, he pays the whore and he's supposed to give me my monthly maintenance payments. No wonder he's anxious to get at our joint account. He's on a spending spree.

This entire scenario blows my mind. I was just beginning to absorb the facts that he gave his bank card and PIN number to the "girlfriend" for the past year to use whenever she wanted at our money; that he filed his taxes as single leaving me delinquent without my knowledge; used my flower fund-raisers as his deductions; and possibly took all the money from the sale of the bonds while giving me half of the capital gains tax. Maybe he bought his new house and his swimming pool with the bonds money, so I get to pay for that too! The word bastard comes up repeatedly and isn't nearly strong enough.

**August 18, 1995**

It's noon on Friday and I'm half way through Pennsylvania on my way home from my vacation to Indiana and Iowa. Armed with Victor's 800 number, I've called him several times to get updates on what my husband was doing and what we could do about it.

Victor sent a letter to Sheila the Monday after the pool phone call incident and said the response was that my husband was putting a 15 by 30 foot above ground pool at the Big House. He claimed he would remove it when he moved. At this date, we don't know if my husband installed the pool yet, and if he did, if he put water in it using the Big House's well and pump.

Yesterday, Victor informed me that my husband answered the interrogatory about his "affair" with the filing clerk and denied everything.

I visited relatives in Indiana and attended a fabulous wedding in Iowa. Interestingly, one friend said he was sure my husband would not admit to infidelity in the interrogatory. He seemed to have a strong sense about it from a male perspective and from a legal aspect.

My nerves are on edge and my anger persists although I've had only occasional outbursts of "God damned bastard," and only a few tears when I've related the stories to my family and friends.

Before I left Iowa, my friends offered anything they could do to help me. They said they would fly to New York to see me soon. I shared some of my writing, the tax problem and the swimming pool weirdness with friends. I showed them a photo of the girlfriend and my husband together taken just after we'd purchased the farmhouse to become his new office. They all agreed that she's chubby and no beauty. My young friend, Jill, referred to the girlfriend as "Poca-hump-us," which made us all laugh. Returning to Indiana, I had dinner with my cousins and my network of support grew again.

So, I'm heading home to renew the legal efforts. The depositions continue on Monday. As much as I like Indiana and Iowa, it was clear to me that I didn't want to live there. I need to get clear about what I do want and where I want to be. It's hard to think about when there are so many loose ends.

## August 20, 1995

I'm back in my home and it feels good. I actually started crying when I turned onto my road last night. I called Nancy and Molly right away. I'm going to visit Molly in Stockbridge today for lunch and tennis. She's planning to take a philosophy course at U. Mass this fall and she's looking for a new apartment. I'm so happy she's making positive moves.

I did the coffee house with Flora on Saturday morning and Pete and Ed invited me for a swim and dinner on Saturday night.

My husband did install the above-ground pool at the Big House even though Victor sent a legal letter asking him not to do it.

**August 21, 1995**

I did some writing this morning while waiting for the deposition to begin:

> *Only one cup of coffee and my nerves are jittery. Pulsating alarms are going off in my entire body -- uneven breathing, pounding heart, a catch in my throat, my stomach tight against my breakfast and my brain scanning its reservoir of memories.*
>
> *Questions asked and answered are fantasy mental exercises for my test under pressure to be clear and honest. Fears of entrapment, my words taken out of context, taunt me in my head.*
>
> *Today it doesn't seem fair to ask God for help; it would be like asking someone to do my job when I should do it myself. Nor can I solicit my family and friends. I am contained in a thermos that takes air from my lawyer. Perhaps life once carried me in a fine tapestry. Now I can only rely on the strength of the thermos and hope it doesn't drop and shatter. The coffee is still hot.*

**Later --**

It's not quite over, my deposition will continue at another meeting scheduled for August 31st. In the midst of it all, Victor showed me a note -- "Relax," and only once did I fall apart. When Sheila questioned me about an $8,000 CD, I said I'd saved it for "a rainy day, which has happened," and "I have a grandson and I wanted to be able to give him something." The combination of thoughts shook me and I broke down in tears.

Victor quickly halted the deposition and we all took a break. After that I was OK. My preparations for financial disclosure seemed adequate and it went fine.

My husband admitted paying more than $7,000 for his swimming pool and said he needed it because "It was hot." Good information for the judge.

## August 24, 1995

Time has its steady march. By perception, time goes quickly, slowly, happily or painfully, but it marches on. What has happened to my time in the past year? 365 days pushing me older, releasing my pain in increments, inviting me to grab onto the acceleration, energize, produce, live!

But I'm reluctant to move quickly. I let my mind drift into the past as time zooms on. I can still go back in memory while the moment moves on. I can only use minutes, hours and days at a partial of their momentum. I let time flow over me, floating to recover on a course not charted. Time has a hold on me.

The only time I can capture is the moment. So at this moment, I'm touching base with friends, extending invitations, setting dates for occasions and writing for my future project, which has its roots in the moment. "Move on, time, I'm coming with you." Let the good times roll.

## September 4, 1995

My final deposition took place in Victor's office last Thursday afternoon. In the morning, the girlfriend was deposed. She was legally represented by Sheila, my husband's lawyer. I did not attend. Victor said Sheila didn't allow her to answer any questions about her sex life or relationship with my husband, so the best he could do on that stuff was to get her to admit to sending the love letter and romantic dinner gift.

After my deposition was completed, Victor took me over to my new CPA's office. The CPA needs me to get my 1099s together. I realize now that my husband took my 1099s and has withheld this information from me even though I must do my own taxes now. I called my banks to get new 1099s sent to me.

Labor Day weekend has been busy and fun for me. A Tanglewood concert, a party at Marty and Kent's, tennis, a great hike with Diane in Stockbridge and I wrote this poem today:

*Why should I cry anymore?*
*It's over.*
*You cut out my heart*
*and trashed me.*
*Why should I cry anymore?*
*You dragged me over the hot coals of humiliation*
*and flaunted your infidelity.*
*Why should I cry anymore?*
*I have survived*
*and still stand tall*
*so*
*Why should I cry anymore?*

--------------------

The deposition last Thursday caused a resurgence in my anger. I was seething when I drove home that day and my emotions were raw on Friday and Saturday. I vented with Nancy and tried to call Debbie but didn't get her. I cry easily again. But this time, I'm also managing to laugh, move in positive directions and accomplish a little.

Tomorrow I'm having my windshield replaced on my car. It's an all day thing in Hudson. So I've packed my bicycle and my day pack and I'm going to spend the day biking along the Hudson river. I can buy a picnic lunch and take my paper and pen to write my memories of my kids growing up. Jeffrey has asked each of his parents and his sisters to write our memories of our kids' childhoods. It will be a Christmas gift to us all, a compilation of our writings describing our thoughts about the time period when the kids were growing up. It's a great idea of his and I am happy to focus on the project.

**September 6, 1995**

Today I shared my writing with our new minister. She was an excellent listener and had constructive comments. Her thoughts were in line with Debbie's and she didn't offer prayers or religious solutions. It was good talking with her. Some of her comments included: "He needs massive counseling," "Keep this thing as just part of your life, let life go on," and "It's good that you can write your feelings."

She told me she was planning a sermon for the next Sunday on the importance of supporting one another and that my situation was inspirational to her.

**September 13, 1995**

My husband has sent four affidavits to the judge asking him to deny me maintenance payments. He was seen taking the girlfriend's daughter to the video store. I have not received maintenance or back pay this month yet and it was due on the 7th. My lawyer is calling my husband's lawyer.

Last week Nancy and I were invited to New York by Marty and Kent. I really allowed myself to experience the city and have fun. I dared to shop in Bergdorf Goodman and bought a fabulous fall outfit, which I spent too much for -- especially since the maintenance payments are constantly being challenged. With all this going on I woke up in the middle of the night and wrote:

*3 a.m. Feelings*

*Held in a straight jacket*

*of acceptable behavior*

*my only weapon - the truth -*

*falls impotent against his bold-faced lies.*

*A noose is drawn around my mind*

*choking the search for words to strike a blow.*

*For anger in its silent screams*

*has not language strong enough*

*to slash the straps of bondage*

*from which only tears escape.*

--------------------

Later today, after receiving more legal paperwork from Victor, I wrote:

*He wants the divorce for Christmas,*

*a tidy package all for him.*

*Call me "Scrooge," but I won't be "Santa."*

*I'm taking a break from "kind and generous,"*

*to try a little "I'll take my share, because*

*I'm worth it."*

*I won't eat shit and he can't trample me.*

*My dander is up! The fight is vicious, the stakes*

*are high, the price is extreme.*

*I will be the winner even though*

*he schemed all the plays.*

*We play by different rules.*

*I will win by virtue of virtue.*

*Easter comes after Christmas -- a time of hope.*

--------------------

Debbie said today that a person needs a level of wellness to seek counseling. She said my husband has a primitive defense in that he won't take responsibility for his actions and needs me to be "the bad guy." Emotionally, it is very unhealthy for him. She reminded me that I am not at fault in any way and nothing I could have done or said would change him.

## September 15, 1995

Even uncertain hope gets squashed. His attempts to deny maintenance payments, my lawyer's responses, threats of court action, seeing the girlfriend at the post office -- it all scrapes open my wounds. I cried hard again and questioned my ability to see this through. Rays of hope boost me above it, but suddenly it hits again, deepening the anger, pain and sadness. Then thoughts return that maybe I can't handle it, I can't go on, how can he do this to me? It isn't right, it isn't fair. He's trying to leave me with no choice but to end it all. Why does he want me dead? Why would he do that to our kids?

I need some good news. I need support. I need to hang on until Monday. I wish my kids could be solidly in my camp, but I know they relate to their father, too.

I'm going to help Molly move today and maybe things will seem better.

## September 17, 1995

**1 a.m.** - My feelings are like they were a year ago -- crying so hard, weak and sick, thinking of how to end it, confused, hopeless and alone.

The hour is not good to call anyone. Monday looms as a threat or a hope. What will happen legally? A maintenance payment or legal action against my husband? What makes any sense? Why do I care what the hell he does? Why do I fume over his part in the youth activities project? Why am I bothered that he takes the girlfriend's daughter into the video store? Why do I look at his house and notice he's using the master bedroom? If he gets the office and the farm, can I stand it? If I am forced to take the Big House, can I stand it? Can I live here in Falls Town with him in my face? If only the legal system will work for me. But what if it doesn't? Will I really be OK anyway, as Debbie says, or as I've even proclaimed for myself during times of feeling stronger?

Debbie always emphasizes, "taking care of myself." She recognizes the extreme emotionalism that surrounds this phase of the divorce process. It must be a time when many people throw in the towel. The battle is accelerating toward destruction. He wants to destroy me and I want to destroy him. If I'm not to have the marriage I believed in, then why should he get a life with anyone else? The fact is my marriage is destroyed, he has a life and he denies me even a pittance. To survive, I must stand up each time I'm trashed -- over and over again.

Writing helps. Now that I've written this I'm not crying. I'm tired. My mind has turned to plans for the upcoming day. I think I can go to sleep now. I'm so grateful I made it through this hour.

**Later --**

With puffy eyes, I went to church anyway. I feel sort of irritable. Little things bother me and it's a drab day. I have tentative plans to see a movie with a friend. I made plans with my cousin, Ann, to see a Broadway show and I made calls to my mother, Jeffrey and Molly, and I think I'll write a letter to Michelle. I also got busy in the kitchen and made salsa and potato salad.

**September 18, 1995**

Details -- call again for my 1099s for my taxes, call Victor for the status of maintenance payments. He says Sheila has sent faxes saying my husband will <u>not</u> pay maintenance. She also demands that I pay the Big House taxes and split all the other properties. I said an emphatic, "No!" Victor will charge my husband with contempt of court and put him jail if he doesn't pay. The battle has sunk to its lowest level so far.

Even Victor is astounded with the poor legal advice my husband is getting and he, too, believes my husband is calling his own shots -- and they are not legal. I told Victor it's all been very hard on me the last few days.

I called the Seymour Tribune to check on the status of an article I wrote about my brother and the editor said it would be printed in a day or two. I invited friends to lunch on Thursday, I'm going to New York City for the Broadway show on Sunday and I took Spooky for a hike in the field today. My week is now somewhat filled with activities. I'll cook and clean and play tennis and write. It's all a good buffer for when more shit hits the fan as my husband hears from Victor. "Jail" is one of his fears and I don't think he'll want to go.

My husband and Sheila have stated in recent letters that they want <u>all</u> of our property and belongings to be sold -- sell everything and split the money. This is his dirty play to hurt me to the "nth" degree. Victor says this may be the ugliest divorce he's ever witnessed.

## September 19, 1995

**3 a.m.** - Sleeping a few hours and awake in the middle of the night is characteristic of the earlier days in this divorce nightmare. Victor always raises my spirits with his guarded optimism. Then my husband's mean responses crush me again. When the scale tips in my favor, I feel strong. Then fear and pain re-surface and I'm back to devastation. I wonder if I'll ever be in love again, waking up happy and secure.

## October 3, 1995

Today, O.J. Simpson was found <u>NOT</u> guilty in the murder of his ex-wife and her friend. The verdict came in while I was having lunch with my tennis group at the Woodlands restaurant. All eight of us felt sure O.J. was guilty, and yet, young boys from a nearby prep school who were in the restaurant cheered at the results.

It hit me especially hard since my husband and I were in L.A. at the time of the murders and the famous white Ford Bronco chase on the freeway. At the time, under phenomenal marital stress of my own, I immediately thought he was guilty and I understood his passion for the crime. My husband, at the same time, said he was sure he was innocent. The acquittal today somehow made me feel like a loser and I cried in my car coming home from the restaurant.

I know I was afraid. The verdict made me distrust the legal system and worry about how unfair it may treat me when right and wrong seem so obvious. Molly said everyone at her work thought O.J. was guilty, too. Perhaps power, celebrity and money paid off. I wonder if I'll be a loser like Nicole and her friend and their families?

In the past few days, I've been helping Molly move into her new apartment. She has a very nice place in Stockbridge and I've worked hard to help her get moved in. Michelle was also here to help with some of the work. The girls had dinner with their father while they were both here. It really hurts me but I didn't say anything.

Legally things keep getting worse. Now in court, awaiting the judge's decision, is the maintenance issue, again. I am astonished that my husband and Sheila have decided just to stop paying maintenance after it was already ordered by the judge to be paid and are asking again to not have to pay it. It seems an absurd and stupid legal move. Victor says we'll attach my husband's car if he doesn't pay.

My cousin, Ann, gave me a day pass to the Canyon Ranch spa. I spent the first two hours with the nurse there. She and I had a frank talk about divorce. She had recently found out that her husband had cheated on her for five years, with a friend of hers, no less. She coined a phrase, "S.O.S.," for "slut on the sly." I laughed. Clever referrals to the whore now are "S.O.S." and "Poca-hump-us." Anyway, she and her husband are trying to resolve their problems and save the marriage.

**October 11, 1995**

Last night I went to the church charge conference, which is a potluck dinner and meeting about church issues. As I was leaving the meeting, a friend mentioned that my husband's car was at the girlfriend's house all day on Monday, which was a holiday. I screamed and wailed in tears on the way home. My car has always been my safe place to scream. I yelled, "You bastard, you Indian-fucker, you son of a bitch, you whore, you slut! How could you do this to me? STOP, STOP, STOP, STOP, STOP!"

When I got home I went to bed and cried some more, then I got up and called Michelle. At first I just said, "Hi, how are you?" Then I told her some of the more recent things. I told her about his refusal to pay maintenance and his contempt of court. She guessed jail was the possible outcome. I told her about his plan to sell everything and how I thought what hurt most now was "being trashed." She said, "You are separate now, so go on." Her response was a cold reminder that it's so difficult for my kids to understand. They just don't get it and I should leave them out of it.

I told Michelle that I couldn't stand it if he tries to take my kids, too. She said he can't do that and they love me and need me.

When I woke up this morning, I dozed off again and I had a nightmare: My husband invited our daughters and the girlfriend to go with him to the coffee house while I was there working. He came in as if he owned the place, chatted with my friends, socialized with our daughters and the girlfriend and ate popcorn. In the nightmare, I lost it. I screamed, "I'll kill you. I'll kill her. I'll kill myself." I was screaming inside my head until I woke up with bolt.

Then a friend called and said my husband was everywhere at the art auction fund-raiser for the youth activities project. He was with the girlfriend and he was happy as a lark. Last night Michelle mentioned he was not happy. "Why," I asked, "because he's guilty that he ruined the family?" I'd rather hear "not happy" than "happy."

Friends are coming today for lunch and tennis. I really need to keep busy with people. It passes time in pleasant ways and inspires me to cook, clean, plan and give. It's a gorgeous fall day. But as I was getting dressed, washing my face with the puffy eyes, I looked with anger into the mirror. I said, "You, bastard" as if he were there. Then I broke down again. I dried my eyes and went to the church house to help Jean clean.

A stop at the post office yielded a big package from Victor with various motions, affidavits and a copy of the deposition of the girlfriend. I shared a little of the legal information with Jean. While we were talking, two flies landed on her shoulder, they moved close together and I swatted them, killing them both. She said, "That was your husband and his girlfriend." We laughed.

Then Nancy and her kids came for lunch. Her daughter Deborah is an actress and her husband, Jonny, is a movie producer. I suggested I had a story for them and said I was willing to tell it. We all learned from Jonny that a "schmuck" is a penis and we had laughs referring to my husband as a "schmuck."

It's 6 p.m. and I'm ready to call Debbie in California. I have a lot to tell her again.

**Later --**

As usual, Debbie was so helpful. She refers to this period as the "Vietnam of divorce." She has such a way of cutting to the heart of the matter and the ability to wrap it up with good sense and parting advice to help me prevent mistakes and to give me courage.

She suggested my conversation with Michelle was about the losses I'm feeling so acutely and said my kids might not respond in a way that feels good to me since they are coming from a different place.

**October 12, 1995**

Today there is more legal mail; opposition papers to motions and vicious accusations in more affidavits from my husband including more cries of his so-called poverty. I'm feeling the battering. I'm even feeling "trashed" today and that's depressing. I am tired and lonely, even though it's gorgeous outside. I've pushed myself to accomplish a few simple tasks. I called Victor to see how we were doing and to point out the specific lies in the affidavit from Sheila and my husband. Victors thinks the judge will see the truth but we don't know.

Debbie had suggested I make an "anger list" of what I've thought of doing to my husband, so here we go:

1. scratch his car with scissors
2. put nails in his driveway
3. put a road kill animal in his swimming pool
4. dump trash on his lawn and at his office
5. spray paint his CPA sign
6. put poison ivy in his bed
7. call his answering machine and let the tape run out
8. take a seat next to him in a public place and grab his "schmuck" and jerk it.
9. ram his car
10. shove him off a steep edge
11. kick him in the balls
12. pour blood on his porch
13. call him an "Indian-fucker"
14. send him an Indian doll in a position called "Poca-hump-us"
15. call him Garrick "sleeps-with-sluts" Belt
16. fight him barehanded
17. scream obscenities at him
18. walk away with a great life of my own

## October 15, 1995

Sleeping is not easy. I wake up in the wee hours of the morning. I need someone to talk to before I go to sleep. Last night I called Lilly and talked for an hour or so. My long distance phone bill concerns me but it didn't make me stop talking.

Saturday was a day of pleasure and stress. The coffee house was good, but two messages were passed to me. A friend said she was told that my husband and the girlfriend were seen at the crafts fair holding hands. That thought made me cry. Then another friend said he had seen them in my husband's car at the post office and you couldn't have put a piece of paper between them they were so closely embraced. I asked him if he would testify to that and he said he would.

Later, at a party hosted by my young friends, I met a few of my husband's new friends gained through the youth activities project and I managed to be jolly. In their earshot and for their benefit I commented to another person that I had an "estranged" husband. I shared some of my legal information with my young friends. They were very supportive and had nothing nice to say about the girlfriend or her daughter and we all bad-mouthed my husband. When my friends are willing to dump on my husband and his friends it feels good to me.

I cried really hard driving home from their party. When I woke up this morning, I was repulsed to think I shared my bed with my husband. In the past months I have sometimes reached over for him in my sleep, but today I withdrew into my space and said, "Don't touch me."

I'm crying as I write this and Spooky came over to me. She knows I'm sad and she wants to help. I said, "Spooky, would you bite him, shake him and break his neck -- just like you did to that rabbit you caught? I would appreciate it." Spooky is the perfect dog for me. She is always a sweet and constant companion. I know she's vital to my sanity.

Today I want to go to church, make a haircut appointment and wrap gifts to mail -- babies and weddings. I think I'll call my mother before 8 a.m.

I wrote this just now and I am a little better:

*Repulsed by tales*

*of hand holding and snuggling,*

*sickened by lies and greed.*

*Feeling trashed raises*

*new levels of anger*

*raging in me.*

*Victor, break his neck, legally.*

--------------------

Where is the light at the end of tunnel? Ignoring the comfort of the couch, I am alone, racked with pain, starved for solace, trapped in the concentration camp of my body and mind. A depraved tension grips a stronghold on my feeble efforts to escape.

## October 16, 1995

At 10 p.m. last night, I "communicated" to Debbie with a letter, not sent:

*Dear Debbie,*

*Since I just called you a couple of days ago, I can't call again only to sob and hope for your words of strength. At times today I pulled myself out. I did just the right things; I talked positively to myself and accomplished a few things. A friend came over and I talked about my property settlement thoughts and tried to become more clear about my wants in that regard. Then I helped Molly move a piece of furniture to her apartment. I became sensitive about her rejection of my ideas which I thought I was offering gently and helpfully. She said that was only my perception. I started to cry. She apologized and I left early. All the way home I wailed in my car, "I can't stand this anymore."*

*I wonder what I can stand? The emotional battering, the existence of my husband with the girlfriend, the divorce proceedings? I feel sick. I want to kill myself but I don't have a plan. I don't want to do that to my kids but I don't feel like I can go on either. If Victor doesn't give me some good news soon, I don't know if I can keep getting up. The stress is unbearable. I had ideas -- drive my car off of a cliff, go to my husband's house and tell him to call the police to take me away, call Molly and tell her I just can't take it anymore. So far, I've just cried and cried.*

*Why do I even care? I don't know. Maybe I am crazy. It's hard to believe there could be a future for me. I am very weak.*

## October 17, 1995

Molly called at 8 a.m. to see if I was OK. I was still in bed. At 10 a.m. I got up and tried to motivate myself. I stayed in my robe and played myself in Scrabble. I see it's a nice day but I can't quite face it yet. If I make the muffin mix I need to buy buttermilk. If I go to town, I need to look good -- I don't.

What is it? Why do I allow myself these feelings? Why can't I act upon the positive stuff I have? What will make me get up and do one of my ideas -- rake leaves, wash my hair, ride my bike to town or even on my road, clean the coach house, take a walk, buy the ingredients and make the muffins, call someone for tennis, buy salt for the water softener -- be alive!

My house is silent except for Spooky breathing. I am very, very sad. I wish Victor would call me with some good news. I need some not just for vengeance, but also for preserving myself from being trashed.

While my head tells me one thing, my emotions don't allow me to move. I don't want anyone to see me. I'm limp. I also feel guilty that for all the help I've had, all the friends and all the support, I am still on the "pity pot." It must be a conscious decision to get off the "pity pot" and move on. Victor says "Move on." OK, I'm going to choose one of my things and get up and do it.

**11 a.m.** - Took a bath and washed my hair. My eyes are puffy but otherwise I look OK. While in the tub, I realized he'd stopped washing my back because he didn't care anymore. I had tried to share my concerns and he turned a cold heart. He is actually using that behavior now, embellished, in the legal battle. So what's the logic in killing myself? He will go on with life, my kids will be devastated and all my assets will pass automatically to my husband and then probably to the whore-girlfriend. So get up, damn it! Fight the bastard! Stand up for my rights! Take action! Seize the moment!

**12 noon** - I paid a month's insurance on my house and reconciled my checking account. I'm down to a less than a thousand dollars but I have a little cash. I'm going to pick up sticks while I walk to use as kindling in my wood burning stove and then eat lunch. It's tuna salad I made yesterday and the last tomato from my garden.

**4 p.m.** - After raking leaves, I took Spooky with me to shop for groceries. I stopped at the church house to drop off some dried flowers and chatted for a few minutes. I bought an angel for my counselor, Debbie, for Christmas.

I said "hellos" to a few people who looked at me in a way that was "knowing." I asked a friend who's a photographer to make an effort to get a photo of my husband with the girlfriend. I noted my husband was not at his office or the Big House. I put gas in my car, bought salt for the water softener and came home to my quiet house.

I'm feeling low but I think I'll take a short bike ride before I mix the muffins. I'm sleepy. One crazy thought went through my head when I saw Halloween decorations out, I could dress up in a complete disguise and go to my husband's house trick or treating. It was just a fantasy.

**5 p.m.** - I rode my bike for several miles and then mixed the pumpkin/apple muffins for the coffee house. I'm going to treat myself to another game of Scrabble, then go to bed and watch TV. I'm almost through the day, not at all exciting, but it passed.

**October 18, 1995**

Lilly called last night and I filled her in on my "coping" problem. I woke up at 2 a.m. and couldn't sleep for a while. I was awakened at 8:30 a.m. by a call from a friend and she said, "Hang in there." Then Michelle called and said her dad had been to visit and she confronted him about the division of property. He told her he wanted to be fair, was willing to hear my proposal and didn't really want everything to be sold.

I totally lost it with Michelle. I relayed all the stuff I've been writing over the past few days. I spared no language in referring to my husband as a lying, cheating, fucking bastard. I said he'd come very close to pushing me to the point where I can't take it and I'll kill myself.

I cried hysterically over the phone. She tried to stay calm and sensible with me saying, "Are you talking with your counselor?" and "Can't you get your lawyer to speed up the process?"

She said her dad told her he's unhappy about the family being split up and he feels guilty. He also said he needs a place to live so he'll stay in the Big House, and he needs an office so he'll keep that, and he wants the land. He is going for exactly what he wanted to begin with -- the Big House, the office and the farmland! He needs, he needs, he needs... Bullshit!!! And he's convinced Michelle that he wants to be fair?! I am seething with anger. What a conniver he is!

Michelle suggested I try to separate my emotions from the business aspect of the divorce. I said, "My lawyer does that."

I have my last CD due today so I'm going to cash it in Great Barrington. It was purchased a long while ago there as my "rainy day" savings. If Michelle tells my husband what I said, he'll use it against me in court, as he has used every outburst of emotion I've ever had to paint me as a lunatic. I am shattered again.

**4:30 p.m.** - I look terrible, I can't go to the post office and I didn't go to Great Barrington. I'm exhausted. I think I'll try to call Victor and ask him if he has time to listen to this. At 6 p.m. I have my scheduled talk with Debbie.

**5:30 p.m.** - I decided that my lawyer is not my counselor. I took Spooky to the post office with me and I ran into Nancy there and cried. I got more legal mail, including a motion to stop the trial date until all the information is in.

**7:30 p.m.** - I just got off the phone with Debbie. She believes my wanting to kill myself was depression turned in on myself and is actually a homicidal wish. She said I had every right to explode with Michelle even though she was not to blame. She's caught in the middle and simply doesn't get it. Debbie said my "losing it" with her was the "real" emotion.

She said I should never discuss the divorce with my kids again. I can tell them I feel horrible, but no details.

**October 20, 1995**

Yesterday was a decent day. I took a walk with Flora and her grandchild. I made the trip to the bank to cash in my last CD I had dinner at another friend's and then my Iowa friend, Betty, called late at night.

Today I stopped by to chat with Russ at the pharmacy and met another friend for lunch. When I came home I thought I saw the girlfriend's car at my husband's parked way in back. I drove up the neighbor's driveway to check it out. I stopped in to see the neighbor and told her I might use her driveway to check on my husband especially if I hire a private detective again. She said, "Fine." Then she told me that at 3:30 p.m. today, a new black sports car with a soft top drove into the garage at my husband's house. She wasn't 100 percent sure, but she thought he was driving it.

While I was visiting with her, the girlfriend backed her car up further to get a view of my car and then returned to her hidden parking spot. We saw her from the window. The neighbor told me she had no respect for my husband or the girlfriend.

After I came home, I called to leave a message for Victor with this information. Then I called Diane and Lilly to vent this new incident.

**October 24, 1995**

I was doing pretty well today until I went to the post office at 10:45 a.m. There was a letter from my husband, with a copy sent to Michelle, of his proposals #1 and #2 for the division of the property. In both proposals he puts the Big House on the market for almost a half million dollars, which it would never sell for, and he lives there all the while -- he seems to have forgotten that I own it!

In proposal #1, he suggests that I keep the marital residence and the unsalable land lots, while he would keep the farm and the office/farmhouse and live in the Big House until it's purchased. He says he would owe me some money to balance out the assets <u>after</u> the sale of the Big House. In proposal #2, <u>he</u> buys the Big House himself, at <u>half</u> of the appraised value, while he lives there and pays me out over 10 years for it. Meanwhile, he also keeps the farm and the office/farmhouse and I'm supposed to keep the marital residence.

The goddamned bastard! Absolutely nothing has changed. What do I get from these proposals -- the sleeves out of a vest!

I am overcome with anger and have placed a call to Victor. My friend is coming over for tennis. I really need a game. I am shaking with anger.

**October 25, 1995**

I feel jittery inside. I'm glad I have an appointment to call Debbie today. Still no news from Victor about maintenance or the divorce trial date. The local paper ran an editorial praising the youth activities project. The group has raised about $20,000.

I tried to find out about the sports car I think my husband bought. I bombed out on each effort. I called a car dealer in Albany with the idea he might have bought a Saab, which is what the neighbor guessed the car was. I called the insurance company and he wasn't listed as having bought a new vehicle. I asked a clever friend if he could find a way to look in the garage and get the license plate number. He said he would think about it, but he was uncomfortable about it. I don't blame him. I would do it myself, but if I get caught I could go to jail. So I'll try other tactics.

I've told Victor that I am willing to give up my house because I really want the farmland with the greenhouse and the farmhouse/office. Victor is dealing with the CPA/lawyer and possibly an actuary to figure lump sum amounts of my husband's pension, etc. We're still waiting on the maintenance payment issue. I also mailed Victor a copy of my husband's recent proposals to distribute the real estate.

I'm living in a nightmare -- floating through the motions of daily living. "Land mines" triggered by deception, bad news and flaring emotions are exploding all around me.

## October 26, 1995

I talked with Debbie for 1 1/2 hours last night. It seems the hour appointment isn't long enough. She feels very strongly that I should hire a private detective again. She also encouraged me to keep on top of things and call Victor frequently with updates -- which I do. She also suggested that I vent some anger toward my kids in a letter, not to be sent. Not that they are at fault, it's just that they don't get it. I am the recipient of their misunderstandings and their alliance with their father sails through unmarred. So I'll try to write my feelings.

Of course, just as I wrote that last sentence, I broke down in tears.

*Dear Kids,*

*You have a lifetime of belief in your father. You know him to be honest and loyal. You think he's fair. You can't understand how or why he would decide to divorce me, but deep down you believe he can't help himself. So you believe your role is to continue to support him and follow his suggestion that I can go on alone, even without financial support.*

*As he denied there was a relationship with him and the whore, you also did. As he admitted he had been infatuated, you agreed, "Well, it happens." His romantic involvement escalated to nearly screwing her in the streets and you said, "You're separate now, just go on and get the divorce over with."*

*Well, I'm telling you your father planned this divorce in minute detail starting with his infatuation with the whore. He did it secretly, dishonestly and with exceptionally selfish and deceitful motives. He has woven a complex game plan that started with helping the whore out of her marriage and paying her thousands of dollars that were extracted out of our joint account to feather his new bed. He masterminded his divorce agenda with a plot to make his eventual love nest in the Big House and to take the farm and the office too. He "generously" proposes to let me have the unsalable lots of land and the marital home, which is worth less than it appears because of the capital gains. His greed almost exceeds his lust and there is no loyalty or even minimal regard or common courtesy for me, the mother of his children and his faithful wife for 39 years.*

*It's not fun to be emotionally battered, shit on and trashed. It does not feel good to have my kids act as if it's OK. Everyone else I know wonders why you would tolerate such behavior from your father. They wonder why you don't stand up to him. They wonder why you're willing to accept his conniving and his abhorrent behavior toward me as if I can take it, no problem.*

*What am I? A doormat to be pushed around and used?*

*In conclusion, I'm going to lay one big judgment on the bastard. He holds the responsibility for your lack of self-esteem. He is the father who placed his priorities to be himself and his job. He is the father who called all the shots. He is the father who spent more for automobiles than he would on your education.*

*He is now trying to hang on to the love of his children and make*
*that work for him as he fucks the whore who is younger than you are.*

*I can tell you honestly that I love you and I'm proud of you as good*
*children, but I'm also angry that you just don't get it.*

*Love, Mom*

During October sometime I wrote these poems:

*The words come from my children*
*"We're having dinner with Dad."*
*Anger strangles my body*
*as I hold my tongue*
*resisting the overwhelming temptation*
*to expose him as I know him.*
*He must reveal himself*
*and they must find their own truths.*

--------------------

*38 years of love and faithfulness*
*drew him to the edge of his*
*fears of growing old,*
*and he tumbled into an abyss*
*beckoned by the siren*
*of perpetual youth and an Indian girl.*
*As he fell, I stood at the edge*
*screaming, devastated and helpless,*
*and when he crashed into her arms,*
*anger, disbelief and sadness shook me.*

*When they walked away,*
*kicking back their dirt on me,*
*I felt trashed.*
*Buried in their muck of words and actions,*
*smeared on me,*
*I gasp for the air of life*
*and the strength to stand alone.*

--------------------

# BECOMING WHOLE

**October 28, 1995**

I sleep poorly these days. I wake up at 2 a.m. and stay awake until 5 a.m. Spooky wakes me up at 5:30 a.m. and then I sleep until 7 a.m. It's routine. I went to the Church Coffee House, my usual Saturday morning activity. My friend stopped by to tell me the license plate number on the black Saab convertible in my husband's possession. I'm thrilled he was able to get it. I hope Victor can do something useful for our case with the information.

Later I received a call from another friend who said there are horrendous stories coming from my husband's cleaning girl, claiming that I'm a bitch and have threatened the girlfriend's life! I am bumming out over this information.

Molly and her friend are coming soon and we're going to the Falls Town Auction for fun tonight. I have a fear of seeing my husband there. I just placed a call to Debbie to get a little encouragement to raise my spirits for tonight.

**Later --**

I used the time waiting for Molly and her friend to arrive to play myself in Scrabble. It's good therapy, scrambling for words in my head instead of wallowing in emotional thoughts.

We enjoyed the auction and Molly bought a few things for her apartment. I came home and tried to reach Debbie again. This time she was home and she helped me tremendously.

I told her how difficult it was to be the recipient of gossip calling me a "bitch" and "life threatening." Debbie said "So what? You know the truth.

Consider the source of this talk -- the cleaning girl and the girlfriend -- who cares?! Besides, isn't it better to be called a bitch than a victim?"

I called Lilly and spoke with Neal. Then I called Nancy. It took that much talking to drain my vexation.

**October 29, 1997**

The basement was hot this morning. I felt the heat on my bare feet from the stairs when I first got up. Then I heard the electric heater running, nonstop. I shut off the power to it and called the electrician. Another expense.

**October 30, 1995**

Lying on the couch waiting for Spooky to come back in the house at 5:30 a.m., I dozed and thought about the date. A year ago as I left Indiana to go to the airport for California, my husband took me in his arms and said, "I feel like hugging you. This is crazy. I'm going to call the marriage counselor when I get home." He kissed me with passion and I proceeded to California. He went home to Falls Town. In his first call to me in California, he said, "I want to talk nice," and I asked him if he'd seen or spoken to the filing clerk. He said, "Yes, from time to time," and I totally lost it. I found my counselor, Debbie, at the YMCA the next day.

Looking back on it today, I'm not crying. I think it was a turning point because it was the last time he could have it both ways -- keep me as the "nice" wife and have the girlfriend when he wanted. Debbie is right when she asks, "Would you rather be a bitch or a victim?"

It's true that my behavior has moved me in a progressive path to refuse to be shit on. That doesn't mean he doesn't sling shit at me -- it just doesn't stick. In a year's time, crying constantly has given way to occasional bouts of depression; spewing obscenities has settled to a rational, "You, bastard."

Anger now finds an outlet on paper and with legal actions. At this moment, I feel pretty strong. I have optimism about the license plate number and what it will show.

**9 a.m.** -- Victor called. The Saab convertible is registered to my husband. Apparently, he leases it. This is good news. It would be better if he'd bought it outright and paid cash, but leasing is expensive, too, especially since he drives his GMC Suburban virtually everyday and still uses his pickup truck. Victor said, "We'll take him to the cleaners," and then modified that with, "We'll at least try to get a fair settlement." I like the "take him to the cleaner's" comment.

I called my friend who got the license plate number and Nancy with the news. I told Victor some of the bits of gossip around town involving the girlfriend's husband's girlfriend and that I'm a bitch and have threatened the girlfriend's life. Victor said that Falls Town is the wrong name; it should be "Peyton Place." He's right. I can't believe that I'm a central figure in such a slimy story. Victor said, "Just keep taking the high road."

**Later --**

Since it's a beautiful day, I took Spooky with me to the post office and then walked on the farmland beyond the greenhouse with her. While I was there, my husband and the girlfriend came to his office. I looked at her and said, just in my head, "You fat bitch."

While on the farmland I explored the best building site for a new house. That was probably a little overconfident. I told Victor I wished my husband would leave town. Victor said it might not happen.

**November 5, 1995**

No news is like good news to me. Nothing has happened legally in several days so I was inspired to design an outline for the course I'll propose to teach at the local junior college. That led to developing an outline for my book. I started typing up my journal notes after I organized the pile of them sequentially. Typing my story clarifies it for me in a clinical way.

The pace of my life is picking up. I'm going to the Amish area of Pennsylvania tomorrow to join my mother and Lilly for a day. We also begin playing indoor tennis on Wednesday and Iowa friends are flying in on Friday. Thanksgiving is being discussed and I have ordered a new passport to be ready if I accept the invitation to go to the Italian Alps for Christmas with my Brazilian friends. I want to go to Asheville in January to see my grandchild, so it's a busy time. I like typing my book and I push other things aside to do it.

**November 12, 1995**

Today is Justin's first birthday. When I spoke with Jeffrey yesterday, he put Justin on the phone and a little voice said, "Hi." What a thrill! It was wonderful to hear his tiny voice speak to me for the first time.

My friends from Iowa ended up canceling their visit due to a mechanical failure on their airplane so I quickly altered my plans. Nancy and two male friends came for dinner on Thursday. We had fun. Friday morning, Anna called to take a hike. We hiked for four hours and had lunch sitting on a log in the woods. Molly, Michelle and Pierre came for dinner on Friday evening. Michelle reported that her creative writing had taken a quantum leap and we all applauded that. We made a plan for Christmas and I ordered airline tickets to Paris for all of us. We are going to visit my Brazilian friends in Italy and Pierre's parents in Paris and at their place in the French Alps. It's pretty exciting and I need to plan the details – a kennel for Spooky and the cat, communicating with our hosts, choosing small gifts to take and walking to get in shape for mountain hiking.

I was concerned that a trip to Europe might have a negative impact on my legal case, but Victor believes it's good for me to do it and that it's important to live in the way I'm used to as much as possible. Fortunately, since we're staying with friends and family, it won't be a very expensive trip anyway.

I had the TV on this morning as I got dressed and the one quick message I heard before I came downstairs to the winter wonderland outside was "It's a sin to worry. The opposite of worry is faith." I passed the message along to Ann when she called later and said, "Here's an example. I've charged the airline tickets because I believe that by the time the bill comes, I'll be receiving maintenance payments again. If I don't, I'll cash a bond."

At the moment, nothing is resolved. There are no maintenance payments until the judge decides on the motions before him. Furthermore, the divorce date may or may not be December 21st, there is no answer for the continuation of discovery regarding calling my husband and the girlfriend before the judge, and there is no decision about who pays the real estate taxes. These are all issues on the judge's desk. I know they will be resolved and I'm not optimistic or pessimistic. It's just stuff on the back burner while life goes on.

Without losing sight of the serious legal battle that swirls around me, I am feeling more enthusiastic about my life. The waves that knock me down are temporary and brief and I get up stronger. I'm dreaming about the last chapter in the book -- at least, what I believe it will be -- dancing free. Sometimes I can taste it; like when I'm feeling comfortable with myself, I look at men in a way that piques my curiosity about them.

Life isn't terribly horrible or perfectly grand. The simple advice of "take care of yourself" is my umbrella against the storm. For me it means talking, crying, saying "no," treating myself and others, healthy food, playing tennis, walking, listening to Debbie and standing up legally.

I smile when I think my becoming whole again is like a new version of "Humpty Dumpty had a great fall." All the queen's horses are Debbie, Victor and my family and friends; but in this version, they are putting me back together again. I was a crumbled mess for a while and some pieces still fall out while others stick, but the glue of honesty, friendships and acceptance is proving stronger than my perfect egg being in one basket of trust and reliance on my husband.

**November 15, 1995**

Since I saw my husband's car at Sheila's office yesterday and then at the girlfriend's house, I figured something was up. I called Victor's office and spoke with his secretary. She said there was a letter from Sheila charging me with "stalking" the girlfriend. It refers to last Saturday night when I drove by the Big House and saw all the floodlights on, which was very unusual. We'd had a torrential rain and windstorm and I thought maybe there was a downed tree or something. So I turned into the neighbor's driveway to see if everything was OK. Then I saw the girlfriend walk across the driveway with her daughter and dog and leave in her car. I figured the lights were on for her. So I turned around and went to the church house to see some friends but they were just about to leave so I drove home.

I absolutely did not "stalk" her. She is flattering herself beyond all comprehension to imagine that. I don't care what the hell she does. My concern was for my house in a storm. I think it stinks I have no rights to even protect my own property. I've heard her dog stays at the Big House a lot and I don't like it.

Anger has returned to me. It's directed at my husband -- he and the girlfriend will stop at nothing to try to do me in. I still find it hard to believe that he would do any of this to me and still not notice what a fat whore his girlfriend is. He's got to be totally nuts. He really makes me angry and I'm determined to fight -- legally.

**Later** --

Within hours I softened in attitude towards this event. It lost its venom and doesn't perturb me now. I think my husband and the girlfriend are in a more vulnerable state -- paranoid.

**November 18, 1995**

Is this a feeling of things to come? I woke up relaxed, peaceful, warm and with "forgiveness" thoughts drifting in and out of my head. I enjoyed the bliss for a bit and then I decided I better write it down even as I told myself, "Beware...Don't compromise. Hang on to the validated anger. Keep going for a fair settlement. Don't slack off."

Over dinner with Nancy last night, I shared the latest legal letters and she asked if I could live in Falls Town after the divorce -- assuming my husband would be staying. I said I did not assume he would stay, although there is good reason to think he will, so I'll do what I want and maybe he'll leave.

Nancy said, "Like what?" I related several scenarios: He left our home when I returned and he left the church when I decided to stay. If I get the farm, he may want to leave the Big House; if the financial settlement favors me, he may not be able to last in the Big House; if he gets bored with the girlfriend, he'll turn somewhere else. I can place myself on the farmland where I want to be, which just happens to be next door to him if he stays in the Big House, and I'll wait. If I can be at peace with myself regularly, like I felt when I woke up today, I won't even look at him.

**November 19, 1995**

This is the thank you note I wrote to my friend, Barbara. She sent me the book, If You Want To Write, by Brenda Ueland.

*Dear Friend,*

*Inspiration has come to me in a mountain of small things -- kind words, good books, telephone calls, friendly visits and moments in nature. I am slowly climbing to the top of that beautiful mountain to stand naked and free.*

*Thank you for sending me a solid stepping-stone. The book is wonderful and I'm pursuing my own story to help others in this situation. When things get bad, my story becomes more interesting.*

*Love to you and your family. Happy Thanksgiving.*

*- Alice*

I sent the note on a card with artwork on it by another woman who also inspires me, Anne Goodchild.

Then I wrote Michelle a letter, although I'm not sure I'm going to send it. I still feel the sting of my husband being able to convince her how "fair" he is to me, while he pulls every maneuver he can to screw me. A portion of the letter I wrote:

His refusal to pay maintenance to me fits in with the long list of actions he's taken against me in the past year. He has denied his love, his honesty and every shred of common decency. He cut off the credit card, telephone and electric and refuses to give me money yet forces bills on me. Meanwhile, he gave his girlfriend his ATM card and pin number and she withdrew thousands from his business account and he keeps her on payroll even though she doesn't work. He paid $8,000 for his swimming pool and is leasing a convertible SAAB sports car when he already has two vehicles.

Without the support of my friends, and of Debbie and Victor, I know I couldn't go on. I wouldn't even want to if not for my children.

I've decided I won't send the letter. I must do my best to not involve my children in my problems with their dad.

**November 20, 1995**

So far I've typed 104 pages for my book. As I type, I relive the daily sequences and the emotions return, but to a much lesser degree. As I read about the pain, sorrow, pity and anger written in my journal notes, I am encouraged by my own statements, realizing I was doing the best I could to find my way through an unknown wilderness.

**November 21, 1995**

My photographer friend wants me to stop by and select one of the photos he's taken of Flora to use for an article I've written about her and the Church Coffee House. As I type my story, I make two copies, one for Debbie and one for my friend who is a writer and has agreed to act as "editor" for my book.

Debbie called to thank me for the angel I sent her and to also say she likes the book so far. Today, I typed through the horn-honking episode and

I'm reluctant to type my notes about Molly's fiancé's suicide, which is coming up next. It's typing that comes simultaneously with our plans to go to his family's home for Thanksgiving dinner. Molly, my cousin, Ann, and I will join his mother, sisters, grandmother, uncle and friends. As I think of this group substituting for what should have been -- Molly and her fiancé, John, his family, me and my husband and our family, all coming together -- it brings tears to my eyes. It's not right, but it is what it is.

Moving on mentally to the Christmas plans, I am pleased with my ability to get it all together. My passport is here, the tickets arrived, the rental car in Paris is arranged and the contact made with the bank to get francs and lira. I sent a letter to my Brazilian friend, Dayse, and will confirm with her in a few weeks. I've also ordered a new holiday outfit for myself and planned my packing and small gifts to take.

If the emotional truck runs over me again, as I suspect it will, I hope I can cope with it and use it to fuel my power in recovery. My young editor said she used to want her and her partner to "grow up" to be like me and my husband. Now she says she wants to "grow up" to be like me. I hope I'll prove to be a role model that meets her expectations.

Observation: I notice that I consciously don't smile at all if I know my husband is anywhere around.

**November 24, 1995**

Thanksgiving with John's family and their friends was a pleasant and stimulating occasion. It was a full day for me with driving Ann back to the train station.

I understand the saying so well now, "No news is good news." It's true that without "news" I have little to fret about. My life in general is very good. It's just the divorce stuff and my husband in my face that kicks up mud. I am grateful that I'm blessed with my kids and my friends. While talking with one of my oldest friends from the 1950's, I said everything was the same with me -- friends, fun, great kids -- just one difference -- the divorce thing and what my husband is willing to do. She wanted to call him if I thought it would help. I said, "No, I don't want him. Call if you like, but not for my sake."

December 8th will be a major day for decisions. Victor and I and Sheila and my husband will have a conference with the judge to discuss the issues between us and determine if there's a possibility of settling the divorce without a trial. I told Nancy if things go poorly for me on December 8th, I'm pretty sure I'll bum out again.

I gave Victor his Christmas gift early -- a quilt, one my mother made recently. I decided he's the best lawyer I could have and I trust him. I believe he will do as much for me as can be done. If it fails, he is not at fault. So I wanted to give him a nice gift now because I believe in him and I don't want to wait for the outcome of the settlement.

**November 25, 1995**

Writing the date reminded me it's my husband's 62nd birthday. I thought of reminding him of the family he destroyed by sending a family photo or packaging the needlepoint wall hanging that proclaims our wedding date and messages of longevity and love. Maybe I should send that on our 40th anniversary date. These are thoughts to strike back, which I know are useless. I am reminded of my son's advice: "Pray for the person who has hurt you and wish them the things you yourself want." This thought makes me cry. If I could do it, perhaps I would already be dancing free.

**Later --**

I dressed in an exciting outfit, a leopard print silk shirt and black silk pants with my best earrings and went to a friend's art show. Tons of people came and I felt alive and interesting. I connected with friends and met a few new people. I was completely comfortable being alone at my friend's party. I loved helping people meet new people.

My dinner was in the oven and I came home to my warm house filled with aromas from my cooking. I put on the Celine Dion CD and danced around my house -- wishing for a partner, but not my husband. Feeling good, strong, healthy and together. I even feel lucky.

**November 29, 1995**

My calendar for December is very full. As I photocopied the first 170 typed pages of my journal notes, I confessed to Nancy that I thought I would title the section I'm currently writing, "Becoming Whole," and I was motivated by that goal. Even though I know there will be hours or days of jolting back to anger or devastation, I want to find the right perspective to let it go.

Yesterday, I received from Victor a copy of a letter he'd written and sent to Sheila advising her that my husband's annuities (or pensions) had been valued by an expert. The letter also stated that my husband was required to submit all documents regarding the purchase/lease of the new Saab because it's marital property and requested Social Security benefits information from my husband.

It's satisfying to read Victor's well-written, logical letters, even though there is usually a response that doesn't feel good from Sheila. If anyone sees my husband's car at Sheila's office, I know some legal action is on the way.

My morning started with shoveling snow. We had several inches last night. It's very pretty -- an extra chore, but kind of exhilarating, too. Spooky ran happy circles in it while I shoveled the walk. Tennis at the indoor courts may be canceled.

**10 a.m.** -- I drove the four of us to tennis and then made banana bread and cookies. My talk with Debbie was excellent. She thinks the latest installment of the book is great. She said she couldn't put it down because it's so honest. She said she was very proud of me. She always says the right thing.

**December 3, 1995**

How long has it been? How much longer will it be? As important dates approach, like December 8th for the conference with the judge, I feel my troops gathering. Debbie scheduled a phone call for that evening. My friends are marking their calendars. We're anxious for good news, but also have that nagging fear of things going awry. I envision myself both coping with the worst news and celebrating the best news. Oddly enough as I write this and focus on the December 8th event, my stomach cramps and I need to go to the bathroom. Fortunately, it's before church and in a few minutes I'll be OK. I'm having some friends over for brunch after church and I'm all ready to go.

**December 4, 1995**

Yesterday's brunch went well; the food was good and we all had a great time. Last night was Falls Town Flowers' annual Christmas tree lighting in town and it was successful. The Flowers' dinner party afterward was fun although the emotional tension of repeating the event that was so scary for me last year did make me cry on my drive home. Otherwise, it was a pleasure to be with this wonderful group of people. My young friends related that one of their friends who met me only briefly referred to me as "effervescent." They thought it was a perfect description and an accurate compliment and I do too.

When I was in Pleasantville last Saturday working with the wreath-making project, I enjoyed building new friendships with people who are young and from different cultures, while in the company of several long time friends. By the end of the day, I'd connected with a Korean woman and several teenagers.

There is barely enough time to do all the things coming up. A friend died so there is a funeral today and the dinner afterward. I'm responsible for making coffee. Another friend is having cataract surgery and expressed her need to talk to me. The church bazaar is next weekend and I need to help my friend pull it together plus make candy and greenery arrangements. Diane from Stockbridge is coming today and we plan to work on her house project, which is almost completed. I am invited to a party tonight and to New York City on Sunday to see "A Christmas Carol" with Ann.

The tree service man was at the office on Sunday removing the big stump left from the tree he cut down two years ago. I was surprised to see him there and I stopped to speak to him. I wanted to tell him about the divorce in case he didn't know -- and he didn't. He said my husband was the "loser" in the situation. Apparently, he just automatically came to do the tree stump. I have an idea my husband will try to shove the bill for the tree man's work off on me since I handled the office renovation and was the one who had contacted him two years ago to take down the dead tree.

**4:45 p.m.** - Victor called. Good news. The judge has ordered my husband to pay all the maintenance, the back pay, plus interest and the motion's legal costs! He also has to appear before the judge to answer the deposition questions. The judge said the girlfriend, however, did not have to appear, but Victor says he will ask the judge again on that point. Also the divorce trial might start on December 21st. Victor will ask to change that, too. I called Lilly, Debbie and several friends before going to the funeral.

## December 7, 1995

When I woke up this morning, I had been dreaming of another man in a romantic way. I wonder what his status is with his lady friend. I wonder if I'll see him again by chance. I remember feeling some chemistry with him in the past, but that could just be his way with anyone.

My husband's lawyer, Sheila, sent a letter to Victor demanding that I pay old Visa bills and complaining in general. In her letter, Sheila responded that my husband is leasing the Saab convertible with his social security money and claimed, therefore, that it isn't marital property.

Victor asked if I minded giving a referral for him to a potential client. I said I would happily call her and I did. I told her I was very pleased with Victor to this point and I had total faith in him to complete the case as well as possible. She was convinced.

Tomorrow we have the conference. A lot of stress has been removed by the judge's recent decision to stick to his order of maintenance. My husband will have to answer the "romantic" questions before December 15th. I made a list of events to give to Victor, like what my husband did on New Year's Eve via the credit card record from a local Inn that I saw, the receipt for a gold ring recorded by the videotaping in the office, his 4th of July date with the girlfriend to watch fireworks, the October crafts fair at Catamount where they were seen holding hands, the numerous dinners and movies they've been seen together at, etc.

Today I am "taking care of myself." Margaret and I did an early morning walk with our dogs. I have a warm fire in my wood stove and I'm writing. I'm going to do a relaxing bath, wash my hair and lend a hand at the church bazaar preparations.

My real project is my divorce and I'm turning all the stones in my mind to be clear, honest and thorough in preparation for tomorrow. Even though I have a terrific lawyer, he uses the information he gets from me. It's true teamwork. Victor is clever and perceptive. I know my husband and his ways. I know what I want. It's important that Victor and I work together as well as we do and it's obvious to me that I am crucial to my own success or failure in this divorce case.

**December 8, 1995**

I waited in one hallway and my husband waited in another while our lawyers met with Judge Connor. Then Victor and Sheila met at Victor's office after the courtroom conference.

Retired Judge Conway will be assigned to the divorce trial. It might start sometime in January; it may not be completed before March. I don't have all the details of the conference yet, but it is certain that we won't be settling and there will be a trial.

A few highlights of the conference: Victor said Judge Connor doesn't want to hear the case -- he cited that "he doesn't have time and he doesn't want to." The retired judge was selected from the list of retired judges who could be used in the new year. The amount of maintenance and back pay with interest is around $25,000. Victor said he writes an order for that and then Judge Connor signs it. According to Sheila, my husband is going to fight about the "exact" amount, using some different math techniques to arrive at his number.

After that, if payments aren't happening, Victor will start contempt proceedings. If my husband still refuses to pay, a lien will be placed on his bank accounts, his car and his office equipment. Sheila says he has no income. Odd, then, isn't it, that he can pay people for not working, have a housekeeper, a lawn and snow removal service, lease a $40,000 convertible sports car, maintain his relatively new GMC Suburban for "every day use," hold on to a late model pick up truck, frequently eat out at restaurants and live a high life.

My husband will have to go to a deposition next Friday to answer the "romance" questions. Victor has the list I made of dates and instances of romantic connections that I'm aware of starting way back in the summer of 1994 with hidden expensive gifts and the secret shopping and dining spree together in New York City straight through to the present.

The main new issue that arose from today's meeting was the concept of refusing the divorce unless I get more than half of the pie. I want the farm and the farmhouse/office. The business is valued at $50,000, his pensions at $163,000 and we can negotiate a lump sum maintenance. My lawyer says if we withdraw our divorce summons, my husband's "cause" for divorcing me would not result in a divorce. Therefore, if he wants a divorce, he'll have to pay.

This is a slightly risky strategy but there's not much to lose since it would be a 50/50 division left up to the judge if we don't agree before hand. Sheila called it "black mail" and my husband will have some thinking to do. It doesn't seem like it was a good day for him.

For me, it's about "hanging in" on the fight -- sticking to Victor's advice and holding out for my rights and my kids' rights. My resolve is strengthened with every lie in my husband's affidavits and my anger is sustained even through devastating emotional battering. I see now that my sad, low points became, and still are, springboards for renewed legal battle. Principle outweighs the cost. It's not exactly a time to celebrate, but I don't have tears either. I do not expect my husband to cooperate. He needs to control the situation.

While waiting in the hallway I wrote my Christmas letter:

*I'm sitting on the bench outside the judge's chambers, listening to the din of conversation from lawyers congregated in the hall waiting their time to speak to the judge. It's friendly talk and the courthouse Christmas tree looks festive behind them. This Christmas I can tell you that despite Garrick's choice to end our 39-year marriage, I have become stronger and more comfortable in my fight for a fair settlement.*

*Garrick's involvement with his filing clerk, a woman half his age, resulted in devastation for me and an amazing change of character for him. He became willing to deny me even the basic courtesies of utilities to my home or maintenance payments, while at the same time he treated himself to a new swimming pool and a Saab convertible plus "keeping" the girlfriend. Needless to say, it's been a bad year. Garrick's wish to be "young" means playing out his fantasies.*

*Another heartbreaking tragedy happened in May with the death of Molly's fiancé. It still hurts deeply as we remember the hope and expectations for their lives together. Molly is healing and our misfortune has allowed us personal growth.*

*Molly, Michelle and Pierre, and I are going to France for Christmas. Jeffrey and Starr and Justin will be at home in Asheville. Justin is 13 months old. He is walking, talking and is the most charming, beautiful little boy. I plan to visit them in January and then get the kids all together in the Smoky Mountains in April.*

*Today, the court has renewed the order of maintenance with back pay and interest to me. The divorce trial will be pushed into the new year and the lawyers are using our "intensely contested" divorce as a legal exercise.*

*My anger sometimes fades into pity, but I have lost all respect for the man I had felt happily married to for almost four decades. The past two years have been extremely difficult for me, but with a good lawyer, excellent counselor, great kids and wonderful family and friends, I am quite blessed.*

*Understanding emotional pain and the value of support, I am grateful for the power of honesty and the strength that comes through friends. Your thoughts and prayers bring me peace and joy. My wish is for great measures of hope and love to return to you and yours.*

*Merry Christmas and a New Year that starts fresh every morning,*

*Love, Alice*

## December 19, 1995

Preparations for Christmas, like travel plans, parties, lunches and the Church Bazaar, have taken up my "writing time." With a mega-snowstorm forecast for tonight and tomorrow, I hurried about 75 Christmas letters and a group of thank you notes to the post office this morning.

The results of the December 8th court-ordered maintenance payments are still hanging. My husband sent a small check to Victor that he rejected and returned with notification stating that the judge was signing an order to force full payment or put a lien on the bank accounts. In his calculations, my husband deducted all the Visa bill charges from the last year along with the penalty interest charges. Victor said he can't do that.

I hope I see a full maintenance check before I leave but I may not. I still don't know the results of my husband's deposition on the 15th. All I noticed was that my husband was scheduled at 9:30 a.m. and I saw his car at the girlfriend's house at 1:30 p.m. and at his lawyer's at 4:45 p.m.

**5 p.m.** - Victor called and said my husband refused to answer many things during the deposition. Victor said he was very hostile and he wouldn't comment on anything that occurred after the divorce proceedings began. He also said he would not allow me the farm in the settlement and it may be that everything will have to be sold.

My anger feelings boiled up as I learned about my husband's refusal to pay maintenance, his obstinate behavior and his utter disdain to be fair in any way.

**December 20, 1995**

It's a "snow day," schools are closed. It's not the 12 inches predicted but a deep, fluffy, drifting snow and very cold. I had some phone calls of the "holiday" nature, well wishes for the trip to Paris and then a call from my broker. He said that my husband had called to say he was writing two checks for total of $15,000 from the joint account and my approval was needed. I saw red and snapped back, "Absolutely not." I told him I'd call my lawyer immediately. The broker said to wait until he was sure and in a few minutes he called back to say it was true.

I called Victor and he'd just received a fax from Sheila saying that my husband was going to write the checks on the joint account. Then, shortly after, he received the checks with a letter from my husband saying I must unfreeze the joint account and cash the checks. I told Victor "No," and he agreed.

Victor sent the checks back with a letter reminding Sheila that although my husband claims he has no funds with which to pay maintenance other than those in the frozen joint account, he managed to find $8,000 to buy a swimming pool, he leases a brand new Saab sports car for occasional use, is receiving Social Security, has a substantial IRA account and keeps his girlfriend on the payroll. Victor wrote, "Clearly, his priorities are confused."

So at this 11th hour before I go to Paris with my kids, there is a flood of legal activity. It seems there will be more tomorrow. Once again, I called Nancy to vent a little of my frustration on her. She's a smart listener, always thinking and has such good sense. Without a doubt, she is one of my best supporters.

As my husband cries "poverty," he keeps his girlfriend on the payroll even though he apparently let Brett go. He keeps his Saab convertible sports car, his GMC Suburban and his truck; he threw a party for the youth activities group; and apparently bought a television for the girlfriend as they were seen purchasing it at Wal-mart. I'm sure paying me puts a crimp in his style but tough cookies. I deserve it, I want it and I don't care if his lifestyle is diminished or embarrassed.

I called the electric company and asked to have the greenhouse electric put in my name. If I start the greenhouse, I think he might shut off the power for spite even though I pay the electric bill. They said they would change it tomorrow.

**December 21, 1995**

Toss all the emotions into the memory bank of life -- it's what actors do to create their roles. I can think of how he once loved me and cry. I can think of how he's betrayed me and become angry. I can recall the joy lost and become sad. Now I'm being trashed while he clings to his power. But I'm willing to fight with tears in my eyes. I never wanted to hurt him, but if I am to stand up for myself, he's the adversary now. I either fight or allow him to trample me. To stop the battle, he must become fair or I must cave in. It's very sad that the man who last year said, "I'll always be your friend," is now my worst enemy.

I pepped myself up to be cheery for the people I would see at the post office and the kennel where I'm boarding my dog and cat. My husband's dog was at the kennel when I arrived and our two dogs, mother and daughter, stayed across from each other in their cages. My husband's dog looked old and sad. She had no spark and she seemed emotionally neglected. I wondered where my husband had gone -- to visit our son? somewhere with the girlfriend? What he has done to Christmas is unforgivable, the bastard.

Melancholy is being pushed aside by anger, which brings resolve, which makes me stronger and willing for action. I'm ready for fun. Paris -- here we come.

**December 23, 1995**

With reminders of the life left behind at every turn, even the bright lights and holiday decorations on the Champs Elysees don't completely erase the loss but it softens the blow. We're settling into our exciting accommodations at Pierre's family's place with happy family talk -- in French! This magnificent city has it all. We took a bus ride to a wonderful museum, Marmottan, to see the Monet exhibit. Then there were croissants and French wine. What's not to like?

**December 24, 1995**

No jet lag yet. Pierre drove the rental car and we went to the French market for the Christmas turkey and the cheese; only dampened a little by rain that didn't last long. Pierre's family traditionally has a big dinner and then they attend midnight church services.

This afternoon, armed with a good city map, I found my way through the charming streets window shopping and admiring the architecture and then back to the apartment on Rue Pigalle.

The Christmas Eve dinner hosted by Pierre's family was a feast for royalty; incredible food and fabulous wine, all served in a gorgeous setting with a lovely French family. Christmas Eve for me this year ends now at 3 a.m.

**December 25, 1995**

Christmas Day was as fantastic as the Eve before. Pierre's parents prepared another gourmet feast and served it in the grandest French tradition. Champagne and pastry hors d'oeuvres, led the way to rabbit pâté and poached salmon stuffed with fish mouse, turkey and stuffing, roasted chestnuts, carrots and peppers, cheese platter, salad, fruit trifle and coffee and more wine. Another four-hour meal. Then we took a drive through the streets of Paris, stunning with white branches, frosted trees, lights and glorious buildings and monuments.

There were many gifts exchanged and appreciated. Everyone enjoyed the company of Pierre's family and the incredible effort that was extended to create a comfortable and beautiful setting, complete with flowers, music, fine china and crystal and wonderful food. In the end, I felt very emotional and started to cry a little as the family bid their good byes and warm wishes.

All over Paris, the popularity of Disney's new animated film, "Pocahontas," was in my face and continued the year long badgering I've felt. It's not a rational placement of my anger and I know it, but it still eats at me. Feeling sad doesn't alter my resolve to go the limit in my efforts to get what is fair to me from my husband. I wonder if Victor has done anything drastic while I've been away. Probably not since it's Christmas.

**December 26, 1995**

Molly's birthday. We drove from Paris to Sallanches in the Alps. Pierre drove most of the way. It took $50 in tolls, $40 in gas, a snowstorm, rain and 400 miles. We arrived at 3:30 p.m. and went for café au lait and bought maps of the area. Flowers were in bloom in Paris, it is more like winter in Sallanches. Pierre's young cousins are joining together for a dinner party and I've been invited to an aunt's for tea. Biting my tongue every time I feel like saying something about my husband takes self-control, but I'm always glad I kept my mouth shut. I hope I can continue to do so.

**10 p.m.** - I spent two hours with Pierre's aunt speaking in very limited English, as I know no French. We managed to speak of vacation plans, grandchildren and her recent accident, which has slowed her down physically for the moment. I told her about my divorce and that it was not completed. She could not understand why and I told her we did not agree and that it may take months. I couldn't stop my tears and I think I made her uncomfortable.

My emotions need an outlet, to be expressed. Being in Sallanches retraces the vacation we did a few years ago with friends when my husband said, "It doesn't get much better than this." In a while, I think it will.

Even though my kids are handling many of the decisions as we travel, I know I can handle these things alone, too. I'm sure I would make mistakes driving in the city, but I would eventually find my way. My preparation time with a map is painfully slow, but I do get it. The kids are much quicker picking up on signs and directions and they are good drivers. So, all in all, I take a back seat, gratefully.

## December 27, 1995

Michelle, Molly and I went hiking in the new snow in the mountains surrounding Sallanches, with a view of Mont Blanc, its peak above a layer of clouds and ice white. We had cheese and French bread and Evian water while sitting in the snow. They've all gone out for dinner now and I've stayed home to sort out my stuff, do some thinking and some writing and prepare for the drive to Courmayeur, Italy, tomorrow.

## December 28, 1995

We've been lucky with weather and traffic. It cost us $35 round trip to drive through the Mont Blanc tunnel and it took another $30 to fill the gas tank. We mailed our postcards in France just before leaving. I sent one to Jeffrey, one to Victor and one to Debbie.

Pierre and Michelle went back to Paris to depart for home from there and Molly and I arrived in Courmayeur around noon. We kept missing Dayse until almost 4 p.m. so we waited by walking, shopping and browsing. It's a very charming resort community although totally tourist-oriented. It is also designed for easy living. All the shops are up and down the same street and the lift to the slopes is a short walk from the hotel. I bought Molly a Fendi silk scarf for her birthday and we both agreed it was just right for her.

We loved seeing Dayse and her family when we caught up with each other later this afternoon. They're such interesting, warm, nice people. We're planning dinner together tonight.

**December 29, 1995**

It started snowing last night and continued most of the day until there was a foot of fresh powder. Cars went sliding down the street and tire chains are being applied on many cars. Molly spent the day skiing in deep powder with Dayse's son and Dayse and I walked with her husband through the village. I told her all my "stuff" and she said I definitely had the makings of a book. Molly and I drove back to Sallanches for our last night in Europe and this evening we're preparing for our Geneva departure.

**December 30, 1995**

The alarm went off at 3:30 a.m. and we had toast and a quick cup of coffee and started out in decent weather conditions even though it was a little icy, foggy and snowy. We seemed to be the only people traveling and we found our way to the airport without a problem.

Unfortunately, I'd misread the tickets and instead of a 6:55 a.m. departure it wasn't until 9:20 a.m. We were 2 1/2 hours early. Molly was a bit disgusted with me and wished she'd checked the schedule herself. Everything was closed, no one else was around, so we just slept on the benches in the airport.

Then there was another delay of three hours in Brussels before our flight to Boston, but at least everything was open. We browsed in the airport gift shops, had lunch and watched people.

Now we're boarded and ready to go to Boston, which will take about 7 hours. Every last cent is spent. While waiting earlier, I calculated the cost of the trip. It looks like about $4,000 total (or $1,000 per person). If I were to have done it alone it would have been at least $2,000, so traveling together as a group was efficient.

**Later --**

On the flight I wrote:

*How was it the tune ended? We swirled around and you stepped forward and I stepped back. We dipped. It should have been graceful but when my balance relied on your support, you dropped me. And the dance floor was empty except for me. The music was gone except for a little life moving in short rhythms of breath. And that simple stirring at the end was the beginning of the next dance.*

*Today, ending a vacation, dreaming of the next, my mind dances, stepping back in time. The past still moves in unsteady rhythms and jerks tears from me until finally my balance returns and my step feels firm. Ice, snow and rain under my gliding steps keep the dance careful but unafraid. Just dance, leap into the air. It will take more practice, more control, more power, more ecstasy. For now, sway with the rhythm, dance in memory, dance in the moment, step forward to dance alone, reach out to partners to join in. Try a new step. Dance.*

**December 31, 1995**

New Year's Eve day and I'm home, tired, but happy to be home alone. I'm sorting out my stuff, marking the little gifts for friends, warmed by my fire and making lists. I'm listening to my new French CD, Christian Morin's "Esquisse." It's romantic clarinet music and it's not sad to be alone.

I was tempted to speak about my husband many times during the vacation, but I bit my tongue and managed not to the entire week. My curiosity is high about whatever happened legally while I was away. But it will be Tuesday before I find out anything.

**January 1, 1996**

Happy New Year! I spent New Year's Eve with my cousin, Ann, at Diane and Stu's party in Stockbridge. I had to leave early because of my jet lag but it was very satisfying to be with these good friends. New Year's day at my house continues to be so comfortable with Ann and Spooky and my friends. We took a short toboggan slide down the neighbor's driveway, had champagne and a Mexican food dinner. I'm off to bed early again.

**January 2, 1996**

At 8:30 a.m. I called Victor to find out what happened while I was away. He said the checks written on the joint account were returned to Sheila and she sent them back to Victor and Victor sent them back to her. Unbelievable. We are still waiting for the judge to sign the judgment against my husband to put a lien on his bank accounts. Victor also sent material to the expert to put a value on my husband's CPA license. Basically nothing is new.

**January 3, 1996**

There's deep drifting snow and more is forecast for tonight. After my driveway was plowed out, I went to town to meet a friend for lunch and to stop at the post office and the bank. Driving past my husband's office I saw him and the girlfriend frolicking in the snow. It brought up such awful pain that I felt paralyzed to function during the afternoon and I came home and cried hard. Spooky tried to console me. Then I called Victor. I had a list of issues to ask him about and I also wondered if there was any news. I told him it was very hard emotionally at times. He was sympathetic and said we'll get it over soon.

I need to talk to Debbie and we have an appointment for 6 p.m. Today, Nancy offered her house to store things if I decide I need to protect personal items in the event everything has to be sold. I cashed in my last two U.S. Savings bonds today, too, $20,000 in cash. The bank manager thought I should change my safety deposit box. She said I was the primary owner and that I could remove my husband's name and access to it. I took her advice. Tomorrow, I'll use my key and see if there's anything in it; I don't think there is.

I wrote a note to my husband's ex-employee, Brett, who was always very friendly to me.

*Dear Brett,*

*Legal letters are my sole means of communication with my husband and I read in them that you have left for "personal reasons." My husband claims he doesn't earn any income from his business and certainly won't now because he can't prepare as many tax returns without you being in his office.*

*I hope your departure means a better opportunity for you. As I know nothing of your circumstances, I only wish you the very best.*

*The divorce process is mysterious, with changing strategies, contempt of courts, a new judge and much "cruel and inhuman" behavior directed at me. I have become more comfortable in the uncertainties of my life. Even now, I am blessed with friends. I have high hopes, great joy (at times), love and laughter. I wish you good health, clarity in purpose, peace and the continuation of your fine characteristics -- and love in your life.*

*Alice*

I recommended Brett to Flora as someone who could do her taxes since she said she would definitely <u>not</u> go back to my husband.

Two hours ago I couldn't stop crying. Now I have talked to Victor, written a lot and typed pages. I'm anxious to speak with Debbie; I'm already feeling better. It's sort of crazy.

## January 9, 1996

The blizzard of '96, the "storm of the century," a state of emergency has been declared in Columbia County and in state after state along the east coast. My doors are blocked by six to eight foot snowdrifts and the total accumulation was a staggering three feet. I climbed out an upper window and dropped into the snow above my shoulders. I managed to roll out of the drift, over to the door and cleared a space to open it.

Now the driveway is plowed and I'm going to drive to the post office and stop at Nancy's for lunch.

My husband sent Victor a malicious letter. I read it and thought, God, he really is demented. His petty letter has stirred up more legal contemplation like requesting a block on any sale of his assets, subpoena of the application for the lease of the Saab and more resolve to stand our ground.

It appears my husband is very angry. What will an angry man do?

## January 12, 1996

A new path, the size of a thin roadway, has been snowplowed to the greenhouse and it originates a couple hundred feet from the existing driveway. As a result, there's a huge pile of snow banked up right in front of the greenhouse door. I think it's the result of the angry man's decision to do something. At this point, I just don't know what it means.

In the last days I've been all over the place -- sad, angry, very depressed. I wake up thinking of things I could do to harass my husband, mean and destructive things. I thought of sending him the cross-stitch wall hanging that proclaims our wedding date and love-ever-after messages. It still hangs in my bedroom but I'm thinking of getting rid of it. Lilly made it years ago. I thought of asking my friends to aggravate him with phone calls. I thought of vandalizing his CPA office sign and I thought of throwing a rock through his window.

As I thought of vandalizing, I wondered if some inner-city kids have these feelings of anger, helplessness and total frustration when they slash tires or destroy property at their schools and in their neighborhoods. I have never acted on any of my thoughts but I wonder what it would take to make me do something. I feel so angry right now.

**January 14, 1995**

The only thing I could imagine about the strange snow plowing at the greenhouse was that perhaps it was an attempt to divert water off the hill to the street. Then I learned that a local contractor used his bulldozer equipment to do it. When I asked him about it, he said, "I don't know why Mr. Belt asked me to do it, I just do what I'm told."

Again, I woke up this morning with vengeance burning in my head and then thinking past that, I realize there is nothing I can do that hurts him more than it hurts me. My only hope for satisfaction in this battle is through Victor and legal means. I think the current unresolved issues, like the maintenance payments, cause me to feel helpless, drifting, out-of-control and I wish for justice.

My logic tells me to fight for everything that is rightfully mine, get it and then dance free. Let him go entirely.

This current limbo stage leaves me on the fence. If it goes OK for me, I'm willing to let it go, but if I get screwed, I'm not sure I will let it go.

Victor says we should have the "judgment" against my husband tomorrow or Tuesday and then we should see some "fur fly." If that happens, I wonder what my husband will do?

Debbie reminded me that since I've chosen to try and keep our kids out of it, my side of the story isn't apparent to them. She suggested he might tell our kids what "terrible" things I'm doing and they might buy his story. I think he'll press a "stalking" charge on me for driving past his house so that I'll have to fight that. He might try to extend the court order against me approaching the Big House and his office to include the farm, therefore my greenhouse.

Trying to use these "snow days" to accomplish unpleasant tasks, I'm getting my tax information together. I have a fairly detailed record of my actual spending in 1995. It was $55,000. Considering that half of my insurance, utilities and health insurance were covered by my husband, my estimate for an ongoing budget to live exactly as I have been is $75,000. Taxes and legal fees are included in this estimate. I figure my husband needs $150,000 to continue the lifestyle he's accustomed to. Clearly this kind of money does not exist for either of us. We used to live on about $100,000 all together.

### January 15, 1996

Yesterday the roof collapsed on the barn behind my husband's office, pulled in by the weight of the snow on it. A local contractor had stored his equipment in the barn and it is buried now. I wonder if there is insurance.

Victor asked me to find out the dates my husband used the safety deposit box. I called the bank -- January 31, 1995, April 21, 1995 and September 6, 1995. When I opened the box last week, he had removed everything but the gold watch for my son and the silver coins marked for the kids. I don't know why Victor is interested in the dates. He says we're getting closer to the trial preparation.

Today, Nancy and I skied at Catamount. We took a free lesson and had lunch there. Then I renewed my driver's license and prepared for dinner with Molly. She and I are celebrating my birthday early.

### January 18, 1995

In my "legal" mail yesterday was the judgment order signed by the judge allowing Victor to pursue the maintenance by putting a lien against my husband's bank accounts. Victor said my husband must pay (not by our joint account, as he's been trying to do) before January 19th. This should mean a $12,000 check tomorrow.

Also in the mail, the Christmas family memories that Jeffrey put together. It is a wonderful document of childhood memories written by each of the kids, me and my husband. My husband's contribution to the project is weak, shallow and poorly written. His memories reflect exactly how little he was involved -- they are of himself and his career and read like a bullet list.

As the family memories drift into my mind, a sudden sting in my nose pushes tears into my eyes and I'm sad.

Nancy is having a birthday lunch for me today. I don't know how many people she's invited but I know it will be very nice. The Falls Town Flowers meeting is tonight and Spooky goes to the kennel for the weekend. I'm off to see Jeffrey and his family in North Carolina. I'm excited to see my grandson.

**January 24, 1996**

My 61st birthday was duly celebrated with a laughter-filled lunch at Nancy's. Then again with a cake and candles at Jeffrey's home and a great weekend with them. Justin is wonderful -- energetic, happy, outgoing and beautiful.

When I arrived at the Albany airport at 9:30 p.m. on Sunday, my car wouldn't start so I had to solve the problem. I rented a car and returned on Monday afternoon to try starting my car again. It started and I did a big release on the way home in my safe haven -- lots of crying.

The maintenance check arrived at Victor's office and I stopped by to get it. It was from his business account, apparently written by the girlfriend with her version of my husband's signature. In the "00/100" part, she wrote "no sense." It bothered me for a while, and even as I write now, it smarts. Oh well. Another reason to keep going on the legal fronts.

Victor is going to suggest unfreezing the joint account in order to take the cash, split it 50/50 immediately, with half to go to me and the other half to go to my husband so he can then use it to pay me. He's still $20,000 in arrears.

**January 25, 1996**

I aired my hurt feelings to Debbie about the check written and signed by the girlfriend. Debbie said, "They can't hurt you if don't let them. Be an actress -- laugh when you see them! Don't let them alter your life in any way."

I had sent Debbie snapshots of Falls Town and she asked to see one of my husband. I found two good snapshots of the two of us in happier times and sent them with a request to return them to me. For some reason I really like the good photos of us together, but I also feel like sending them to my husband. He'd probably use them as "harassment." It's all so bizarre.

**January 29, 1996**

Victor called to say the new judge sent a message saying that he would like to start the divorce trial in February. Victor says he has personal plans in mid-February and another trial in late February, so it sounds like it will be March instead.

We are going to meet this Thursday to talk about property distribution and I'm to be prepared with a list of my assets as of March 3, 1995. I'm supposed to think hard about this marital house I live in now in regards to our proposal for distribution. I've said I want "the farm," which is the farmland, the greenhouse and the farmhouse/office; and if it makes sense to sell this home, I will. I can't see myself living here for more than five years so I might as well make the decision now. I called the farmer who rents the farmland for his crops and he said he had sent my husband a check but had not signed a new lease contract yet.

My social life is as active as ever. I invited friends over for dinner on Thursday and we went to see the movie, "Mr. Holland's Opus." I did the church coffee house on Saturday morning, church on Sunday morning, a matinee with friends to see "Sense and Sensibilities," and then a pre-game and Super Bowl party.

I was hoping to see a male friend that I think I might be interested in at the party and he was there, with his long time lady friend. He quickly connected to me with a hug and compliments and we chatted for a while. He looks good to me and I have a feeling he might be interested too, but I don't know what the status is with his relationship. I said I'd noticed that he wasn't around (although he said he has been) and I volunteered to grow him some begonias for the summer. He said the plants he bought from my greenhouse last summer were gorgeous and that people stopped to photograph them.

I ordered the seeds, soil mix and the propane for my greenhouse and by Friday, everything will be there. I'll start the cleanup next week.

I stopped by the greenhouse to check on the status of the work to do. I saw my husband go out at lunchtime and come back with a bag that looked to be lunch for him and the girlfriend. I muttered "bitch," and came home teaming with thoughts of another man. I feel a little like a teenager changing boyfriends; the same sort of pipe dream and uncertainty about what to do or how to do it. Basically, I think I'll do nothing and see if anything happens.

The idea of possible romance takes the focus off my husband and changes the pain and anger to anticipation of something, someone, else. It's sort of fun.

Pete and Ed came home today from their winter trip. It is so good to see them.

**January 31, 1996**

A message came from the new judge assigned to the divorce trial saying that he wants to schedule the trial in February. A scurry of activity pertaining to maintenance and proposals for property settlement is underway. I'm to think hard about my wishes for real estate division.

The weird possibility of choosing my own future is clouded with fate, luck and salable scenarios. I will choose the farm with the greenhouse and the farmhouse/office. My husband is likely to choose exactly the same thing as I think he'd like to control this whole end of town by keeping the Big House, his office and the farm too.

I don't want the Big House. It has bad vibes for me. My husband's romance with the girlfriend began in that house when his office was still there. When I walked into that house I could smell her. My stomach would cramp and I'd feel sick. The house is also 5,000 square feet with a several-acre lawn. It's way too much for me alone to afford, maintain or use.

Who gets what will boil down to the lawyers' skills and the judge's penchant. And it may be a moot point if the divorce is denied.

With my future hanging in so many hands, I escape, mostly thinking about my chances of romance with another man. I have no idea what to expect. My husband has been my only serious "boyfriend" in my whole life. I've never had sex with anyone but him. My imagination flies. I want to lie in bed with this new man and talk. I want him to hold me. And if it feels really good, I want to make love with him and then sleep wrapped up in each other. And if it's good, I want to do it again. And if it's really good, then I will be loyal to this new man. I wonder if he dances?

**February 1, 1996**

I awoke with a start at 7:45 a.m. thinking, "Did I miss my wake-up call?" I didn't hear Spooky at the foot of the stairs whining to go out. At first I thought I'd slept too soundly, but then when I came downstairs she was lying on her bed in the living room. I looked around for signs of an accident, but there was nothing. She didn't jump up or get excited to go out or eat. When she did get up and go out, she sat down in the snow. No energy. It seemed hard for her to come up the steps and then she dropped to the floor next to me. I called the vet.

By 11 a.m. they were tapping her chest cavity for what looks to be fluid around her heart. The two suspicions are congenital heart failure or rat poisoning. Of the two, rat poisoning has a better prognosis. At noon, they're pretty sure it's rat poisoning. I can't believe she found more of the stuff. It's terrible.

She's been given Vitamin K to coagulate her blood and she's in the vet's office with VIP treatment.

**February 4, 1996**

Very scary, touch and go for a few days but Spooky bounced at the foot of the stairs this morning at 6:30 a.m. - my usual wake-up call. Thank God. I slept on the couch for three nights to monitor her breathing and her recovery was swift once the bleeding stopped. The vet says it will take a week to overcome the anemia.

During these past days, I have kept Spooky at my side at all times. I asked permission to bring her to my meeting with Victor. She quietly lay on her mat beside my chair as Victor and I went over finances. My husband listed my mother's quilts in the list of assets to be divided -- a new low.

As we reviewed the scenarios, the only one that is good for me has not a chance in hell of being agreed on. The scenario after that has very negative downsides. I choose the farm, greenhouse and farmhouse/office and to remain in my home, the marital residence. If that is not agreed on, we withdraw our summons and my husband has to prove me to be "cruel and inhuman." If he cannot, there is no divorce. If there is no divorce, we predict he will piss away all of his assets and there will be nothing to divide in the future trial when I again charge him with infidelity.

As I left the meeting with Victor, I said I must be true to myself. The money is important, but not important enough to capitulate to my husband's cruel and inhuman treatment of me. The letter not sent to him that I wrote last February holds true for me today, "Rot in hell, you bastard."

Luckily, my health has been excellent and I can deal with my life -- my taxes, my car problems, my dog and the harsh winter. I also want to be with Nancy who just broke her leg skiing. I hope I can be a friend in a way that truly helps her. She's been there for me constantly throughout my whole ordeal.

I asked Victor if I can publish my legal letters and he said I could. They clearly represent how my husband's ugly allegations have battered me for the past year.

**February 7, 1996**

As I passed through town on Monday evening, about 6:45 p.m., I saw my husband going into Sheila's office. From the road, I could see a group assembled around her conference table. If I were to guess who those people were, I'd say Sheila's husband, the girlfriend, my husband's cleaning girl and Sheila. That is a totally paranoid thought -- thinking they'd gather to prepare their "story" for the trial regarding our "fight" incident. I plan to tell Victor what went through my head even if it's way off base.

Nancy had surgery on her broken leg and I'll be spending time with her at the hospital and helping out at her house for the next few days. My greenhouse is cleaned up and ready to start. I'll turn on the heat in another week or two.

It's nearly a year since the divorce summonses were issued; even I can see that I've come a long way. When I wake up in the morning, my awareness is for Spooky and what's on the morning news. Sometimes I get a "catch" in my voice as I relate painful parts of the divorce process, but I don't cry too much and often I laugh. Sometimes it doesn't even feel like me somehow. It's as if I'm an actor who's a central player in a bizarre drama. My part is "the woman getting a divorce."

I did not receive the electric bill for the greenhouse so I asked the meter man how the meter was listed and he said, "Under your husband's name." I called the electric company to ask why it hadn't been put in my name as I'd requested. They said on the same day I made my request, my husband also called and said it should remain in his name and could not be changed without his "code" name. It infuriates me that the electric company would take his direction over mine and didn't even notify me about it. When I called Victor about it, he advised me to call NYSEG and ask them to notify me if my husband tries to cancel the electric or doesn't pay the bill. Victor also said that he had received a fax from Sheila saying my husband would not agree to our proposal regarding the joint account and he sent a check from that frozen account once again. And once again, the handwriting on the check appears to be the girlfriend's. Sheila says my husband plans to pay all the taxes, the Visa bill and the fee for the appraisals of all the properties he arranged for from the joint account, too. I said, "Absolutely not." His gall is outrageous.

Every Wednesday at 6 p.m., I have a pile of topics to discuss with Debbie. It's an incredible adventure through this web of treacherous explosive issues.

**February 12, 1996**

I'm feeling emotionally battered by the legal letters in the mail, checks written on the frozen joint account and the maintenance check in the girlfriend's handwriting to "Ms. Alice Schneck Belt," and signed by my husband. They used "Ms." instead of "Mrs." They included my maiden name (which I don't use) written in large letters and wrote the "Belt" in little shrunken letters. Their actions are laughable and childish, but it still makes me ache deep inside.

I shared the humor and the pain with my friends and my minister, and just at the moment my tears dried, a neighbor, Anne, stopped at the church house and handed me a book, "The First Wives Club." She said it was very funny and somewhat relevant to my situation.

Now I feel like pursuing my writing to document my story that goes on and on. I wrote a note to a young friend who is also getting a divorce; he has a three-year-old son. I found a card that says: "May you always find new roads to travel, new horizons to explore and new dreams to call your own." I added my own note:

*You are surrounded by caring friends and family. You will be amazed at your own strength and fine characteristics. You will find your way through what may seem an impossible wilderness now. Be good to yourself. Make choices that are good for you. My experience with a good lawyer, a great counselor and wonderful friends has worked for me because I became willing to be honest with all of them. When advice doesn't feel right, it probably isn't. My counselor and my lawyer make the best sense to me and I'm grateful for my loving friends.*

*If you feel good vibes coming from the east, it is me thinking of you and your son and wishing you joy as the sun rises.*

*Love,*

*Alice*

Stopping at the greenhouse, I noticed a flower delivery from a local florist at the office. I came home and called the florist and asked if the delivery was meant for me and they said no. I asked if it was for the girlfriend and they said maybe. Of course, it makes sense. Her valentine flowers delivered to her at work. How romantic.

I felt a curdling go through my whole body. The good news is that it seems the romance is still hot and heavy. That should mean he really wants the divorce and that could be good for me in the settlement. Or it might not, since their greed may outweigh their lust.

At 3 p.m. a phone call came from a classmate of mine from 40 years ago. She said she had a terrible dream. I was in it and she had called other classmates to get my phone number and to inquire into my well-being. I asked her what exactly she dreamt. She said in her dream we were in California and there was an earthquake. She said that she and the others held on to one another and survived -- I died. She awakened in fear for me and cried. She decided to call to find out if I was OK.

After we talked, she decided the "death" was my marriage and she had dreamed about it without knowing anything. I told her I continue to feel very connected to my friends, past and present.

**February 16, 1996**

For a while now I have felt urges to "dance free." I'm feeling comfortable and even happy with myself. I rise to dance to music on my radio, loving my home but willing to move on to new challenges, thinking of changes with some excitement. Courage to stand up pushes away my fears. I'm laughing and feeling healthy, acknowledging pain in life, but allowing for the bright side that is always there.

How can I dance free, if I'm not yet divorced? And will I dance free when that decree is signed? Will tears come to my eyes even as I'm dancing free and a sad memory moves me? My music for dancing free is not one tune, not all rock and roll, or country or classical. I can choose it, create it and share it. I can be moved by it.

Knowing I'm powerless to change my husband doesn't mean I didn't want to. Boy, I pulled out all the stops I could dream up in my attempts to arouse him and to save our marriage. Recently, I've taken to calling those past efforts -- as well as my _new_ way of being me -- "dancing naked." It reflects my willingness to expose myself in every way. I have nothing left but me and nothing but my true honest self to offer, and it's fine. So here I am -- raw, unguarded, uninhibited, dancing naked.

**February 22, 1996**

We've been notified that the trial will begin on March 12th. At a meeting with Victor a few days ago, we reviewed our proposal for the division of the assets and I detailed for Victor exactly how I supported my husband in his career for 38 years. I felt jubilant at the end of it all. The good feelings since have lasted for days even though I know there will be repercussions to our proposal. As long as I don't know what they are, or until I do, I feel great.

I've been walking in the field every morning with Spooky and Margaret, one of my neighbors, and her Labrador puppy, Daisy. Margaret is bright, beautiful and unusually perceptive. The morning walk gives me confidence to make plans and assume leadership.

I'm taking in stride the natural ups and downs that are a part of daily life and seeing the possibilities in problems that create positive actions.

Tomorrow I'll bring Nancy home from the hospital and I'll stay with her at her place for a couple of days.

This afternoon I cranked up the volume on my radio and I danced to the music in my kitchen.

**February 28, 1996**

After a great game of tennis, I stopped at the deli to get stuff for a sandwich for lunch. The girlfriend was there and she looked at me and sheepishly said, "Hi." I didn't speak. I stood next to her at the counter and stared at her. She smirked. I stared until she left the store. I said nothing to her or about her. I ordered my sliced turkey, paid for it, thanked the sales clerk and left. The girlfriend is unattractive and fat, but as Debbie says, "She has balls."

The next thing I see while driving home is my husband crawling out of the passenger side of the girlfriend's small car to go into his office -- he's laughing. I came home and cried so hard even Spooky couldn't console me.

I kept checking the time to see how many hours to go before I can call Debbie. I decided to buckle down and do my tasks. I forged ahead with my call to Macy's to correct a mistake in my purchase from yesterday. I'll type for a while and then maybe I'll call Nancy. I'm thinking I had better arrange for a lot of moral support during the divorce trial.

**Later --**

After my talk with Debbie, Molly called to say my husband claims I did something to the girlfriend at the deli. Molly wanted to hear my version. It seems especially devious to me that my husband would go through Molly to get at me. There were other people in the deli, of course, if he wants an eyewitness account. Anyway, I told her what happened and then I cried. I told Molly that Debbie applauded my strength to stand my ground and suggested that if I am silent and only "stare" and the girlfriend responds, I can say, "Are you harassing me? If you are, then I'm calling the police."

I'll call Victor tomorrow morning.

**February 29, 1996**

When I shared some of yesterday's events with Margaret on a morning field walk with our dogs, I cried again. I thought I couldn't go out and face the community, but I took a long bath, washed my hair and chose a perky outfit -- a skirt and a red sweater.

Victor said he mailed me the financial proposal from my husband and we would discuss it next week. I told him about the "deli incident," and he said, "It's fine. Staring is not illegal."

I decided to solicit donations for the auction fund-raiser to be held during the annual Falls Town Flowers dinner by going to some of my husband's clients. I called Oblong, the local bookstore, announced I was Mrs. Belt and requested a gardening book for the benefit. They said yes. Then I went to the florist my husband used to send the girlfriend Valentine's Day flowers and they gave me a $20 gift certificate. Then I thought of his swimming pool and drove to Hudson to request a gift for my fund-raiser. I found a "Closed" sign on the door -- darn! But there was also a date when they'd reopen. I'll march in and say, "I'm Mrs. Belt. You installed a pool at my house in Falls Town. I'm sure you'd like to be well represented at our local charity fund-raiser."

Relating my "justice" fundraising adventure to my friends, we all laughed ourselves silly. Flora suggested a kiddie pool with Miss Piggy in it. We decided we might do it as our own contribution if the pool business fails to come through.

**Later --**

I'm so glad I allowed myself a great day before I read the proposal from my husband. Again, my imagination is not vivid enough to have predicted how ruthless he can be. And once again, the proposal is filled with erroneous financial calculations and slanted property and asset values insidiously calculated to benefit him.

**March 5, 1996**

It's snowing again. It's been a record snowy winter and unusually windy. I've had some problems with my Jeep, but overall it has gotten me everywhere I've wanted to go. It's also become Spooky's home away from home. She likes to go with me and she sleeps on the front seat. I probably smell a little "doggy" sometimes.

Today Victor and I meet to go over the property proposal and trial plans. I feel jittery and very sleepy. I think I want to sleep to escape whatever is out there for me.

When I woke up this morning I was dreaming of being in a beautiful spot in the grass next to a big beech tree. A male friend was there and we were talking. In the dream I wondered if I should ask him to come to the church's corn beef and cabbage dinner that's actually happening in real life.

Tears are running down my face from wrenching confusion and I just did my makeup. I'd better get on a different track and move on.

**March 6, 1996**

Nancy reminded me of the funny comment that was made at Victor's office when I took sick Spooky to my appointment there. The secretary came into the conference room and said, "Everyone is asking, 'Who is that woman with the good-looking dog?'"

When this is over I'll miss my encounters at Victor's office, the people there are really wonderful. But I won't miss being emotionally drained, like I was yesterday as we rehearsed my taking the stand in the trial. I said, "Geez, this is practice and look at me -- I'm crying way too much."

**March 8, 1996**

I'm feeling shit on and I'm weeping as if I've lost everything, just because Victor called and said there's no agreement on the farm property, the judge may say to sell the farm and my husband still has a chance to get it. I said to Victor, "I can't stand it if I don't get the farm."

Overcome with depression from the news from Victor's phone call, I stayed too long on the couch crying, Spooky along side passing her paw to me. Finally, I got up to take a bath and re-do my face.

I called Victor back to ask about taxes and insurance that my husband was responsible for, hoping I'm not stuck with even more expenses. I started making mental adjustments to whatever happens next week. Victor said I should make a list of the furniture I want.

Molly is coming tomorrow to plant in my greenhouse -- at least it still feels like my greenhouse. Really it's planting on a sinking ship.

## March 11, 1996

Awake but still in bed, I could hear my heart beat in my ear against the pillow and my chest tightened every time it skipped a beat. My closed eyes became moist with only a few tears and my thoughts were on the trial.

I don't want to study my deposition or be clear about my finances. I'm not sure I can ever be accurate, close maybe, but not exactly perfect. That scares me because I know my husband's lawyer will try to nail me. There's nothing to "nail," but there are things to distort. I'll see Victor today and at 11 p.m. tonight I call Debbie.

## March 12, 1996

It's sunny and cold, but the forecast of rising temperatures and a wish for spring clinched my plan to wear the pink sweater set and blue and pink flowered skirt for the trial. I picked up Nancy at 7:45 a.m. and Spooky settled into the back seat. We drove to Victor's office. There were only a few last minute details, then huge brief cases were packed and we trundled down to the courthouse. The security men at the door assumed I was legal staff and asked "What case?" I said, "A divorce case -- mine."

We arrived exactly on time, 9 a.m. and now at 11 a.m. I'm alone in the courtroom waiting for Victor, Sheila and the judge to finish their pre-trial conference. On a trip to the bathroom, I saw my husband standing in the hallway reading the newspaper. It was a very characteristic thing for him to be doing. His face looked puffy and red and he didn't look at me.

I also saw his lawyer, Sheila, briefly, this morning before they went into their meeting. She did not look well to me.

My nerves are kicking in as I wait so I've decided to clear my head of what might be said and just relate on paper what's going on for me. OK. Actually, I'm hungry. My 6 a.m. breakfast of oatmeal and a banana is gone. At 11:30 a.m., I started chatting with the male court stenographer who was also waiting in the courtroom.

Victor came out and gave me the update. "Constructive abandonment" is what the lawyers will change the "cause" to in order to guarantee that the divorce will happen. I consented. I will be divorcing my husband.

Nancy, Victor and I ate sandwiches at Victor's office during the lunch break. When we got back to courthouse, Victor went back into the conference with Sheila and the judge, but came out soon after and said I would be taking the stand first and the trial would begin this afternoon. Victor had said before that my husband would testify first, but that changed somewhere along the way.

**Later --**

Court ended about 5 p.m. and I'd been on the witness stand for two and a half hours. Victor said I could not have been better. I cried here and there, but not out of control. Before I was called to the stand, I let my mind drift across the names of all my friends who I knew were supporting me. That little mental exercise brought me the clear head I needed to speak well. I was so grateful for my friends.

Nancy sat on the bench on the main floor near the concessions/newsstand area and near the bathroom, as she is still recovering from her broken leg and using a walker to get around. Her companionship all day and especially on the way home was invaluable. My husband was in the courtroom during my testimony but he never looked at me.

Victor asked questions that revealed what our married life was like and my contributions to our relationship, our family and my husband's career. Victor was also very effective in nailing down the financial aspects of my situation. For example, I am due half of the $20,000 that my husband took for the barn roof repair, half of the pension money that my husband received last year and payments of the back pay maintenance and interest.

It's been a long, grueling day and I'm exhausted in a way I'm not sure I've felt before.

## March 14, 1996

We had yesterday off from the trial due to other appointments that the lawyers had. I caught up on some rest. It was Nancy's birthday, too, so we celebrated with friends last night.

Today we go back for the second day of the trial. I'll still be on the stand with Victor asking questions and then I'll be cross-examined by Sheila. I'm taking my financial information.

I called Molly to tell her the divorce would be over soon.

## March 15, 1996

Five hours on the stand yesterday carried me through every emotion I have -- I cried, I laughed, I was angry, I felt pity. The day ended with my mind overwhelmed.

An expert witness went first and testified about the value and financial workings of my husband's business. Then I was back on the stand first with Victor's questions and then Sheila's cross-examination.

Eventually my testimony lead into the issues behind the divorce -- how the marriage disintegrated with my husband's turn of affection for his filing clerk, his locked file cabinet, secret and expensive gifts, clandestine trips, our money given to her and my emotional distress.

Sheila asked if I wanted to live next door to my husband since I've requested the farm and he wants the Big House and the farm. I said, "Yes, I can. I will." Sheila asked if it was my preference to live next door to him.

I said, "I wouldn't prefer to live next door, but I will. I live in the same town, it's a small town."

Her question was annoying because it assumed that I was moving into his "territory" just because he's living in the Big House right now and that somehow he has first rights to the area. If I get the farm and move into the farmhouse and he chooses to stay in the Big House, it is not that I have chosen to move next door to him. We will have both agreed to the property division and he will have chosen to live next door to me as much I have chosen to live next door to him. He doesn't have "first dibs" on anything or any place, especially since he's the one who's busted up our marriage with his philandering. I agree with my kids; he should leave town.

Sheila had me go over the events leading up to our "fight," and I had to describe what happened that night several times. Sheila asked me if before our so-called fight in November if we'd ever had a physical fight. I said, "No, we never fought and he always loved me. I was nice and known to be nice. We never, ever fought -- only after I couldn't deny these feelings about his relationship with this girl and I know now that when I have these feelings they are accurate. We weren't fighters, we were lovers."

Sheila asked me if there was a time that I threatened my husband and said I'd call all of this clients and tell them what a shit he was. I said, "No. I told him in Indiana that I was going to do him in. I said I had a weapon and the weapon -- my weapon -- was the truth. And the truth of my weapon was I can tell everyone we know and your clients what you have done and how you have acted. And he said, 'If you do, it's over.'" Of course, I never did it.

Sheila worked very hard during her questioning of me to try and make me sound like a crazy lunatic or something. She asked me over and over again "Did you get hysterical?" Finally I just said, "My feelings are normal. If you don't have these feelings you are really not normal. I mean if I didn't care about my marriage or what difference it would make, who would care?"

It was as if being married to the same man for nearly 40 years who suddenly becomes totally infatuated with his filing clerk, hides it, sneaks around with her and lies about it to me was such ordinary stuff, it couldn't have possibly triggered some hysterical crying! I'm so glad I don't have those feelings of urgent desperation and utter despair anymore.

I also described the horn-honking incident and Sheila asked if I'd run the girlfriend off the road. I said that I had more accurately run my husband off the road as he trailed after his girlfriend. I said I pulled into his lane, forcing him onto the shoulder, rolled down my window and had something to say to him. Sheila asked, "What did you say?"

I looked at Victor and he nodded his head to go ahead, and I looked at the judge and he said, "Say it." Then I looked at the court stenographer and said, "Are you ready for this?" He nodded. I focused on my husband and said, "Go ahead and fuck the whore! Tell your goddamn lawyer I'm crazy - - You bastard!"

Later the judge told Victor that he thought it was good I got that off my chest. He also told Victor he was leaning toward giving me the farm. Today my husband takes the stand.

**Later --**

It's after the lunch break and I'm waiting alone in the courtroom for the judge and the lawyers to have a conference in the judge's chambers. My husband is sitting in the hall chatting with the stenographer.

So far my husband's testimony has supported mine with minor exceptions of his recall of incidents, which he described, of course, from his perspective -- like his professional career, his description of events leading up to our "fight," and his characterization of that event.

Then he depicted his fear of me and how scared he was to be near me. This testimony was designed to show how we could not possibly be neighbors and how he should have the Big House and the farm because he thinks I'm so dangerous.

It was hard to believe what he was doing to me. I could have just sobbed right then and there, but I held it together in the courtroom. I've managed to stay composed and never showed my emotions while my husband was testifying. I just looked at him.

In his testimony, my husband conveniently forgot our conversation in the car driving home from Vermont when he told me his passion comes and goes and that he wanted "space," to which I said, "Fine, I'll leave and give you space." Instead, he stated that I just announced, "I'm leaving," like it was out of the blue!

He said that I didn't leave until the next day, when, in fact, I left about 30 minutes after we arrived home. My husband also claimed, under oath, that he had no idea where I'd gone and didn't know until my testimony the day before that I'd spent the second night at Michelle's. He was "forgetting," of course, that he knew I was at the Big House the first night and that he came and saw me there.

It was shocking. Even Sheila got the story straight when she was questioning me the day before. She said, "Garrick told you he wanted his space and you accommodated him by moving out for a month, correct?" I said, "That's right."

My husband was emotional a couple of times on the stand this morning, but generally, he was OK. He testified that the girlfriend was "a diamond in the rough," he was trying to help her develop her potential and that he's always done that with young employees. He made a big deal of how I objected to the "candy sucking" behavior that went on in his office with him and the girlfriend and that I looked in his trash baskets for discarded candy wrappers.

I laughed silently to myself -- it was so ludicrous to talk about in trial -- paying our lawyers and stenographer probably more than $400 an hour to have the judge listen to charges of romantic music in the office, candy sucking and wrappers in the trash.

It's incredulous to think a 40-year marriage went up in smoke with him believing he was mentoring "a diamond in the rough," and me believing he was infatuated and proceeded to an affair. I trust my instincts and know I'm right. I'm totally validated in my intense feelings of his breach of fidelity.

At lunch over sandwiches at Victor's office, Nancy asked about the conclusion of the case and Victor said, "The divorce will be granted, but it may take months to have a formal judgment of the settlement from the judge." To me, this felt like a weather report; it might rain today or it might not, but it will someday and it is what it is.

My husband was supposed to be cross-examined by Victor after lunch, but when we came back the lawyers and the judge went into a conference in the private chamber near the courtroom. It's now 3 p.m. and they're still going at it -- bickering, I assume. Maybe they're trying to work out a settlement.

It's beginning to look like we won't finish today. The adrenaline is running out of me and I feel very sleepy. I'm drained. I hope I don't have to go back on the stand. I think I'll put my head on the table and shut my eyes.

At 3:30 p.m., Victor came to me and said, "The judge has decided everything is to be sold." Apparently, the judge has been expressing his thoughts about the case to Sheila and Victor as it rolls along. He leans one way and then the other. At this point, it's not firm; it's still just "talk" amongst the judge, Sheila and Victor.

We do have a chance to bid for ourselves. I pointed out how I would be out of a home because my house will sell and the Big House, where my husband is living, will not sell quickly, if at all. I might also lose the bid on the farm. My annoyance and frustration were clear. My concerns made sense to Victor and it seemed to give him incentive and worthwhile stuff to go back and fight for and negotiate around. It's good teamwork.

**4 p.m.** -- Overwhelmingly tired. I'm fighting to keep my composure. The word now is that we must begin our bidding for the farm at the offering price, which is based on the appraisal, or we can't get it. Now I think my husband will let the girlfriend get the Big House as it slides to lower prices once it's on the market for a while.

**March 16, 1996**

Yesterday was such a long day. Late in the afternoon, after consulting with my husband, Sheila walked back through the courtroom and looked at me with venom in her eyes. Perhaps they'd decided they were ready for the kill and she was doing her best to look mean.

The lawyers continued, cloistered in the private conference room. Victor came out several more times with details of the negotiations. At one point I said, "It sounds like I'm losing; giving up $25,000 on the value of his business, hearing they won't pay maintenance, thinking my husband will be left in the Big House which won't sell, leaving me without a home because the marital house will sell quickly, not having money to buy the farm, wondering how much I can possibly afford to bid on it!" I was totally bummed out. I felt defeated.

I started crying a little driving home and Nancy was very empathetic and helpful, as always. I dropped her off at her place, but by the time I got home, I was screaming in agony from being trashed.

Then Molly came for dinner last night. I was a basket case. Finally, at the end of the evening, I called Debbie in California. She said, "Go back and fight."

### March 17, 1995

It's Sunday and I'm focusing on "adjusting." I'm easing into the notion of selling everything rather than dividing up our possessions. Even if the losses to me are horrendous, monetarily and emotionally, Debbie says she's positive that I'm going to emerge a "whole person."

I'm not so afraid about the losses anymore, not even as much as I was a couple of days ago. I'm grateful for the gains. I realize my worst-case scenario is a totally fresh start. Not too bad.

### March 19, 1996

This day began with Sheila announcing that they wanted to negotiate. Victor came out from the conference early on this morning and said my husband is ready to negotiate. Victor said it means my husband wants to settle, that everything doesn't have to be sold and that my husband does not want to be cross-examined. I think Victor would have liked to have cross-examined him, but Victor also wants to finish the deal with this decision from my husband in hand because it is a stronger negotiating position for us.

I don't know why my husband did not want to be cross-examined by Victor. He must have believed it would not serve his case in a positive way to have to answer Victor's questions. It feels like a point of capitulation for my husband. He seems to be throwing in the towel. Whatever the reason, the negotiating is a tedious item-by-item process that Victor is very good at. I hope they can settle all the issues before 5 p.m.

**2 p.m.** -- Well, it's now five hours later and they're still going at it. While waiting in the courtroom today I chatted some more with the stenographer. He was sitting around waiting and reading like I was. It certainly passed the time to talk with him and he was interesting because he has an unusual hobby -- scuba diving. He's had a few short conversations with my husband, too, and at one point he said to me, "You know, he seems like a pretty nice guy."

At 2:30 p.m., Nancy, Victor and I ate tuna salad sandwiches for lunch at his office, kind of our ritual during these trial days. The negotiations are sounding positive for me. It seems that I might get the farm and that my husband was considering taking the Big House for himself.

**3:45 p.m.** -- Victor just came out reported that it's an even swap and the deal is done. The marital residence will be sold, he'll get the Big House and I get the farm. We'll be next-door neighbors. Wow.

It feels good to have the farm, but not happy, not yet.

Victor's gone back in. Splitting the unpaid taxes, devising a plan to split the Visa bill and offering to give my husband the video camera is our next move.

Victor seemed thrilled about the farm and Big House swap. He knew I was willing to pay a lot to get it. I'd told him that I wanted a clean break; I didn't want to rely on my husband for anything. I would rather have a lump sum now, even if it's smaller than monthly maintenance payments would add up to be, than to count on him for anything in my future.

Now Victor just came out and said my husband agreed to pay my health insurance until I'm 65, it's cheaper for him than a lump sum. I'll pay half of the $3,000 Visa advance and I'll give my husband the video camera, which he's been adamant about. Fine with me. I reminded Victor about the furniture and it's next on the negotiating list.

When I walked to the ladies room moments later, I saw my husband sitting on the bench in the hallway. He looked very glum and pursed his lips as he actually looked at me for the first time. His look wasn't angry or depressed. It seemed to be one of frustration and resignation; that he's done. I looked at him but I didn't stop. It's interesting to me that he finally looked at me now. I believe he did because now he can stand it. How could he have looked at me before?

I've been calmer today because before the negotiating began this morning I repeated the mental exercise of remembering the names of all the people who are thinking of me and supporting me. I also recalled "The Lord's Prayer" and the "Serenity Prayer."

**4:30 p.m.** -- I feel pity for my husband and I have lost my desire to fight any more. The settlement is in my favor. At this moment, I've done my job. I stood up, I didn't eat shit and I stayed the course. There is satisfaction but no joy. I think I can go on.

I will proceed carefully and slowly until I feel comfortable in my new living situation. I believe the farm, farmhouse and greenhouse are perfect for me, but I'm not sure I'll be able to be his next-door neighbor. I need to test myself. Debbie said it's OK to change my mind if it doesn't seem to be working for me -- if I find myself obsessing over it, paranoid or nervous, or always crying. These reactions would certainly be a sign. Debbie believes that if I'm aware of the pitfalls, then no matter what, I will be fine. I must be aware. I can always make another choice and move on.

**Later --**

The divorce was granted at 6 p.m., with agreements having been reached on everything. Nancy was invited into the courtroom by the judge to hear the full settlement decision and details. I had introduced the judge to Nancy when we were all in the lobby on one of the "recesses." The judge had noted the friendship and trust and saw Nancy sitting in the hall each day of the trial.

Nancy hobbled in on her walker and seated herself near the conference table. My husband looked exasperated with Nancy's presence, but he surrendered with no choice. At the conclusion of the judge's reading of all the distribution of assets, he stated with finality that it would all be "put on record." I thanked Victor and told him I'd speak to him later. I bid farewell to the judge and Nancy and I descended the courthouse stairs to arrive at my car with Spooky inside wagging her tail.

We drove to the Hillsdale House Restaurant and Nancy treated me to dinner. We reviewed all the details we had heard in the settlement decision. We spoke of friendships and how nice it was of Margaret to stop by the courthouse and give her support and how wonderful the support from all my friends has been. Nancy congratulated me with her magnificent and irrepressible smile for getting what I wanted -- the farm.

# DANCING FREE

**March 20, 1996**

Now that the plug is pulled on our almost 40-year marriage, the pain is draining away and I awoke this morning with excitement filling my head. I'm actually feeling curious about my next adventures.

I made calls to family and friends and to Debbie, spreading the word that my ordeal is over. I'm struck, once again, by my fortune in having such good friends.

Many offered to come to the courthouse and wait in the hall to offer me support during the trial, but it was Nancy who filled that spot. Each day she'd hobble in with her broken leg and set herself up on the bench in the downstairs hallway. Armed with a bag attached to her walker, she had her day's necessities -- a book and material for her current project. She used some of her time to research the history of her house since the office that has the records of property titles is also in the courthouse.

And she would be there for me with her clear head and solid support. Each time I stepped out of the courtroom, I could immediately exhale all the minutia of the last hours, inhale her encouragement and we'd exchange observations. Nancy's friendship is much more than a pat on the back and a listening ear; she has intelligence, honesty and a wise perspective that keeps molehills from becoming mountains. Knowing this great friend was only steps away smoothed whatever emotions had bubbled up.

Also, having Spooky waiting patiently in my car with her simple needs for fresh air, water and brief walks, allowed me the opportunity to care for her. This pure and rewarding activity helped to minimize my sense of loss during the trial ordeal. I welcomed her joyful love.

So, I jumped into my new life today. I made a list -- things I need in the farmhouse, demolition of the collapsed barn, price to build a tennis court and to add a pergola to the front of my greenhouse, call the farmer who rents the land, plan to put a picket fence around the house. I asked the Town Supervisor to think about putting their new town hall on a portion of my land, which I will give to them, so that it would adjoin the town's businesses. Should that project happen, I would suggest that I be chairman of the project.

I did some more typing of my journal notes. I've decided on a title for my book, "Dancing Naked."

**March 22, 1997**

I'm still calling and writing notes to friends who are in my support system, notifying everyone that it's ended with a fair settlement.

I'd like to catch up on sleep but I'm motivated to take action on my ideas and also to write about my feelings. I want to save time to put my publishing goals together and to organize and pack up my divorce legal papers.

Greeting friends yesterday, they said, "You always smiled, but now your eyes are smiling too." And yet, when asked the details of the settlement, tears still well up.

When Judy comes tomorrow, I plan to burn the Indian voodoo doll that Stu and Diane gave to me. Actually, it was Stu's idea and he instigated it with great flair. They'd picked up the Indian doll during their travels in the Southwest. Stu stuck pins in it and on the plane ride home, wrote an entire page of witty "instructions" on how to use the created Indian Voodoo doll. He stated that the doll was given with the hope that it will rid my past and present of all evil spirits while creating a bright future. He detailed how to stick the pins in for different effects and stated that it would be terrific therapy, with a recommended use of twice a day. Finally, he said I should burn the doll in my fireplace to cleanse my home and life, once and for all, of any kind of meanness or wickedness.

It was a strong and positive dose of Stu and Diane's solid support of me. So, per his "instructions," Judy and I lit a lovely roaring fire and burned the doll. It was an appropriate conclusion and we filled the room with laughter.

Spooky and I have been invited to dinner tonight at Margaret and Michael's, and I have a tennis party tomorrow night. My mother and Lilly are coming for a few days next week, and the Realtor called today to ask to look at the house. I have a lot of typing to do and a spring cleanup. I feel good.

## March 27, 1996

Mom and Lilly are reading my unedited book. They can't stop and they're amazed that I endured such horrendous treatment before I knew there was really no hope left.

My mother has been on a fascinating journey with respect to my marriage falling apart. At first, she was embarrassed that she had a child who would be divorced. She felt she'd failed as a mother for having raised a child with a bad marriage. She thought it was somehow her fault, something she didn't provide to me as my mother.

Then there was her "denial" phase, when she thought it might be best if I just ignore my husband's lack of affection to me and ignore his surge in affection for his filing clerk. My mother and a couple of my older aunts suggested I just learn to live with my husband's "little affairs," because I should think about the future and his pension.

On this visit, however, my mother demonstrated her strongest outburst of anger. She said, "I'm old now and if I had a gun, I could take that gun and shoot him." Of course, she would never do it, but it is the sentiment a mother might have when her child has been raped, beaten or killed. For my mother, it was a valid expression of her hurt and fury and it settled that she was fully in support of me and my actions. Her healing process, I believe, began that moment.

Lilly read nonstop for hours. Near the end, she said, "I think you put up and hung in there for an eternity."

Next week I'll meet with my friend, Lyrysa. She's a journalist and has agreed to be my "editor." We're going to discuss a strategy for publishing, which is very exciting. Now, with lots of irons in the fire, I want to accomplish many, many tasks and I want to celebrate. When the settlement papers are signed and the deeds are transferred, I want to be ready for action -- work and play. I hope Debbie can come here for a visit and I'll plan a big party to celebrate.

**March 28, 1996**

OOOPS! The music stopped with news from Victor. I was in the midst of sorting out all the legal papers that had accumulated for more than a year, getting them stacked sequentially and putting the bills in a pile. It felt like going through the closet of a dead person, not pleasant, sometimes interesting, but most of all, just time to do it and get it done. A closure, of sorts.

Then Victor called and said he'd talked to Sheila ("more like a shouting match," he said) and that my ex-husband was now trying to change all the provisions of the settlement. He disagrees with the back pay, the division established for the joint account, the price of the real estate and the amount of the pension payments. Victor asked me how I felt and I said, "Tell them to go to hell."

A little later, Victor called back to read me his response letter to Sheila. He stated he'd read her letter with disbelief. He said after lengthy and exhausting negotiations with a settlement reached and placed on the record before the judge, that their attempts "to renegotiate the terms of the settlement now were nothing less than contemptuous."

I was OK seeing the girlfriend drive up his driveway to the Big House today and the thought of her moving in there didn't bother me too much. But this nasty attempt to screw me over again definitely makes me furious. I called Nancy and told her I felt like kicking my ex in the balls.

I called the Realtor to cancel the appointment for her to look at the house. My ex had selected the Realtor so I told her I didn't know her and that I had zero respect for my ex and was not comfortable with people that he is comfortable with. She was impressive in the face of my pronouncement. She stated she was a client of my husband's, not a social friend, and she promised me she'd be fair to both of us. She said she'd been through a divorce herself so she understood my position and was glad I was upfront with her. I gave her high marks after our conversation; she was very professional.

Nancy invited me over to watch a video tonight and I'm bringing the pizza. My ex can't stop the fun and he can't keep the music away from me no matter how hard he tries. I believe in Victor and I am going to dance free.

**March 31, 1996**

Palm Sunday, a gorgeous day. After church, Nancy and I decided to do a picnic at my greenhouse. On the way out of church, our friend, Millie, mentioned she'd made an appointment with Sheila a couple of months ago to do her will. Sheila told Millie that she was very busy with a big trial, Belt vs. Belt. Millie assumed that Sheila was my lawyer and shared how everyone was praying for Alice. Sheila admitted that, actually, she was representing my ex and said, "Well, somebody has to."

We all had a good laugh. The odd part is that she distanced herself from her client and spoke unprofessionally about it.

## April 1, 1996

The letter from Sheila to Victor said my ex "has decided to agree to the stipulation as submitted by you. He does not wish to prolong this matter any further." So we're scheduled to sign the official papers on Thursday.

My neighbors, Pete and Ed, came for dinner tonight. Such wonderful neighbors will be impossible to replicate. Of course, our friendship will not be affected by my move, it's just one more sad note.

## April 3, 1996

Spring is struggling between sun and snow, but the daffodils and tulips are emerging and the ticks are out. I've already removed a tick and taken it to the doctor to be tested for Lyme disease. Fortunately, I feel robust and I walk happily in the fields with Spooky and my friends.

Plans for Easter and the Pastor's invitation that I do a reading for the Good Friday service are hopeful and invigorating activities. My willingness to express myself honestly also makes me feel healthy. I'm even thinking about a nude photo of myself dancing for the cover of my book.

The days are longer and there are so many exciting things to do and decisions to make. What junk to save out of the collapsed barn? Should I buy some work gloves and remove the stuff myself? I can always use some extra boards but I don't know about those old windows.

**April 6, 1996**

Victor noticed I was a little snippy in my referrals to my ex during Thursday's "signing off" meeting with my ex and the lawyers. My testiness subsided during the next day, Good Friday. I participated in the readings at our church service, and even though the service was poorly attended, the impact of the message was not diminished, a solemn preparation for Easter. I was grateful to be a part of it.

My house showed well to the Realtor. She was complimentary and suggested a high amount for the "asking price." I told her I wanted the price to be realistic and that it was not to my advantage to have it on the market for a long time. I'm wondering if it will be difficult for us to agree on the asking price. I have a suspicion that my ex might try to manipulate this part of the settlement, too.

Today I'll get a demolition permit for the collapsed barn. Easter plans include Molly, my cousin, Ann, and Nancy. I'm feeling up.

**April 7, 1996**

Easter! And it's not the snowy day predicted, just a little rain, clouds and 40 degrees. The birds chirping at the early dawn were indeed a joyful sound. As I listened to them, I recalled the chirping birds in my bad dream that mocked me by mimicking my ex's special family whistle to call the girlfriend. At least that awful nightmare is over.

My table is set for a lamb chop dinner after church. My house exudes country charm and friendship -- flowers on the table, green plants around the rooms and Spooky curled in peaceful slumber on her cushion. If a buyer were to come in today, they would be tempted to "buy" these intangible things.

**April 12, 1996**

A beautiful sunrise at 6:30 a.m. and then the clouds covered and the day couldn't be drearier. Rain, snow, wind and cold have not deterred Margaret and me from our morning walks with our dogs. So at 8 a.m., Spooky and I hike up the hill to meet them. As Margaret and I walk and talk through acres of fields, our dogs run and frolic on the magnificent land. One short hour in the day spent appreciating nature and conversation, laughing and developing a healthy body is so positive.

Margaret has become an amazing friend. She really listens and "gets it" in down-to-earth language. She offers advice in a straightforward way. She's given me courage. She has a way of flattery that is very appealing. She's a keen observer and sees more than most because of her own varied and unexpected personal experiences.

**April 14, 1996**

"Do you know what he did <u>now</u>?" That was the familiar question I posed to my friends during the divorce proceedings. Of course, now we are divorced and there are still lingering details of settlement that erupt and my friends and I say, "I can't believe he would do that!"

My ex has the right to stay in the office until the end of September and he's responsible to pay the carrying charges until then. It didn't occur to me that he'd extract the office building from the farm as a whole and cancel the insurance on the land and the greenhouse portion, but he did. So I'm scurrying to find insurance with another agent. The joint account has yet to be divided due to difficulties in separating the bonds. I also learned that my ex refuses to speak to the broker.

My fluid cash is to come from that account so I'm skating on thin ice for now. I believe the joint account issue will be settled soon, but if it isn't, I'll think of something to tide me over. Cash extension and conservation is something I've become quite good at as a result of this experience.

My water softener conked out and flooded a part of the basement so I had to have the plumber in on an emergency situation. All the expenses at my home are mine and I've had plenty of them in the past one and a half years. No big deal, that's life. Now that real estate agents are showing my house, I keep it very tidy and presentable all the time. I really enjoy this home, but I believe I'll enjoy my next space, the farmhouse, as much, maybe even more.

**April 15, 1996**

Church has been an important part of my recovery. Being open to the "word" as spoken from the pulpit and expressed in song always helps me to soften anger and feel forgiveness.

To forgive the man who is still striving to hurt me is not a solid act of compassion or generosity on my part. I <u>want</u> to forgive the "mythical man," the one who has the girlfriend, denies it, but proclaims his wrongdoing and begs for forgiveness. But the man I <u>must</u> forgive is, by every action, still my enemy. Lack of trust and anger distort the separation of feelings necessary to forgive. Amazingly enough, the Lord's Prayer, repeated often, helps keep forgiveness viable to me.

For my own peace, and for my kids, I hope I can reach total forgiveness. I want to and I wish for it. It would be a miracle, though. I still believe in miracles. I don't believe, however, that I'll ever have respect for him again.

## April 18, 1996

Today the collapsed barn is being demolished and buried at the farm. The 6 X 6 posts have been salvaged to build the pergola at my greenhouse. My contractor stopped by to mark where the posts are to go and we discussed the plans to build a garage/barn near the farmhouse/office.

Still no money from the settlement so I'm very low on cash, but I know it will work out soon. The stock market has been in a slump ever since the divorce date so the joint account has less total value.

I found a new insurance agent to cover the farm and greenhouse, but when I went to my former local agent to tell him, he resisted my taking the business away from him. I explained that it didn't have anything at all to do with him, personally. Then I said, "It's just that Garrick is a total asshole and I won't be connected with him in anyway." The agent visibly shuddered at my words announced in front of all his employees in the small office. His wife, standing near by, tossed her head and stormed away. I placed all my insurance, including my car and the marital residence, with the new agent.

"Taking sides" happens in this process. I'm surrounding myself with people clearly on my side. I can be cordial to others. But I don't have to be "nice" anymore. I like being genuine.

## April 21, 1996

Well, yesterday was interesting. The morning began with sprucing up the house so the Realtor could show it. Then I was off to my activities -- the greenhouse, the coffee house and the post office.

I've stopped fearing the mail, but there was legal mail again. From it, I learned that my ex is still trying to renegotiate the settlement. The bond and stock market have gone down in the weeks that my ex has been disputing the settlement and now he's attempting to recalculate the settlement so that he can have half of what it used to be rather than half of what it is currently. Of course, that would negatively alter my share. It's horrendous.

He wants to believe he's some financial wizard, but he isn't. It's really a last ditch angle of control that he's digging at. Victor responded with the suggestion that we either sue my ex for breach of honoring the divorce agreement or wait to split the account until the market goes up.

I came home and played tennis outdoors for the first time this season with Ana and George.

The Realtor called as I was taking a bath and getting ready to go out for dinner. She reported that my house had been shown while I was out today and she signed an offer for the full price -- in cash! There was no problem with the prospective buyers for me to stay in the house until the end of September and she planned to notify my ex next.

Before joining my friends for dinner I called Pete and Ed, Nancy, Lilly, Victor and Michelle. Since things are not signed, sealed and delivered, my emotions are a bit guarded. I'm not sad but there are some sentimental memories wrapped up in this house. But it seems things are working out. The Realtor certainly sounded positive and I'm optimistic and excited.

Earlier today I was hashing out my cash problems with Nancy. I decided I could sell some stock that I had purchased from my B&B money and held in my name. It will help me stay strong in my legal battle and keep me afloat for a few months. Before the news that my house sold, I'd been working on more ways to manage financially in the face of an extended period without adequate income. One idea is to step up the process to publish. I'm very pleased with my editor for my book and I'm enthusiastic about the prospects to publish.

I want to end the book on a high note. This feeling of wanting the high note is one I remember from my childhood. I am at school, running on the track with hurdles. When I go airborne and clear the highest one, I'm soaring. Limitless. My mind leaves my body.

**Later --**

I'm marveling at how lucky I am. The forsythia around my house is almost bursting in bloom. I am standing my ground with creative flexibility. My optimism is tempered with common sense and the support of my great sounding boards, my friends.

While I was working at my greenhouse, I was very curious about the party going on at my ex's house. I walked through the field with Spooky to take a look. Rock and roll music was blaring from the Big House and kids were running around in their bathing suits with the hose spraying water. The girlfriend's barking dog was tied to a wire between two trees, a tacky umbrella was open and bent over the patio table and my ex was standing at the fence talking with a young guest. The ages at his party ranged from 3 to 30-something, and then the old man -- 62. I laughed. And when they all loaded up in his Saab convertible with the top down and honked at the neighbors as they drove through town -- it was a sight!

I decided it was time to get my furniture out of the Big House. My Oriental rug and Victorian couch may already have stains from sticky fingers, muddy feet and dog doo.

Witnessing the party, a mix of feelings washed over me; humor, revenge and pity. I felt sorry for my kids and hoped they wouldn't allow themselves to be tainted by their father's behavior. Today, he reveled in youth, rock and roll and fancy cars; I planted perennial plants, discussed the crops to be planted on my farm with the farmer, worked on my book, took a long walk with Spooky and listened to public radio. Even though I too can enjoy young people, rock and roll and fancy cars, I am very happy with my lifestyle choices.

**April 22, 1996**

A morning of discussion about the editing of the book proved again how much fun it is to work with my editor. She told me that her computer spell-check program balked at several of my words -- "whore" and "fucking," among others. She issued commands for the spell-check program to "learn" those words. We laughed a lot.

When we have a few chapters completed, an outline of the rest of the book and a strong cover letter, we'll send it all out as a query package to agents and publishers. I'm even excited about "rejection" letters. We chuckle when we fantasize about the big advance we'll get. Dreamers!

I sold my MCI, Reebock and USG stock and the check will arrive in a few days. Victor is dealing with the binder for the sale of the house, the insurance on the farm, the separate deeds for the two lots next to the house and the exchange of the furniture arrangement.

Diane and Stu are bringing pizza for dinner tonight on their way from Stockbridge to Pleasantville. They have been very supportive of me throughout this saga of a soap opera. Diane said to me recently, "You know, I thought before that you were very nice. But now, now you're really interesting and exciting."

**April 24, 1996**

So far today, things are falling into place. An early call from Mike scheduled the exchange of furniture between the Big House and the marital residence to happen right away. The quick plan resulted in a quick move this morning. I started to cry when the family photograph portrait was stacked in my barn with the other items coming from the Big House. I said, "I wonder how he felt when he passed that over?" Mike said, "It doesn't matter how he felt. Don't look over your shoulder. You are going on."

The last time I was in the Big House, I saw that the family photo was off the wall and stashed in a closet. He clearly didn't care about it. Later, I asked for it in my list of items from the Big House. He didn't resist at all.

It's OK to be sad about this detail of closure. I don't want to wallow, but I'm balancing the reality of Mike's statement with my own sorrow. I only felt weepy for a moment.

Then a piece of my tooth broke off and I was lucky to get an appointment with a new dentist. I haven't had a dentist for a couple of years so I'm glad to get going on this aspect of my health care. When I called an eye doctor about a recent vision problem I'm having, he seemed concerned and scheduled me for today. That was quick and again, something I've needed to do.

Finally, the tick bite from four weeks ago requires a blood test for Lyme disease and I'll do that tomorrow. I have selected a new dentist, a new ophthalmologist and a new doctor. Debbie says that responsible medical attention is an important part of taking care of myself.

The joint account is about to be settled, finally. Victor called to say my ex has agreed to the distribution of stocks and bonds so I'm to sign off on that this afternoon. I'm looking forward to my scheduled telephone session with Debbie tonight. It's been two weeks since we've talked.

Tomorrow, Spooky and Chicken Feet go to the kennel. Molly comes to spend the night and then we're off to North Carolina for a weekend together with all of my kids. Hooray!

**April 26, 1996**

The vision problem turned out to be a severely torn retina, close to being detached and quite dangerous. Immediate laser surgery took place in the doctor's office and then I drove home. Doctor's orders were "to do nothing" -- don't bend over, lift anything, twist or strain or even walk, except to slide across the floor gently without my feet leaving the ground.

Of course, it killed my plans to go to North Carolina and on vacation with the kids. Molly took the cabin reservation I'd made and drove herself to the airport.

My eye is a lot better today but not quite normal yet, so it's been the right thing to stay home, lie in bed and try to do nothing. I told Pete and Ed that I felt lucky to have discovered the problem before it progressed to a fully detached retina and blindness. Ed said, "I don't want your luck."

**April 27, 1996**

The kids called from Bryson City, North Carolina, last night to say they had all arrived safely and were waiting in the lodge for their luggage to arrive. Severe turbulence and delayed flights caused late arrivals and even later luggage so the airline was making a delivery to the lodge. They had to literally run to catch their connecting flight in Charlotte, so it's more clear than ever that I made the right choice to stay home and "do nothing."

My friends have all helped me by bringing meals and calling me on the phone to find out what I need. If I haven't said it a million times, I am so lucky to have such a wonderful network of friends. I love my friends.

## May 1, 1996

The results of my eye checkup yesterday left me bummed out. The doctor said that no healing had taken place so far and that I must continue "to do nothing." He said I was in danger of losing my sight. I canceled my appointments and social calendar.

Nancy brought a wonderful dinner and I'm wondering if I should get another opinion about my eye.

To "dance free" these days, I must keep both my feet on the floor and glide and try not to move my torso at all. Doctor's orders are that I'm not to jar my head even slightly by stepping, bending over or turning suddenly.

## May 3, 1996

Six weeks after the divorce and I awoke in the middle of the night. I was once again struck with the acute pain of what he'd done to me. I wailed into the silence of my room.

Now my emotional pressure valve is released and logic is setting in. I'm probably feeling sorry for myself and without good reason. Most things are working well for me. It's premature to fret about my retina failing. The laser surgery hasn't worked yet, but that doesn't mean it won't. I have a good plan to deal with it if things get worse: With the help of my friends, I have an appointment with a retina eye specialist in Boston the day after my next appointment locally. Should an emergency arise, like a totally detached retina, I'll go the emergency room in the Eye Infirmary in Boston. It took me a while to get this plan in place, not to mention unwinding all the plans I couldn't keep.

The parade of friends to my house and the many phone calls keep my "doing nothing" life fairly busy and fun. My friends have been bringing lunch and dinner and join me to eat. Other friends are doing the shopping,

taking Spooky on walks and getting the mail. Everything is taken care of --
cleaning my house and doing little repairs, work in the greenhouse and
books on tape! Spooky was even taken to the vet for her annual checkup. I
am extremely lucky to have such great friends.

I've said "Yes" to my contractor for building the garage and porch at
the farmhouse/office, which will soon be my new home.

It's now 5 a.m. and the birds are chirping. I'm not blind, I have good
plans and I have reasons to celebrate this new dawn and little cause to look
back.

## May 4, 1996

Pinch me. Is it true that Chip and David Selby actually called last night
and asked for the "rights" to my book so that they can create a movie
project from it? They're doing projects with Shirley MacLaine, John
Updike and Joyce Carrol Oates, and they want the rights to my story? It's
like a dream!

With my ear to the phone, I became weightless on a cloud that still left
my feet on the floor. "Yes, I can have something to you next week. Thank
you for the call."

I hung up. Turning to my friends who had come for dinner and were
seated around the coffee table, my arms floated up with the glass of wine
still in my hand and I said, "Guess what, guys? That was Hollywood and
they want my book!" It was about 8 p.m. and Molly, Nancy, Marty and
Kent, and I clinked our glasses, laughed and enjoyed a superb dinner.

Even as we talked of many things through the night, I felt spontaneous
smiles break out on my face. I wanted to keep celebrating; it felt glorious
to be dancing free. I called Lyrysa, Victor, Debbie, Ann and Flora, and
completed my day as David Letterman was going off the air.

**Sunday, May 12, 1996**

Dawn came quietly, peacefully and with gentle rain as my waking thoughts passed from this date, May 12, Mother's Day and the 40th anniversary, to focus on this day. Feeling good, physically and mentally, rising early to be greeted by Spooky, listening to birds, noticing the apple tree in blossom, I am happy for this day. A day with plans. My cousin, Ann, is here and Molly is coming to prepare brunch with us. We want to work in my greenhouse and take a walk.

My life is exciting and visible to all. The community is taking frames of exposures and piecing them together to view a progressing and moving picture. It's a serial to be continued. My ex is installing a tall stockade fence along the property line that will separate his Big House from the farmhouse/office that will be my home. But his fence is not high enough to obstruct the view to his house or to his aboveground pool that sits up on a slight hill. It has everyone laughing and we call it the "spite fence."

His plans to celebrate the girlfriend's graduation from college with a party at his Big House on June 2nd changes the laughter to disgust. The news that elicits cheers is that the manuscript for the first three chapters of my book has been sent to California.

**May 19, 1996**

Even some of my friends received invitations to the girlfriend's graduation party being hosted by my ex. She received an award given to American Indians and her degree is in "public affairs." How appropriate.

I confess I am not always comfortable with their "public affair" in my face or the idea that we have mutual friends. I know it's unrealistic to think every friend would take my side and reject my ex. When all my nerves retreat from abrasive reactions to the hearsay around town, I need a time out to focus elsewhere. Time out to take care of myself, spew a few obscenities, order a summer dress, choose to be with people I'm most comfortable with, let a few things slide and stay aloof, but civil to people who appear to be sucking up to my ex and his girlfriend.

I want my kids to have a father even as it hurts to know their interaction with him is centered in his new world. Life has these emotional thorns, but the rose is not diminished. I'm just aware to either clip the thorns or hold the stem carefully. I'm trying not to make a big deal over what others choose.

I am excited about my prospects to sell my book and the potential movie project it may create. The summer promises to be very busy with tennis, walks, social functions, my greenhouse and garden projects, as well as building the new garage and porch and moving into my next home. Life is too wonderful to be pissed by what others do. Let go. Writing helps me to let go.

**May 25, 1996**

Since I'm expecting calls from the Selbys in Hollywood, I ordered voice mail to be put on my phone. I may need it as well for other "business" calls and my friends are thrilled to finally be able to leave me a message.

When I tell my friends about the prospects for my book to become a movie, the response is always the same -- a burst of joyous laughter that does the heart good. My network alone is the best publicity a movie could get. Everyone is excited and they have all told someone else, and so it goes with word of mouth, especially in a small town.

## May 28, 1996

When a friend asked how I felt about his being asked to be the bartender at the catered party my ex is hosting for the girlfriend's graduation, I said, "To be honest, I am uncomfortable with my friends participating socially with my ex, but I do understand that it's a separate issue from my friendship and logically it's OK. It just doesn't feel good."

My friend replied that was enough said and he would not go to the party or be a bartender for it

Even though I know some people straddle both sides, the best support from my friends is steeped in loyalty that includes a clear choice exhibited by word, deed and action.

Friends and neighbors stopped by all through the holiday weekend. I have given away a lot of plants and planted more of my garden. We played tennis, walked to the top of the field with Spooky and laughed at my ex's tacky aboveground pool and his behavior. We all speculate about the movie: Who will play my ex or the girlfriend? We talk about the cinematography and how it could enhance the story. We marvel at the natural beauty of our location and rejoice in the quality of our friendships. Sharing the new excitement in my life has given all my friends a stake in the adventure.

Debbie says she'll try to come to Falls Town for my outdoor gala in September. I'm planning a major party to celebrate moving to the farm, the book, hopefully the movie, too and my new life.

## June 1, 1996

When he broke his ankle, I wished for ice and snow to make it a difficult winter for him, but instead it was the mildest winter we'd had in many years. Now today, the eve of his graduation party for her, I wished for rain and storms, but it's a gorgeous day and will be a gorgeous weekend. But it's gorgeous for everybody -- including me. The days are perfect for reveling in the gifts of nature. I enjoyed the afternoon at a church picnic.

**June 3, 1996**

It's odd that I should have such a hard time sleeping the night of my ex's party for the girlfriend. I'm not sure if Spooky woke up several times because she sensed I was awake, but letting her out was a reality check for me as I connected to my dog's dependence on me and my need for her. Looking in the mirror this morning, I saw pain etched in my face and I couldn't erase it.

Soon I will move into the house next door to my ex. Our lives will be in plain view of each other. That thought at this moment makes me awash in nausea and erodes my energy. In my bumpy sleep last night, I dreamed I was in bed raising and lowering the TV's volume using the remote as I searched for a station. All the programs seemed to have variations on the same story: The young girlfriend blaring, "You are fat and ugly, old woman," and then laughing. My voice was barely audible, half asleep and even I couldn't hear what I said to defend myself.

Just now as I write, Spooky sits next to the bed and pushes her head closer to mine and licks the salt from my face.

Yesterday, in a phone conversation arranged by David Selby, the author, Elizabeth Hailey, encouraged me and Lyrysa to continue our book project and gave us plenty of constructive criticism to keep us busy. David had given her his copy of the rough draft to read.

We're working through what we're calling the "Devastation" chapter to pull up additional vivid details that were not included in my writing of the journal entry at the time. Rethinking and reconstructing the events is reliving them to a degree for me. For particular scenes, it is like breaking open a still fresh wound.

**June 4, 1996**

Has only one day passed? At 7:30 a.m., I met my contractor to mark the location for the new garage and porch I'm building. At 8:30 a.m., my car was serviced. At 9:30 a.m., I was at the courthouse getting the release form for my discontinued B&B. Then I ordered the chicken for the dinner after the church concert on the 22nd. Poor Spooky pooped on the inside of my car so I drove home to clean that up.

After I received about 10 phone calls, had my roof checked for a leak, called the exterminator for ants and walked for an hour in the field with Margaret and our dogs, I reviewed the results of my recent Lyme disease test. I had a total blood analysis done and I'm thrilled with the good news - - I am completely healthy.

**June 5, 1996**

Talking with Debbie is an amazing affirmation of her value to me. Last night I told her of Elizabeth Hailey's constructive criticism and she responded with her own comments and insights. In regard to my efforts to write about the nature of the characters in my story, Debbie said, "How other people respond is central to the issues in a divorce. There are always the reactions of people close to the situation and people do make judgments of others."

She said that going back to the painful places to add vivid storytelling details is a wonderful way to validate where I am at this moment. Responding to a past crisis has a different ring to it now.

To help me understand the anger I felt over my ex's party for the girl, Debbie said, "He's trying to do it over again, to rewrite the script. A voice in him says it's a 'cool' thing to do. He has to keep the engine going himself now. He'll think it's his own idea, but it's your piece. You were the part of his life that gave the parties. It's as if he's in 7th grade and you are his rival."

Debbie also said I should expect that there will be a baby. She theorized that he'll want to create a new beginning as if he were young. I cringed at the thought of him with a new child and my children gaining a half-brother or sister. God, that will be a lot to swallow if it happens.

Debbie is sending a release form for me to sign that will grant her permission to speak openly about her counseling of me for our purpose of publishing a book and producing a film about my life.

## June 11, 1996

A funny one I heard today was that my ex and the girlfriend went to have lunch in a local spot. My ex tapped on the shoulder of my very elderly friend who was there and said to him, "Don't you know me anymore?" My friend got to see the girlfriend up close and later told a group of us, "I'm pretty old and decrepit, but even I could do better than that!" The town got another laugh, as did I.

## June 16, 1996

As soon as I was awake this morning a pall of lethargy overcame me and I began to dwell on it being Father's Day. Lying on the couch waiting for the dogs (Michelle's and mine) to eat their breakfast, melancholy washed over me in tears. Michelle and Pierre stopped by yesterday on their way to New York City where they spent last night with friends. They said they'd be back sometime this afternoon, but never specifically stated what they'd be doing today. Knowing my children, I guessed that along with Molly, they'd all have brunch with my ex.

The idea bothered me a great deal and it seemed unfair that I'm "dog sitting" for his "occasion" with our kids. But it's the way it's always been and it's what the kids are used to. I'm the caretaker and he does the fun stuff. For my part, I have consistently assumed the role and performed it well for decades.

I began to visualize them going to the Big House and preparing brunch for him. Having my kids see him on neutral turf is painful enough, but to go to his house with the evidence of the girlfriend all over the premises really freaked me out.

Margaret noticed my "sleepy" eyes when we met early to do a photo session with me and Spooky. She's taking photographs so that I can use one for my party invitation. At 9 a.m., I met other friends for the Father's Day breakfast fund-raiser at the firehouse. I was still feeling very depressed. I continued with my shopping plans to go get the groceries I need for next week's concert. On the way, I drove over to the Sheffield Auction to check out a brass bed that Nancy told me about and thought I might want to purchase for my new place.

On the way home in my car, my safe haven, I erupted in crying and foul language. I needed the release. Then, remarkably, as I turned a corner, my sunglasses flew out my open car window. I pulled over and stopped to try and find them. Searching along the roadside in the weeds, I could barely see through my blurry, tear-filled eyes.

Just then, Molly came around the same corner. It was immediately obvious that she was on her way to my ex's for brunch. The top of her convertible was down and I could see the grocery bags of food in the back seat. In the instant I was putting this together, Molly had jumped out of her car and was saying, "Mom?! What are you doing?" I felt my shoulders slump and my spirits collapse. For a few seconds, I began to explain about my sunglasses, but I crumbled. I was swept in a downward spiral that I could not reverse. Through my sobs, I said, "Intellectually, I know it's OK for you to go to your father's house, but emotionally, it's not OK at all." I let it all out. I said, "At this moment, I can't go on. I can't stand this, I want to kill myself."

Molly was calm and hugged me. She said, "It's a nice day. Enjoy it. Make a plan. He's our father. We don't like what he did, but he's still our father."

I recognized she was trying to be rational so that I'd be rational. It's her way of trying to handle the family situation, by taking responsibility for my emotional stability.

She glanced down and picked up my sunglasses saying, "Look, Mom, here they are." I thought, well, at least it confirms that I was looking for them; proof that I'm not totally whacked out.

I got home around 1 p.m. with my groceries and Michelle hadn't come yet to get her dog. I decided to take the dogs to my farm field that goes behind the Big House. I would drive right up and let the dogs run.

En route to the Big House, I passed Michelle and Pierre on the road so we pulled over and transferred her dog to their car. I told her I was having a big problem with their "party" for their dad at his place. I told Michelle I would watch the party from my field. She said, "Oh, Mom...," which for Michelle's communication style meant, "We can't help this."

Totally obsessed and distraught, the only thought going through my mind was, "I'm not going to have it, I'm not going to have it!" I drove up on my land to the field right behind his pool and let Spooky out. I stood by the fence staring at my family who had just gathered around the picnic table outside. They didn't look at me, but they all knew I was there. Within moments, they all got up and left -- each in their own cars.

As I felt more and more despondent, I wandered through my greenhouse. It was too hot to hoe my garden, so I decided to wash my empty pots to get organized for next season. I washed pots for a while and then decided I should write since my emotions continued to rage.

So here I am. If I'd had a gun when my kids got in their cars and drove down his driveway, I think I would have shot myself. I'm remembering a lifeline that a friend gave me several months ago when I was barely hanging on. He told me that at the worst point in the breakup of his first marriage, he sat in his barn with a gun to his head. The only thing that kept him from pulling the trigger was thoughts of his children. When he told me the story, he said, "What if I'd done that? I wouldn't have fallen in love again; I wouldn't have this wonderful life that I have."

Sometimes though, there seems to be no amount of rational thought or logic that can overcome the angst. The solution pounding in my head is to end my life.

It would be a pathetic, senseless ending to my book.

It's just a day. When it passes everything will be fine. Maybe I will laugh again and I won't care what he does. Maybe I'll be grateful that I'm free. Maybe I'll forgive my kids. Maybe they'll forgive me. Maybe life will be exciting and I'll have fun again. Maybe I'll do good and make life better for someone else. I don't know.

**Later --**

Around 5 p.m. while talking with Nancy on the telephone, the call forwarding beep (new on my phone) came through and I took the call. It was my Michelle and Molly calling from Molly's place. They were checking in on me and struggling for what to say. They suggested I call Debbie. I said I'd be OK. I told them my emotions were stronger than my logic and I'd keep talking to my friends and writing. They labeled this a "bad day" for everyone.

When I called Debbie she commented that often what I want to hear is some negative comment about my ex. But it will come from my friends, not my kids.

As I write, I realize that poor communication has long been a problem in our family. I realize, too, that I did all the wrong things today. I created real psychological problems for myself; every button was punched up and I was totally primed. And lots of other "wrong things" just happened as well. And the irony -- what are the chances of it all happening the way it did? The way our paths intersected and the timing? It was meant to happen.

**June 17, 1996**

Still simmering in yesterday's turmoil, the early morning walk with Margaret and our dogs brought some relief. Then a heart-to-heart talk with Nancy released most of everything toxic left in me.

Before having lunch with Gerry, I made a quick stop to see how my garage construction project was going. As I was leaving, my ex drove up to the office and gave me a dirty look. I did a U-turn and gave him a cold stare right back and mouthed, "You bastard." I wanted him know that I can look at my own property whenever I want. Just then I noticed that the girlfriend had come out of the office and was taping me with the video camera! I drove straight home and called the police station and said, "I want to report harassment."

About an hour later, Gerry and I invited the Sheriff Deputy into my home to tell him what had happened. I told him that I felt threatened by her harassment and that I'd called my lawyer. The deputy said he would talk to the girlfriend and ask her to stop videotaping me and he'd call me later today.

I believe I did the right thing. I think she's trying to build a harassment case against me by whipping out the video camera each time I'm in their vicinity. I guess she videotaped my mean look and angry curse to my ex.

I have a right to be on my own property and look at anything I want. I told the deputy, "I don't want to be pushed around by them. I am standing my ground."

At 2 p.m., the deputy called to say they must take long lunch breaks because they still hadn't returned. He is going to try to talk to the girlfriend, again, tomorrow. My anger is alive and kicking.

**June 18, 1996**

Here are this morning's thoughts about how my ex has injured our family for his own "youth pleasures."

*Garrick,*

*Even an apology to your children cannot erase the painful scar you inflicted. Your immoral relationship with a girl younger than your daughters has embarrassed and humiliated your children. We all walk with a tomahawk lodged in our backs. But as long as I have life, I'll stand my ground.*

*Allowing your girlfriend to videotape me standing my ground while on my own land vividly contradicts the intended use of the video camera since I had purchased it to give to Jeffrey to film his happy, innocent baby, Justin.*

*Just look at yourself.*

**June 19, 1996**

It's been two weeks since I've spoken with Debbie and I'm really anxious to talk to her tonight. Molly told me she'd called Debbie to get help on the Father's Day disaster. Molly wants to talk about it next week.

**June 20, 1996**

The upshot of my talk with Debbie last night:

*Dear Michelle, Pierre, Molly,*

*I am neither proud nor ashamed of my honest emotions. The problem is that I need to find a way to throw them off track by my own intellectual coercion.*

*My feelings are legitimate, but I know they don't work for me. Taken to the last degree, they still don't work for me. What has happened to me absolutely sucks -- that's why my story will make an interesting book and movie.*

*On the other hand, my recovery has progressed in the face of a monstrous situation; with the help of my counselor, my lawyer, my friends and my own honesty. To let go of the monstrous situation, I have to defy my feelings and pretend I accept this life -- warts and all. In so doing, I do it for your sake, but I'll also do it for my own sake. Some day all Father's Days will be filled with something good for me.*

*Dancing free is the best revenge, but for some reason, I haven't been able to dance completely free until you all really know how very hard it is for me to learn the steps.*

*I love you,*

*Mom*

*P.S. May life's most complex steps come easily and gracefully to you.*

**June 24, 1996**

The Sheriff Deputy's red and white patrol car was still in my driveway when Chip and David Selby drove up yesterday at noon. The deputy had come to my house to tell me what had happened with my complaint from last week. He said, "I called the town police and they said Garrick had demanded my arrest on harassment charges." The deputy explained to them that I had also complained of being harassed by the girlfriend with the video camera and that neither Garrick's charges nor mine were really valid "harassment." The officers all decided they weren't going to arrest me or get in the middle of the situation.

I referred to my ex as "That bastard," said, "Thank you very much," to the deputy and we walked to his car and met the Selbys just emerging from theirs.

This latest entry to my story was a rather dramatic scene on a gorgeous day -- and the timing was incredible. Pastoral views, perfect 75 degree temperature, Spooky cheerfully greeting the guests, serenity all around us and yet, jabbed in the middle of it all, was the deputy's patrol car in my driveway and his nerve-rattling visit regarding my ex's threat to have me arrested.

The beautiful day won control of the happenings, nonetheless, and we went on to have a wonderful day. We toured the locations mentioned in the book, visited with Lyrysa about the editing and writing of the book and had dinner at the Swiss Hutte with our mutual good friends, Stu and Diane Benedict.

News from Michelle that her dog had died following surgery made for a very sad phone call at the end of the day and my heart ached for my daughter's loss. She loved her dog very much.

I'm satisfied with the world on this glorious morning at 6 a.m.; sounds of birds, more perfect weather, a relaxed Spooky, a good cup of coffee, lounging on my couch in my home that I love and writing. The Selby's spent the night and are still sleeping. It is quite possible that nature will entertain us with wild turkey, deer and breathtaking scenery as we trek over the farm fields with Margaret and our dogs at 7:30 a.m., our first plan for the day.

Drifting back in thought to the "harassment" charges, it seems that my ex actually views himself as a victim and that his ears are offended when "bastard" is directed at him. He doesn't like me calling him bastard, giving him dirty looks, standing my ground, fighting for my rights. Perhaps he justifies his behavior with his own perception of how "right" he is to have what he wants, no matter how he goes about getting it. Therefore, he believes everyone should accept his choices and even support him. I think he finds my dirty look threatening because it doesn't give him the approval he seeks. He wants total control and everything his way. In the end, he cannot.

**June 23, 1996**

For the first time that I can recall, Debbie got tough and "talked turkey" with me last night. She said that for my kids' sake, for their mental health, they need a relationship with their father and I must allow it to happen.

She expressed sympathy with my kids' position and stressed to me that she didn't want me to display such negative behavior again. She said, "That behavior from you won't be tolerated. It's not acceptable."

Debbie also gave me solid advice. She said, "Don't allow him to come between you and your kids. It puts them in a triangle and they can't 'fix it.'" She reminded me that only I can change myself, fill up my spaces and relieve myself of a destiny of pain and anger.

I have the power to let go. I'm confident that now my kids better understand what I have experienced and I am not diminished in any way by communicating my emotions to them.

Instead of being locked in a depressing dungeon, I can think about forgiving my ex for the escalating list of actions that have betrayed my every confidence and beliefs I've developed over a lifetime. I am grateful for the gift of children and the joy of freedom. I live well with myself.

I did laugh when a friend related a snippet of conversation overheard at a recent party. Someone asked, "Who is that over there?" Glancing across the room at my ex and the girlfriend, someone else said, "Oh, that's Garrick Belt and his cow."

For today, I do not wish my ex well nor do I wish him bad.

**June 30, 1996**

Excellent visits with Michelle and Molly this past week perhaps put to rest another piece of my recovery. Molly invited me to lunch on Tuesday at the Red Lion Inn. She brought up the Father's Day stuff early on and we didn't allow emotions to get in the way of a good discussion or a good meal.

Molly was very skillful. Debbie had told her that I have a right to express myself and that I'm sane and my feelings are real. Molly displayed much more empathy and sympathy for me. I spoke about how I can manage my feelings differently. We both recognized things we could have done better. Our discussion was helpful and very loving.

And I've just returned from visiting Michelle. It's invigorating to be with my kids in ways that are about them. I learned a lot about what's currently going on in their lives. It's gratifying to be more resolved.

**July 4, 1996**

Rain fouled our plans for tennis, but I loved having a quiet day to plan.

While straightening up my desk, I ran across a list I'd made several months ago:

### 12 STEPS TO RECOVERING FROM A DIVORCE

1. *Find an effective counselor.*
2. *Lean on a strong network of family and friends.*
3. *Get a good lawyer.*
4. *Begin journaling, writing or keeping a diary.*
5. *Nurture a pet or plants.*
6. *Engage in a hobby, crafts or sports.*
7. *Explore honesty, feel the feelings.*
8. *Try something new, take a class.*
9. *Discover creative ways to deal with problems.*
10. *Treat yourself special.*
11. *Set small goals and enjoy the accomplishments to rebuild self-esteem.*
12. *Help someone else as soon as you can, let go of your own pain, let life go on.*

I felt revitalized after reading my list again.

## July 11, 1996

Too much radon, too much bacteria in the well water, some carpenter ants and a leak in the roof were the negative points from the house inspector's report. None of it must be too bad or I must be lucky to be alive! Still, it's a little discouraging to have these faults show up in the tests. Victor is taking charge of the various corrections and repairs. He's the best. He keeps everything in clear perspective and he's so rational. I know these are serious faults to be dealt with before the sale of house, but it's all stuff that can be fixed. Hopefully, the buyers will be equally optimistic.

Plans are underway for my big party on September 7th. I'm going to host the party on my newly acquired farmland; a cookout and potluck supper with dancing. The fire department is going to grill chicken and corn-on-the-cob, I've rented a big tent, I'm inquiring about a good disc jockey for dancing and Margaret is making photo postcards of me and Spooky for the invitations.

For me, this party is a gesture of my gratitude to my friends and a celebration of my new life. I've decided an appropriate theme is "Independence Day -- a little late!" I'd love to have fireworks at the end of the evening but I'm reluctant to spend the money. I really don't have a clear handle on my current or future budget yet. There have been so many extras that could erode my principal. I want to be secure but still choose some "risks." So fireworks are not a good choice for me now, but it's fun to imagine them.

## July 22, 1996

My Winterhawk guests have just departed. When I operated the summer weekend B&B at the Big House, I developed friendships with some of the regular guests including Barry, Nan and Ben. They are connected with the annual three-day bluegrass music event -- The Winterhawk Festival -- held on a farm field a few miles from Falls Town. Bluegrass fans from around the country come to enjoy live performances from their favorite musicians. Most of the festival-goers pitch their tents on the huge field and camp out, while the others quickly fill every available hotel, motel and guest room in the area.

For years, Barry and his friends have relied on me for housing during the festival and we have stayed in contact through the other seasons, too. Without the B&B the past few summers, I have invited Barry, Nan and Ben to stay at my house. We talk, play tennis, eat together and have a wonderful time. I've shared my ongoing story with them and they've met many of my friends. So even though we see each other only once a year, the bonds of our friendship are very strong.

**August 9, 1996**

I've spent the last four days in Maine at Flora and Herb's summer camp. Herb was away taking care of some work, so Flora and I could do whatever struck our fancy, not to mention a few solid days of "girl talk." We enjoyed perfect weather, the gorgeous lake, delicious meals, wine and delightful conversations. Then we discovered the sailboat! It took us a little while to get it out and up and running but then came the exciting fun. Once Flora and I were "at sea," the wind carried us skimming across the big clear lake, bordered, naturally, with boulders, large trees and rocks. Flora insisted that I could effectively guide the sailboat using the rudder and the sail and for a while she was right. But as I was trying to direct us to return to her dock, the boat suddenly flipped, tossing me and Flora out. The sailboat slid away and crashed into the rocks on her shore. Our heads popped out of the water and we quickly noted everything, including us and the boat, was still intact. Then we laughed ourselves silly.

**August 11, 1996**

For weeks now, Flora has been clipping G.B. Trudeau's "Doonesbury" comic strips for me from her newspaper. It's a hilarious parallel of my experience. The main character, Mike, becomes involved with a very young woman, Kim. I think Mike is divorced already, or at least separated, but it's the age difference between Mike and Kim where Trudeau finds the funny stuff.

The characters are generations apart so they frequently don't understand each other's vocabulary. They bungle and humorously explain to each other their own terminology and lingo. All the while, doubt is cast on the viability of their relationship. Eventually, Mike and Kim get married. Their wedding reception becomes an awkward event because of the comments from their guests about the couple's age difference and personality splits. Even when making their champagne toasts, Mike and Kim find some bumps in their relationship.

Anyway, Flora brings the cartoons into the coffee house on Saturday mornings and we read them and laugh and laugh. The similarity to my story is uncanny at times. Flora and I have jokingly wondered how Trudeau manages to get firsthand information about my situation!

**August 18, 1996**

An older couple who've been my friends for years had a dual birthday party at the Swiss Hutte restaurant tonight. Their combined ages were an impressive three-digit number, but it was their expression of love for one another that touched me. When he read a beautiful love poem to her before this group of friends and family, I swallowed a lump in my throat. In our community, they reign as the models for wit, charm, wisdom, devotion, longevity and love.

**September 6, 1996**

A couple of weeks ago I learned that Debbie won't be able to make it here from California after all, but with only a few other exceptions, most of my friends plan to attend my party tomorrow.

I rented a tent from the man I have rented from before and he brought his brand new, fancy, white, big tent. He and his crew put it up today next to my greenhouse on my farm.

Flora has baked a cake decorated with "4th of July" sparklers. The farmer who rents my farmland brought in hay bales for seating. So everything is set for tomorrow. It's exciting!

**September 8, 1996**

It was a PARTY! Fabulous music, wonderful food and most of all, great people. My friends brought tomatoes, salads, cookies and beer and wine. The fire department's barbecue chicken was terrific. We all kicked back and cut loose. And we danced and danced. In fact, the party was a blast because everybody cut loose and people danced like maniacs for hours! George, from the Falls Town Flowers group, was the star on the dance floor. We all had a ton of fun watching him, joining in with him and trying to keep up with him!

It was a light-drinking party; no one got drunk. People were drunk on joy for me and there was a huge amount of happiness expressed overall.

The DJ I hired was talented at getting everybody up and dancing. The folks from the church danced, Pastor Esther danced, all the little kids danced, Lilly, Nancy and Flora danced. Victor came and most of the staff from his office did too, so all the paralegals and secretaries danced. My friends and I celebrated vivaciously. People stayed until 11 p.m. or so until the music was done.

For several hours before the party began it seemed that nature was not going to cooperate. High winds and a storm brushed through the area. The tent poles kept blowing down and a few people didn't show because of the weather. But an hour or so before the party, the clouds moved away, the air calmed and the evening was beautiful.

## September 9, 1996

It was only a hug, but I felt it for 20 minutes -- all the way to my shopping destination in Great Barrington. I had stopped by to see Paul at his house and he was underneath his RV working on it. He slid out from underneath when he saw my feet approaching. I asked him if he might consider doing the plumbing on the farmhouse in my conversion of it from the office into my home. I said, "I know you're officially retired, but maybe you'd do it for old time's sake." He smiled sideways at me and said, "But I don't have my tools anymore." Nevertheless, he said he'd think about it and maybe he could do it along with another plumber. Just before I got in my car, he gave me a hug.

Paul is the one man I have an interest in, but he's a question that needs exploring. Is he involved with someone else? He did have a lady friend, but I don't know if they're still together. Does he have the characteristics I want? Would he be interested in me? So far, I like what I see <u>and feel</u>, but I really don't know. On the rare occasions that I see him, we have nice chitchat and he always hugs me. I think these hugs feel more intimate each time; but that's it, that's all I'm going on.

## September 11, 1996

On my way to visit a sick friend in the hospital and bring him flowers from my garden, I saw Paul in his driveway so I pulled in to say hello. Paul saw the flowers in my car and wanted to cut a few from his garden to add to my bouquet. He led me around the back of his house and into his garden. It felt romantic and private. He cut a few more flowers and as I was turning to leave he hugged me and gave me a pat on the rear. I was surprised, but his familiarity has fueled my interest.

## September 13, 1996

September 27th is the date being mentioned for the closing on my house, but it's not set. I'm going ahead with my move and I'll complete it on Sunday with Chris' help if the weather is OK. I'll sleep over at Nancy's until the office, my home-to-be, is vacated by my ex and the girlfriend at the end of this month. Today, I sold the king size bed I've been sleeping on, which had been "ours," with no regrets and some relief. It was too darn big and I was done with it.

With the news of the possible closing on the 27th, I stopped by to tell Paul because he plans to be traveling to visit his children in the next couple of weeks and the bathtub installation will be my top plumbing priority once I move in.

We stood in his driveway and talked about the plumbing schedule. He said the last time I was there, people saw me as they drove past and asked who that white-haired woman was. He told them, "My grandmother."

He said, "People will talk, but I don't care." I said, "If it involves me, they will for sure."

The hug we exchanged as we parted left me wishing for more. He patted Spooky and nothing else happened. I'm going to Flora's for dinner.

**September 14, 1996**

I'm giggling to myself because I'm using every little piece of new information on my farmhouse project to stop by Paul's place and "update" him -- as the project's plumber, of course. Little bits like potential house closing dates, carpentry schedules, bathtub ordering details, etc. It's all an excuse to visit him and I know I'm creating reasons to see him.

**September 20, 1996**

I'm having a natural wood picket fence installed around the parameters of my farm property so that Spooky will have a safe place to be outside and to give the farmhouse some landscaping distinction. It's looking beautiful but the fence installers have had their share of problems. Twice they've hit phone wires that run underground on the farm property. The lines were laid very shallowly a pretty long time ago and there weren't maps of where the lines were located. They must have figured back then that the field would stay a field and they ran them every which way. Each time the fence installers have hit the wires, the area's phone service has been out for hours! The phone outages even made the local paper. I knew they were a serious problem and I felt terrible, but they were accidents.

After the second time it happened and everyone was going haywire, I sighed deeply and said to Lyrysa, "Look at me, I'm fine. I can't be penetrated by severe problems anymore."

Meanwhile, my ex continues to be pigheaded and is causing more headaches for the fence installers. He and the girlfriend park their cars right up next to the farmhouse building in an area that I plan to enclose within the fence. The fence installers asked if they would please move their vehicles so they could finish installing the fence without enclosing their vehicles. It meant parking their vehicles about 20 feet further from the door. My ex said, "Absolutely not! And if you complete the fence, I'll ram it down with my truck."

His obstinacy knows no bounds. So, in about eleven days, when my ex and the girlfriend are finally out of the office for good, the fence installers can return and complete the fence.

**September 23, 1996**

Imagining the book and its cover, I asked Brian, Lyrysa's boyfriend, to take some pictures. Brian is not only a fine photographer, but also a young, spirited friend and I'm very comfortable with him. Brian selected the date in late September as the ideal time for my concept to be achieved. We had already explored the site -- my farmland on the hill, in the uppermost hay field. The land is planted alternately with a wide strip of hay and a wide strip of cow corn, which gives the hill a striped appearance from afar. The top hay field has beautiful views of the valley, the village of Falls Town and the mountain range stretching all the way to the Berkshires foothills. It also has a little privacy because of the tall corn stalks.

Judy was visiting yesterday so I asked her to joined Brian, Lyrysa and me for our risqué evening shoot. Spooky came along, too. The sky was beautiful, just before sunset and the corn is tassel-topped and ready to harvest. Brian and Lyrysa established the best location for me to stand. I slipped off my hiking boots, dropped my robe and raised my arms "dancing free." Brian clicked away, Judy kept a look out, Lyrysa choreographed my moves, Spooky bounded back and forth and I danced naked in the field. As we hiked down the hill, we were all a little giddy and pleased with contemplating the results.

We were concerned that the evening light was a little flat so we decided to repeat the process this morning at 6 a.m. Nature cooperated perfectly.

There was mist in the air, fog on the mountains, a dewy twinkle to the earth and the clouds broke to reveal a gorgeous orange and pink sunrise. We all felt confident that we got the cover shot for the book.

**September 30, 1996**

Today they must be out. What a relief. The house closed on the 27th and it's a done deal. I shouldn't be surprised that my ex would deny me the ability to enter the farmhouse office until he received the check at the closing, but now that he has his check, it does make me shake my head in astonishment.

At any rate, I was left with almost zero time to execute my physical "move" from the house to the office -- my new home.

Little by little, over the past couple of weeks, the overwhelming task of moving was managed with the help of my dear friends. Fortunately, the new garage that I had built behind the farmhouse is complete so basically everything I own has been moved into it. Back at my old house, Ann helped me clean out the attic and move some heavy stuff from the barn. Ed gave us a hand with his trailer. Ana and George came with their pickup truck one day last week and we moved the stuff I'd stored in the coach house. All my tennis friends loaded up their cars with boxes when they came to play tennis at my old house for the last time.

**October 6, 1996**

My new smaller mattress was still on the floor of my house during the closing. Ed and the new owners (who I think will be new friends) helped me get it over to my new home. The first night, October 1st, I stayed with Nancy. Then over the past week, just as friends had helped me move out, they also helped me move in.

Friends stop by and we spend a few minutes lugging boxes or a piece of furniture from the garage to the house. Chris and I managed the heaviest pieces for my upstairs bedroom and office a few days ago. Shirley was sure that she and I could handle the big Oriental rug for the guest bedroom. We did get it in place but only after she fell backwards and was pinned down by the heavy rug on top of her. We were weak with laughter and very glad she wasn't hurt.

Kent sawed the legs off the dining room table to make a grand coffee table. Cathy stopped by more than once to cart boxes into the house and cheered me with humorous conversation and interesting treats -- like root beer and ice cream floats.

Currently, my house has no kitchen, no tub or shower, no laundry room -- just a tiny sink. But my church friends gave me a microwave, Marty and Kent gave me a stove and refrigerator they no longer needed from their New York City apartment and Brian gave me a perfectly wonderful kitchen sink that someone else was getting rid of. The bathtub, a large luxurious claw foot, has been ordered and hopefully Paul will do the installation plumbing once it arrives.

**October 14, 1996**

Life is so exciting, I'm bubbling inside and out. My new home is wonderful. My long holiday weekend was great. The tag sale that Debbie, Cathy, Margaret, Shirley and I held in the greenhouse was successful. It felt good to sell off some stuff. The fall foliage is fantastic. The fence installers returned to finish off the last piece of fence and now the wooden fence around the house and farm property is complete. And Paul has agreed to install the claw foot bathtub I've ordered.

When I stopped by to ask him, he looked incredibly good to me and his hug surged a renewal of all the chemistry I feel for him and coming from him. I can't remember when I've felt such excitement for a man. It's schoolgirl stuff that I can't explain, it's just what it is.

He's going to stop by my house soon to check out the plumbing. I have no idea if this is just a one-sided interest but it's so good to be tingling with romantic possibilities.

**October 15, 1996**

I'm thinking about Paul and remembering how I first met him many years ago. In 1983, after I'd ordered the plans for our house (the one I just sold) and we'd purchased the property, I found a great local builder, Don, who was my contractor for that project (and all my projects since). He gathered the construction crew that built the house and Paul was the plumber. After the house was finished, we hosted a little party for the contractor and subcontractors and their wives. Paul came with his wife and I found quick friendship with her. Two weeks later she died suddenly. I was shocked. I expressed my sorrow to Paul at the funeral home.

Over the next dozen years, Paul has been the plumber on a number of projects that I've been involved with. I have never known him well, I only knew he maintained a pretty home and garden, he was a respected member of the church and community, he had a nice family and was occasionally seen with a lady friend. I liked him and found him attractive, as, perhaps, many people did.

**October 16, 1996**

I'm trying to focus on the projects for my new home. I got propane gas installed for the stove and I've selected kitchen cabinets. My priority list after that includes getting the tub installed and the bathroom complete. It will be nice to get clean at home. Later on, I plan to build a tennis court, install a stereo system using the in-wall speakers left by my ex and convert the old office's mini-kitchen space into a laundry room.

## October 21, 1996

A realization for today: I've been learning through my recovery to love myself and in so doing, I have grown more accepting of all kinds of other people -- different ages, backgrounds, economic levels. At the same time, I have become clearer and more able to direct my "wants." I can be civil to people I do not respect. But I don't eat shit. I've come a long way and I'm happy with my choices.

## October 25, 1996

At the end of our telephone counseling session last night, Debbie said, "You know, you don't need me anymore." I said, "I'm noticing that, but it's fun to talk to you." We agreed to talk again in two weeks to update the "Paul situation." She's rooting for me to establish a relationship with a man for whom I have tons of chemistry, but she says if this one doesn't work out, there will be others. She emphasized if it doesn't work out, it doesn't mean that I'm not desirable. Many other factors could enter in to it for either person. I agree.

My sense is that he shares the chemistry and feels it too, but perhaps is not able to act on it. I have laid all my cards on the table face up and it feels good to be alive! Just the thought of Paul sends ripples of heat and sensations through my body. I told Debbie that I have more chemistry for Paul than I ever remember having for my ex. This chemistry exists even without ever having sex with him. I don't understand it.

**October 28, 1996**

Lyrysa and Brian came for dinner armed with the "Dancing Naked" photos that Brian had taken for the book cover. I had to laugh at myself -- 61 years old, nude, somewhat misshapen, head tossed back, arms to the sky, Spooky at my side, on my hill, next to the cornfield, overlooking the quaint village of Falls Town!

The photographs display the mountains perfectly and the misty morning air and early golden light are beautiful. We managed to find a couple of angles of me that seem to represent the right spirit and message of my book.

We called California to touch base with Chip and David Selby. The most current piece of news from them was that a letter had been sent to Joanne Woodward regarding another project, but including an inquiry for our project, too. I'm so flattered that they visualize Joanne Woodward playing me in the movie -- what a wonderful compliment.

They are waiting to receive more chapters of the book and the transcripts of the trial that are being printed before they begin working on a screenplay. David said he remains very optimistic about the book and its potential because it has "great soul."

As terrible as it's been to live through, my present joy obliterates the pain. I have no qualms in telling the story.

Sometimes, it definitely seems I'm in fantasyland, but, what the hell, it's fun.

**October 29, 1996**

When I woke up this morning, I said, "Today is the day. I know Paul will come over." And at 10:30 a.m., he did. He stayed long enough to check out the space where the bathtub will be installed, he explored the feasibility of my kitchen sink plans and then he hugged me. Well, it was a little more than one hug. We hugged when he arrived, then again in the kitchen and the bathroom and the basement. Then before he left, I got the really big body hug, plus a kiss and now I'm totally charged. Every hormone I have is racing through my body like fast, powerful, sleek, sexy sports cars. Just when the excitement quiets down a bit, it reignites, hot, with just a thought.

I can't believe I have this much sexuality. I haven't even had sex! He knows he turns me on or, at least, I certainly think he's picked up on it by my actions and reactions. I'm practically palpitating when I'm near him. For now, we've agreed to see what happens next.

Before he left, he said, "We're worlds apart." I asked, "What do you mean?" He said, "You're so social and I'm not." I said, "I'm country -- I love a hike in the woods and a campfire."

We stood in an embrace in the kitchen while my boom box played Tracy Lawrence's "Stars Over Texas" -- Lilly's gift to encourage my romantic life.

I asked, "Are you a dancer?" He said, "I used to be."

The notion of dancing with him in my kitchen is wildly appealing -- dancing alone in my kitchen is tremendous, too. I am OK on my own, but I'm sure I can be an awesome partner in every way. Somebody out there is going to get lucky. Maybe it will be Paul.

I'm brimming with tantalizing soul-stirrings. I told Nancy, Lilly, Lyrysa and Debbie about what's going on. Everyone is thrilled for me. I'm smiling from the inside out.

## October 30, 1996

Celine Dion's "The Power of Love," the Righteous Brothers' "Unchained Melody," and Tracy Lawrence's "Stars Over Texas," are the songs that send romantic sensations through me for Paul. I am so physically attracted to him. And I still don't know if he's right for me in other ways, but I can't wait to find out. I feel fabulous just knowing that I still "have it" -- hormones, attraction, lustiness, spine-tingles, fun and the ability to pull them together with a little creative planning.

Margaret has been a wonderful sounding board for my total inexperience in the "men" department. She has a depth of knowledge with the gutsy honesty to share it. Our morning walks with our dogs have proven to be an incredible piece of my recovery and a solid forging of our friendship.

My house is transforming each day into a beautiful cozy home. I ordered the kitchen cabinets and Don, my longtime contractor, is willing to do the carpentry. Paul is committed to doing the plumbing. He plans to visit his son in Virginia again and I'm willing to wait until his return. Never mind that I still have no tub or shower or kitchen sink. Washing at the little bathroom sink is working and with occasional showers at Nancy's and Margaret's, I'm keeping somewhat clean. I really miss getting in a tub to soak so I bought myself some great bubble bath in anticipation of that luxury.

## October 31, 1996

Waking up in the middle of the night, I reached over for Paul, but, of course, no one was there. But he was in my mind to be there. I wonder if my imagination is totally unrealistic? Do I believe what I believe because I want to believe it? Debbie says, "Trust your instincts. You're right on target, you're instincts have been right." But is this instinct or desire?

I need to keep all parts of my life balanced, but I admit, I have Paul on my mind a good share of the time, which brings surges of sensuality and romantic emotions rippling through my body.

I've hired a cleaning service to clean the basement and I set up the delivery of the soil mix for my greenhouse. Sarah and her helper worked in my perennial flowerbed next to the house and I've raked most of my leaves. I'm carving out this good life and I'm very pleased with my new home.

**November 1, 1996**

More than 200 kids came to my house "trick or treating" for Halloween last night. I ran out of candy and then out of dimes and nickels and quarters, so I turned out my lights to discourage any more. I loved having the kids and their parents come to my house; next year I'll get more candy.

Today, I signed up for Social Security. I'll get $430 per month from my ex's Social Security and if he dies, I'll get his full share automatically. I drove past Paul's house and his car was there but I didn't stop. I don't want to be "pushy," but I hope he'll stop by my house sometime today. I have planned my day to be relative free, so we'll see.

**12:30 p.m.** -- I called Paul and asked how his tick bite looked. He'd mentioned it when I last saw him.

He said, "I was going to call when I finished my lunch. Are you home this afternoon?" Perfect. He'll be here soon.

OK, I've done a few things in preparation. I brushed my teeth -- again, and freshened up a bit at my tiny sink with my Evelyn Crabtree body gel.

I also put on the Celine Dion CD. As I put the disk in the machine, I realized the irony of me using this recording. It's the CD I took from my husband's office to find out what type of music he was playing there when he was alone with the filing clerk. I discovered the case was empty when I got it home, the disk still in the machine at his office. So I bought the CD to hear what it was like. It is, in fact, wonderfully romantic.

I'm remembering Margaret's advice, "Don't go for the 'mercy screw.'" I'm pretty sure that wouldn't be me. I don't have desire for a man simply to "have a man." It's just that Paul really charges me.

Debbie says, "You'll know when it's right." I'll decide if the opportunity comes up.

**2 p.m.** -- Paul looked kind of cute when he stopped by, wearing his funky baseball cap, work shirt and he looks particularly good in his jeans. After a few good hugs, I asked if he wanted to "talk." He said, "Not now... on Monday." He said his daughter's birthday celebration was coming up over the weekend and he was getting ready for it by cleaning up his house.

He showed me where the tick had bitten him on his leg. In fact, he undid his belt, unzipped his jeans and dropped them to his knees to show me the place on his thigh. It was an amazingly bad bite with some infection, but I also noticed he has great legs. It seemed a very bold move to show me in the way he did, but I'm trying not to make too much of it. It just shows he's comfortable with me.

After he left, I felt a little disappointed. I'm slightly frustrated with not enough affirmation of his physical or emotional feelings for me. My reality check: I suspect his weekend birthday party may include his lady friend. Perhaps he has a conversation planned. Perhaps he feels awkward dealing with two women.

My friends advise me to go slow. I say it's hard for me, but I'm trying. Paul said he woke up in the middle of the night and I <u>didn't</u> say, "So did I," even though I did.

**November 4, 1996**

Paul called to say he and Dick (another plumber) would be over around noon to plan the plumbing for the tub, which is due to arrive this week. His voice sounded wonderful. So far, I like the way he looks, sounds, smells, tastes and feels. We still haven't "talked" and he leaves tomorrow for another two weeks at his son's in Virginia. Margaret gave me breath freshener to be ready, just in case, and my friends have given me all kinds of advice and encouragement.

**12:30 p.m.** -- They came together in the same car. Paul didn't touch me until they were leaving; then he looked me in the eye and squeezed my hand on the way out the door. My gut instinct is that he'll come back but that could just be my wish. My entire body tingles with desire for him. He looked so incredibly good to me. His attitude toward me was happy and connected. Oh, who knows? I feel a little sad.

After sharing my feelings with Lyrysa on the phone, my best logical conclusion is that he's backing off, but still has the feelings. Lyrysa said, "The day's not over," meaning it both literally and figuratively. But we both thought it's probably "over" as far as something happening today with him. I'm reluctant to fill the space in the rest of my day by making a different plan, though. That's my shred of hope.

I learned today that one of my school classmates died this week. She was 61 years old, like me. She was vivacious and happy and died of cancer too soon in life. Nancy went to one of her friend's funeral this week, too.

And yet, I am, and my friends are, healthy and energetic and alive, and we have fun by simply planning it. There is no reason to focus on such a slight disappointment as "Paul's decision." I really have everything I could ever want right now. I have every reason to enjoy the good life I have to the hilt. I'm glad to be taking this renewed look at myself and my life. It's something the dead give us, like a gift.

I put a peppier CD on the boom box and now I'm looking forward to seeing Lyrysa again later to work on the book.

**November 14, 1996**

I am bursting from the inside out, heart pounding -- I rise to dance and smile, it's beyond contentment. It's as much as I can hold in happy excitement. The day had many possibilities even before Paul called at 7:30 a.m., but his call from Virginia set my spirits soaring. The power of his voice traveled spontaneously through my body, igniting every sensation along the way. He said, "It's good to hear your voice." I asked, "When are you coming home?" He said, "Probably Sunday, I'll call you." I said, "Good."

If that wasn't enough to start my day, the next call I made to the local newspaper filled my head with creative excitement. My suggestion to put a different slant on the press release to promote the church's annual Christmas Bazaar was met with praise for my "great concept." Within an hour, plans with the editor were underway to feature my story in as much length as I choose to make it and with photos to accompany it. Now I have an important writing assignment. It's a great day.

Later on, we're going to load up our tag sale leftovers for the battered women's shelter in our area. The items will help the women create their "fresh start" in different living situations. I am so pleased to contribute to this cause.

## November 18, 1996

Today I woke up still dreaming. In my dream, Jean initiated a warm conversation with my ex. I balked momentarily with thoughts of her as a traitor and then I accepted the reality that people will talk to both me and my ex. Lying awake, wondering about the dream, I consciously took some responsibility for the breakup of my marriage without assuming any blame. It felt like squeezing the last drops out of a wet rag.

Then my mood shifted and my emotions flooded over to Paul. Watching the sunrise from my kitchen window just now, I like myself.

**11 a.m.** -- The mail today included the first words from Garrick in more than a year. They were:

> *Alice,*
>
> *Rather than you hearing it on the street, I wanted to tell you that I will be getting engaged the first of the year. I have also informed the kids.*
>
> *Garrick*

I am completely validated.

## November 22, 1996

It's been two nights since I had sex with the second man in my life -- Paul. I know it was absolutely great because I can't stop smiling and yet, I cannot recall the details. We had nothing to drink and I don't understand why I can't recall exactly what happened. When I told my counselor, Debbie, about it, she couldn't explain it either. She theorized it might be something like what happens to trauma victims -- a super strong emotional burst that shuts down memory.

**November 23, 1996**

Working on the "Discovery" chapter for book is a minor torture treatment. Lyrysa has asked me to do some fill-in writing. I'm to flush out my precise behavior and provide more details of my actions and thought processes at the time when I found the key for the locked file cabinet and opened it. It's making me sick again as I vividly recall that experience. At the very same time as I'm putting myself in that painful place of more than two years ago, I'm wondering if Paul will call.

I just washed my face. The tears were burning on my cheeks and I want to look my best -- just in case. I'll deal with working on the scenic bits and emotional details for my story when I recover a little. Sometimes Lyrysa and I write together to better "paint the picture" of key events in the past. Other times it's up to me to recall and relive the moments and write about them myself. I've done enough for today. I can only do a little at a time. It's wrenching.

**6 p.m.** -- Paul called. God, it was good to hear his voice. He can't see me until Monday, but he said nothing has hit him this hard in a very long time. I said, "Paul, for some reason, I am also completely overwhelmed." We'd both spent the day thinking about each other. I was so relieved to get his call and I'm more secure now about my instincts about our mutual feelings for each other. I was beginning to fear that he was having second thoughts and I was bracing myself to "get over it." Excitement is flourishing in me again.

## November 26, 1996

On my own, I've made good decisions. I love my choice of property, I made smart financial moves and I decided I'd have sex if the opportunity to be with a wonderful man came along. So, I'm smiling and he's whistling. I admitted to Paul that I couldn't remember the details of the first time we made love together. I asked him last night, "Did I do this?" He said, "Oh yeah!" And we laughed and cuddled through the most incredible sex I've ever had.

I'm 61 and amazingly free. It's hard to say where it's all going, but I think I'm the best thing that could happen to him and I know he's very good for me, too. I'm not worried about getting hurt by him, no matter what happens. He's making my good life better. How lucky I am.

A friend sent me the book "All Things Are Possible, Pass The Word" by Barbara Milo Ohrback. I particularly liked the Old English prayer on page 64:

*Take time to be friendly,*
*It is the road to happiness.*
*Take time to dream,*
*It is hitching your wagon to a star.*
*Take time to love and be loved,*
*It is the privilege of the gods.*
*Take time to look around,*
*It is too short a day to be selfish.*
*Take time to laugh,*
*It is the music of the soul.*

**December 1, 1996**

*Dear Michelle,*

*A strange result of being so profoundly hurt is a payoff in boundless spirited optimism that spreads across every aspect of my life. I can't help it that I am left without prejudice, I am clear about who my enemies are. I can stand naked, I am sexually without bounds and there is no more failure for me. No one would choose to be so "lucky," nor would have I, but my honesty and realness are how I've earned my good fortune. Now I have something that is priceless. If I can pass on what I have experienced in order to help other people, then just think of its value.*

*Michelle, I don't think I'll be settling into my old age in a rocking chair in a sleepy town. I think this town will "rock" on what I'm going to do for it. I am bringing honesty to grassroots America and hope will seep into hearts as fears and prejudices will drain out. For this role, as a mover-and-shaker, a person who can make things happen, I am perfect -- old enough, smart enough, pretty enough and rich enough. I am affecting people everyday with my story and I have no doubt that I have a "best seller." And, yes, I am thinking of what I'll wear to "opening night" of the movie.*

*I love you,*

*Mom*

*P.S. I'm even thinking of rebuilding the old movie theater in Falls Town to premiere the movie!*

**December 2, 1996**

I wrote Michelle that letter yesterday after a conversation we had on the telephone. She seems to view all of my excitement about the book and movie possibilities as a "mom-thing." I think she cautions me to not get "too excited" to protect me from being disappointed. But why should I be guarded? It's an element of Michelle's personality. In fact, I think she is so guarded that she stifles herself. Some people are so cautious they can't find a disappointment in their lives. I'm not worried about disappointments that may come my way and I'll continue to try to express that to her. I don't think I'll send the letter, though. I needed to get it off my chest and organize my thoughts and it's served that purpose well.

**December 5, 1996**

Tonight's the night. Paul will soon be here for his first "overnight." I'm playing one of my most romantic CDs, the French clarinetist, Christian Morin Equisse, and I'm wearing my pale blue cashmere sweater. Paul and I plan to "christen" my new tub together tonight and then he's sleeping over.

How did I get so lucky? To be in this place with this man at this time in my life is a heavenly gift to please every particle of my being. So complete in mind, body and soul; every sense filled with life, passion and peace. I am overwhelmed with serenity and gratefulness. Thank you, God.

**December 7, 1996**

My Christmas letter for this year:

*In this season of miracles, I have cause to celebrate. Having made great quantities of lemonade from life's lemons, the party is at my house.*

*Divorced in March after a four-day trial, my good lawyer secured my choice of the farm, the greenhouse and the farmhouse (the former office) for my new home. Garrick chose the Big House right next door and, as he plans to marry the 30-something filing clerk, we are estranged neighbors.*

*I have recovered from one of life's great traumas. I am comfortable here and my life has taken wonderful turns in exciting directions.*

*Not only am I writing a book from my journal notes, detailing the events of the last couple of years, a Hollywood producer is securing the rights to make a movie. The project is on its way and I'm connected with the best people in the business.*

*My blessings have me glowing with love for my children, my grandchild, my family and my many wonderful friends.*

*Optimism without bounds -- laughter and love are mine. I wish each of you the miracles of this season -- joy and hope.*

*Love,*

*Alice*

When I read this letter to Debbie she said, "Do you realize what a difference this year's letter is from last year's?" It gave me pause to recall sitting on the bench outside the courtroom writing my letter last year. My world was uncertain and full of dark corners. A year can fly by so quickly and still feel like a lifetime away.

## December 10, 1996

Thinking about Paul this morning after a great night making love, laughing, a little talking -- I believe in many ways he's not the second man in my life, but the first. Even though I thought I had a satisfying married life, that life is a distant second to my experience with Paul. Passionate kisses, physical ecstasy, insatiable desire for closeness, are all at new levels in this amazing relationship. I say it's him, he says it's us. I can't explain it.

I have learned a lot about Paul. I know he loved his wife deeply. He also adores his children and grandchildren and is very devoted to them. Although he is retired, he is still something of a "workaholic." He enjoys being busy and he has the talent to do any trade. He restores antique cars, renovates old cabins and shacks into livable spaces, builds beautiful birdhouses and loves bluebirds, in particular. He is self-made, patriotic, practical, honest and sexy.

He's described his relationship before me as being "not serious-serious," which confirmed to me my observations of that friendship over the years. He chose to officially end it with her and fortunately, they are still friends. He sat with me at church recently and joined in the socializing afterwards which was a visible sign of his affection for me.

When I claim that the physical attraction is really him not me, he says, "It takes two to tango." He recalled that at first he thought I might be "stiff." I guess he's learned now that I can be about as "un-stiff" as anyone could be.

I am free to be myself freely. I view this as the positive element to come from my situation over the past three years. It's been a definite choice I've made to redefine my life. When I wonder about how it is that one is "set free," I realize my ex could have chosen to be honest with me to set me free. I think of other examples of "setting free" -- a child growing more independent as the parent releases control and steps away from guidance; a caged animal released into the wild again; an inmate released from a prison; an unappreciated employee fired from a stagnant job; or a kidnapped victim, beaten up but thrown from a car alive. But without honesty, kindness, respect, fairness or any regard for my well being -- in fact, in many cases, deliberate actions to be dishonest, deceptive and hurtful -- my ex <u>was</u> successful in thoroughly setting me free. I choose to call it a gift -- that I am emancipated, independent and strong. And yet, it's my choice to seize the opportunity, test my wings, feel my feelings, let go and fly.

**December 16, 1996**

I'm not writing as much as I used to. Perhaps because I'm happy, I'm busy and I need it less for therapy. It's a monumental stack of journal notes that I look at now, near the end of another year. My editor and I continue to work together toward the goal of publishing my story and I stay motivated by hoping that my experience might help someone else.

Looking at the pile of pages on my desk, I realize that my writings from the past three and a half years document that my instincts were on target, even while my belief systems, which were constructed over a lifetime, were shattered.

Learning to live alone and cope alone in a place so foreign at age 60 was a brutal blow. But I'm proud of my choice to "go on" and be active about life. Recovery is a process, but it is real. I measure my recovery in how I feel, what I say, how I look, what my responses are -- like a dipstick into my growth, strength and happiness.

**December 25, 1996**

It's Christmas Day and me and my all my kids and my grandson are in Vermont. They worked out a plan to have their father visit a few days before I arrived, so they've had a kind of double Christmas. Our activities revolve around Justin -- ice skating at a community ice rink, Disney videos and playing with toys. Paul called me yesterday and the kids now know that I have a beau.

**December 28, 1996**

Paul seemed to really enjoy my Christmas gift to him. His enthusiasm for his recently acquired camp on a lake in the Adirondacks prompted my idea -- two lifesaver vests for the canoe. Besides being a fun gift, they are needed and practical. I thought they would represent my hope for a continuing relationship, the "lifesaving" message and the anticipation for fun in the canoe at his place.

Paul and I arrived in Virginia yesterday to spend a couple of days with his son and daughter-in-law. I think I got a "stamp of approval" from them. I love this opportunity to get to know more of his family members.

**January 1, 1997**

Happy, Happy New Year. Ignoring the pitiful lack of snow and our ages, I convinced Paul to stay awake last night until midnight. Then we dragged the toboggan up the hill behind my house and SLID into the New Year! Spooky danced around us as we rolled off the toboggan at the bottom in a heap of laughter. Toasting ourselves and the New Year with champagne, we laughed and loved some more.

**January 5, 1997**

"Lights on, lights off -- I just can't figure what you're up to," my neighbor said to me at a recent party. I started to laugh as I gave Nancy a "knowing" glance and she rolled her eyes and smiled. This neighbor is around my age, but she's very prim and proper. Nancy and I know the lights are on when Paul arrives and we turn them off or light candles as the romantic evening progresses. Reluctant to share the reason to this neighbor, Pastor Esther created an escape for me using an antiquated phrase I hadn't heard in decades. She turned to me and said, "Well, Alice, you're 21, white and free!" I laughed so hard and couldn't wait to share this tidbit with Paul.

My life is thinly veiled on Church Street. Even with my new window shades and curtains, I am easily visible to the surrounding town and passersby, like living in a fish bowl. I can be seen in my house if the shades are up. I'm in plain view if I'm on the lawn or on the front porch. With just a glance, townspeople can look to see whose car is in my driveway, which lights are on in the house or what I'm up to in the yard.

The gossip volume is turned up high. I hear I'm not a homewrecker and by all accounts, I'm "glowing." My friends are thrilled for me.

**January 6, 1997**

Victor called and said he'd received a letter from my husband's lawyer, Sheila. She said the word around Falls Town was that I'm writing a book that "trashes" my ex and his girlfriend and that he "won't like it at all." In her letter she stated,

> *"In the event that the word around town is accurate, Ms. Belt can expect litigation. Mr. Belt is seriously concerned about this matter. Please notify me as to the status of Ms. Belt's creative endeavors."*

Victor said he would respond to the letter and didn't think it was anything to worry about. He stressed that I have a right to my opinions and the right of free speech. Then he said, "After all, truth is not defamation."

**January 9, 1996**

In today's mail I received a copy of the letter that Victor sent to Sheila. I'm glad Victor is on my side. He really does have a way with words. He stated,

*"Whether a book is published or a film is made remains to be seen. In any event, as I understand the libel law, a derogatory statement is only libelous if it is false."*

## January 21, 1996

We had a wonderful group birthday party yesterday afternoon for two of Paul's grandchildren, who are twins, a boy and a girl, and for me. The twins are 10-years-old; I'm 62. Last night, Paul brought me a bouquet of roses and a romantic card and we went out for dinner.

My self-esteem and confidence have never been better in my 62 years. I have become comfortable with myself. What an incredible feeling it is!

I am decent and strong. I will not be controlled. I have tremendous energy. I stand tall, laugh a lot, cry, curse, pray, love and now, I dance naked -- living, really living, happily in a tiny farm town in upstate New York.

## February 6, 1997

It's become clear to everyone that there is something going on between me and Paul, and the responses over the past few weeks have been mostly positive. Flora said, "Good choice!" My mom said, "I'm glad you have someone to go to dinner with." I said, "Mom, he sleeps over."

My kids have given me their approval, one by one. Molly was amazed that I could be in love "so quickly." I guess time really is a matter of personal perspective.

My friends, all anxious to include Paul in social plans, have accepted my wish to allow him to integrate as he chooses. It is important to me that he meet my kids and get to know them and for me to get to know his kids. All the social functions are optional.

**February 13, 1997**

Last night, lying in bed, cuddling and nuzzling, Paul kneeled back on the bed, whipped the sheet back and said, "You're built like a brick shithouse and every brick is in place." This is not something I've ever heard before. I was a little stunned when he said it and then I laughed. And I have to laugh now as I consider this flattery for a 62-year-old woman!

When I mentioned it to Debbie today during our phone conversation, she said her grandfather used to say that. We thought maybe it's Navy terminology since both men served in that part of the armed forces.

There are a few things that Paul says that I never had spoken to me before. He says, for instance, that I have "great tits" or "great gams." His background is so different than mine and what I'm used to. It took some adjusting at first, but it wasn't hard. I'm open to how he wants to express himself and I would never want him to be inhibited in anything he thinks or feels. Besides, I find it refreshing, titillating, lusty and fun.

**February 28, 1997**

Snuggled in Paul's arms, I say, "I love your eyes and your hands feel so good to me." We exchange every scrap of news and what we did while we were apart. We exchange many "I love yous." Then we plot a few new plans for fun.

Today, I'm marveling at the cycles and growth in life. Back in the 1950's, The Righteous Brothers' had a hit song, "Unchained Melody." When we got married in 1956, and for the nearly 40 years of my marriage, it was "our song."

Now, the young country singer, LeAnn Rimes, has recorded her own beautiful version of the song. When I heard her rendition recently on the radio it really stirred my romantic feelings for Paul so I purchased her CD.

Yesterday, Paul mentioned that while he was in Virginia at his son's, he heard a great love song on a country music radio station, sung by a woman. Although he heard it a couple of times, he didn't know the name of the singer or the song. He said the song made him think of me and miss me.

Just on a whim, with the CD at my fingertips, I pressed the stereo buttons to play LeAnn Rime's "Unchained Melody." I said, "Is this it?" Astonished, Paul said, "Yes, that's it!"

And before we sat down to a candlelight dinner, already on the kitchen table, he beckoned me to dance.

## POSTSCRIPT

My ex and his girlfriend were married on June 7, 1997. They reside in the Big House next door to me.

The same weekend, Paul and I were at his camp on a lake in the Adirondacks. We went hiking and canoeing. The gentle water lapped the rocks on the shore and sunlight sprinkled down through the trees.

In the evening, sweet smoke drifted from the log fire. Held in a dream, we never dreamed could be, our pillows muffled giggles as we made music under the dancing stars.

## 12 STEPS TO SURVIVING A DIVORCE

1.     Find an effective counselor

2.     Lean on a strong network of family and friends

3.     Get a good lawyer

4.     Begin journaling, writing or keeping a diary

5.     Nurture a pet or plants

6.     Engage in a hobby, crafts or sports

7.     Explore honesty, feel the feelings

8.     Try something new, take a class

9.     Discover creative ways to deal with problems

10.    Treat yourself special

11.    Set small goals, rebuild self-esteem

12.    Help someone else as soon as you can, let go of your own pain, let life go on.

While living in a tiny farm town in upstate New York, I had visions of living "happily ever after;" instead, a divorce summons officially declared the end of my 39-year marriage as well as my previous perceptions of what this stage of my life might have been. The news spread mouth to ear on Main and Church streets. Chance meetings at the post office sped the gossip, postage-free, express delivery through the town and countryside. I paid 87 cents postage for a small package containing my rings to be sent to my estranged husband. I wrote a little poem he never saw:

*Return to original owner*
*Used rings in a box*
*87 cents postage*
*Tarnished with deceit*
*After 39 years on her finger*
*Fool's gold!*

--------------------

Having been controlled by a loving husband all my adult life, learning to live alone at age 60 came as a brutal blow. The choice to "go on" left me in a place so foreign that I could take only one step at a time.

There were many clues that his affections were turning to his 30-year-old filing clerk. He acted like an infatuated schoolboy but always denied it. He developed a sudden and unusual interest in her culture, American Indian. He purchased expensive gifts for her that he hid. He began to view her as a brilliant goddess and spent time "mentoring" her to encourage her education. She draped herself at his office door and held his eyes with hers while they made small talk. They sucked on hot cinnamon candies that they kept in her desk drawer.

As I exhibited ugly behavior in accusations and hysteria, I personally suffered health ailments (diarrhea, nausea, headaches and jitters) and a crushing loss of my self-esteem. My husband withdrew from me physically and emotionally, even though I was doing everything I could think of to show him my love for him and reignite his interest in me. All the while, he portrayed me as difficult and he refused to admit that anything was unusual.

Our almost four-decades-long marriage blew up in my face when I unlocked the file cabinet next to his desk after searching for and finding the key, which had been deliberately hidden. In the cabinet, I found the proof of my feelings. There was another gift stashed away for her, an Indian portrait purchased for $400. There were books on how to survive divorce, an appointment for him to see her marriage counselor, secret payments made to her off the books and his own handwritten notes about his plans to divorce me. That was the day I took my first step.

Devastated and lost, I looked in the Yellow Pages under "marriage counselor." Finding a listing for the Option Institute in a nearby town, I drove in search of their rural location. "It looks like you could use a hug," Willow said, when she looked up from her desk and saw my face. She called Richard from his office and he immediately came to walk and talk with me. In the next 50 minutes, I gained enough strength to start to deal with the shattering news that I had unlocked and I became clear about my desire to save my marriage.

A second dialogue session with a counselor helped me articulate my need to have it all -- trust, love and good sex. I encouraged my husband to join me in choosing happiness through this program of self-help, but he vacillated about his feelings for me, staying on the fence for weeks until he announced he wanted his "space." I packed the bare essentials to survive and left my home that night. I spent one night at my daughter Michelle's house in Vermont and determined that I must be on my own even if it meant camping.

The second night I slept in my car in a campground and then I found a cottage to rent. Later I learned from my guidance counselor that there were legal implications to "moving out" and that I had suffered extreme emotional battering at the hands of my husband. The Option Institute sessions were my crutch until I found my counselor, Deborah Mendelsohn, M.S.W., in California four weeks later.

During the month I rented the cottage, I tried to let go of my judgments regarding his behavior and I took my second step. I reached out to my family and friends. The telephone next to my bed was my lifeline. Sometimes my daughter, Molly, would talk to me until my tears dried and sleep came. Emotions raged as I desperately tried to sustain my life.

Knowing I was powerless to change my husband didn't mean I didn't want to. I pulled out all the stops in my attempts to arouse him. Later, in my emotional "journaling," I called these efforts "dancing naked," which reflected my willingness to expose myself in every way. He said he pitied me.

But my friends were there for me. They called, wrote, visited and listened. I talked and talked. At first, I had protected my husband and the girl with my silence because I had hope of resolving our problem, but as he marched on toward infidelity, I became more and more open with my friends. Pure honesty works towards bonding relationships and my humiliation diminished as I felt totally accepted by my friends. Every word of encouragement they gave me was magnified by my desperate need to be OK.

Months later, sitting in the hallway at one of my court hearings, a friend happened to walk by. She stopped and said, "You know, cream rises to the top and you're cream." Only words, but powerful encouragement given at the right time.

Some of the effective actions my friends did that helped me were a brown bag picnic, a hike in the woods, gathering supplies and making

Christmas decorations together, joining me to paddle my canoe and brightening my rental cottage with flowers and plants.

Friends also began to encourage me to get a good lawyer. Back to the Yellow Pages, I located the name of a lawyer I had met once at a dinner party. Recalling that he seemed sharp and fun to talk with, I decided to call him. The first visit to the law office was like my first visit to a liquor store -- a place that made me feel uncomfortable and somehow like a bad person. Months later my litigation lawyer, the receptionist, the secretary and the paralegals seemed like old friends.

There were signs that my friends noticed and that I became aware of, that demonstrated my need for a lawyer. I was emotionally lost and utterly devastated. I had little knowledge of and no control over our family finances. I was not looking for a divorce, but I knew my husband was. Furthermore, he had been thinking about and even planning for our divorce for some time; I was caught by surprise.

My husband failed to prove himself trustworthy by action, word or deed. I knew I had to rely on professional help for guidance. Selecting a reputable law firm with a broad base of expertise and located in my county, not too far away, in hindsight, seems to have been a decision of dumb luck. But it was a saving grace.

The period of "amicable settlement" passed after my husband failed to demonstrate any willingness to be fair to me. During this period, I believe he began fulfilling his sexual fantasies with his girlfriend, still on his payroll even though she didn't work at his office any longer.

My hardest blow came after I returned from a trip to California to witness the birth of our first grandchild. While there, I took advantage of an opportunity to have a counseling session at the Y.M.C.A. with Deborah.

It was my good fortune to have her as my guide when my husband dropped the guillotine blade. My husband had finally consented to the request of our children to go to couples' counseling with me, but he announced at our second session, "I want to end the marriage." It severed my last strand of hope.

Words can't describe the anguish that tore through me. I managed to walk out of the counselor's building, gripped in shock and drive 45 minutes home, alone. Clenching the steering wheel, I screamed as if being tortured.

At home and drowning in an emotional abyss, I telephoned my husband for help. He sent my neighbors to help me and I knew I could never count on my husband again for anything. He extracted himself from our marriage with lies, cheating, emotional battering, financial coercion and no physical or emotional support whatsoever.

With my daughter, Molly, at my side, I survived the worst days of my life. The advice from my California counselor, Deborah, now by telephone, was to take care of myself. She said, "What has happened to you is horrendous, but the worst is over. It's OK to stay in bed, cry and feel the feelings. Treat yourself special, take a hot bath; be very, very good to yourself."

In the year that passed, I surrounded myself with family and friends, leaned on my counselor, worked with my lawyer, moved back into my own home (which caused my husband to move out), resumed my projects, brought my dog into the house and took care of myself. By choosing healthy foods and an active lifestyle, I lost weight, looked good and felt better.

I also began to write daily. Journaling has proven to be an essential tool in my recovery. Writing has allowed my feelings a safe place to go -- on paper! For example, anger on paper:

*Brutal allegations crush me*

*With threats and lies*

*Responding to his daily battering*

*to pay his bills*

*I feel stalked by a beast*

*who wants to kill me.*

--------------------

As he burned his bridges, I was the Phoenix up from the ashes. Rebuilding my self-esteem was a team effort -- my counselor, family and friends were my fellow players. Setting small goals that could be accomplished successfully without stress started with picking up litter and progressed to re-entering my greenhouse for a season of growing flowers for the town and to sell for charitable causes.

Unconditional love from my constant and wonderful companion, my black Labrador, Spooky, was, and still is, a powerful affirmation of the goodness of life. The power of prayer, as it emanates from the hearts of friends, transcends the miles of separation and empowers me with support. Interacting with local friends, playing tennis, planning a fund-raiser for the church and taking a writing course at the local community college (which included learning how to write a query letter to a publisher) helped to establish a calendar of life that becomes more interesting each day.

In response to my husband's threats to turn off the electricity and disconnect the phone, I stocked wood for my woodstove and I bottled water to last for days. I refused to assume responsibility for bills that were not mine, even though my husband tried to press them on me. And I managed to keep going financially without any maintenance payments from him or a settlement.

My husband has proven himself to be "cruel and inhuman," ironically his charge for me in his summons for divorce. When his threat of disconnecting my phone became a reality, living alone in the country called for a communication system with my network of friends. Dozens of friends offered their phones to me and messages were relayed by visits and notes. My support network grew stronger even though my newfound strength resulted in more strong-arming from him.

The first affidavit I received was more distressing than a physical beating and far more hurtful than a disconnected phone. My counselor's advice was to keep my anger on paper and in legal actions. Unfortunately, I acted on an instinct when by coincidence my husband was driving out of his driveway and his girlfriend was driving out behind his car. I was on my way to pick up a friend. There we were, at exactly the same time in three different cars on the same road and I followed them. When he turned off, I continued following her and I honked my horn and continued honking, until she drove out of town. I stopped my husband on the road moments later as he was pursuing her. I had a few choice words: "Go ahead and fuck the whore, tell your goddamned lawyer I'm crazy, you bastard." My counselor said it was good that I was getting the anger out, although she agreed it was not a great way to do it.

A police officer pulled me over a few days later and said, "I have some bad news for you. Come to the station to get the papers." I knew it was about the honking incident. The girlfriend charged me with reckless driving and I was assigned a court date. I called my lawyer from the police station and drove straight to my friend's house to tell her. After telling a few more friends, I actually felt OK about it.

My smart lawyer viewed the incident as a potential opportunity since the girlfriend stated in her charge that she was a full-time student and my husband stated in his affidavit that she was a full-time employee, since, of course, he was paying her as if she was and then some.

In the aftermath of this event, all my "Recovery Steps" really came into play. I needed my lawyer, my counselor, my kids, my friends, my dog and my journaling. Interestingly, my tennis game improved substantially. I have found some humor in it all and the incident adds a little excitement in the chapter of the book I've written.

Feeling less angry and more resolved, I wanted to face my opposition (my husband and the girlfriend) with more neutral and controlled emotions. So, I stood my ground firmly.

Even during all of this, I submitted my first newspaper article to get a byline, which helps to establish my writing credits for later publishing my divorce story. I also helped a friend establish a coffee house as a fund-raiser for the church and it has been a success. I continue to set small goals and accomplish them which keeps life worthwhile and intriguing.

With court dates and legal actions and even with no phone, no credit card, no settlement agreement, no maintenance money from him and the divorce still months away, I nevertheless felt a freedom and I didn't feel stupid anymore. As I displayed my honest emotions, my pain subsided.

My relationships with my kids and friends are wonderful experiences in personal growth. I am unafraid and I feel healthy. I can't claim recovery, but I feel I'm on the road and it is possible that my counselor is right when she says, "I promise you, you will be OK."

On May 12, 1995, my 39th wedding anniversary, I was notified that my daughter's fiancé had committed suicide. With the fragile new imprints of my own steps toward recovery in place, I could be there to help Molly. Thank God.

## CONTINUING WITH THE STEPS

After a year, each step was still essential in my recovery. My weekly telephone talks with my counselor helped me deal with old issues, current issues and new issues. More than anyone, my counselor helped put my progress and my concerns into perspective. She applauded my strength and convinced me that the best way I can help my kids and my friends is to show them my recovery.

Recovery is a process, but it is real. It is measured in how I feel, what I say, how I look; like a dipstick in my emotional pain. Tears still erupted with the slightest prodding, but I could hear appalling revelations about my husband's actions (present and past) and I knew to look to my lawyer for my legal response.

Designing my days with activities that were healthy, helpful and fun required taking some action. Publishing articles which focused on good news in the local newspaper gave me bylines that friends were enthusiastic about. They said they believed I'd be able to share my divorce story in time. When I shared some of my writing about it with friends, they responded with cheers and tears and commented, "You have a best seller."

In the same week that my husband petitioned the court to deny me maintenance payments that the judge had already ordered him to pay me, he spent more than $8,000 on a swimming pool for himself. He filed his income taxes singly for the previous year, before we were separated, rather than jointly and didn't tell me. I was left delinquent in paying my taxes without even knowing it. This further eroded his image in my lawyer's eyes and prompted the need for a CPA of my own.

While the divorce legal workings slogged on, there were weddings, babies, deaths, holidays, vacations, seasons, parties, projects and plans. My daughter took steps towards recovery in her own way. My children are stronger, my friendships are treasures, my husband has to live with himself and I am a capable, independent woman.

In September 1995, the divorce trial was still not scheduled. But through the discovery legal process, it was proved that he transferred our money to the girlfriend by giving her his ATM banking card and PIN number. He also became "in contempt of court" by refusing to pay me the court-ordered maintenance payments. Believing that he could control all the decisions, he also said everything would have to be sold as a condition of settlement, rather than us dividing up our possessions. Even if the losses to me are horrendous monetarily and emotionally, my counselor said she was positive that I would emerge a "whole person." I am not so afraid about the losses anymore. I'm grateful for the gains. I now realize that my worst-case scenario is a fresh start. Not too bad.

On March 19, 1996, the divorce was granted on the grounds, "constructive abandonment," after a four-day trial. I was satisfied with the eventual settlement, pleased with my lawyer and celebrated that evening with my wonderful friend, Nancy. Filled with excitement for life and my next adventures, I spread the word that my ordeal was over and I started typing the last chapter in my book.

My self-esteem and confidence have never been better. I have become comfortable with myself. I feel decent and strong. I will not be controlled or shit on. I stand taller, laugh often, cry, curse, pray and dance -- living happily in a tiny farm town in upstate New York.

Printed in the United States
90962LV00006B/13/A